DATA LINEAGE
FROM A BUSINESS PERSPECTIVE

To my family, Kalina, Natalia, and Adri, who have always supported me

in my professional endeavors.

Published by Data Crossroads.
www.datacrossroads.nl

First edition, 2021.

Book design by Natalia Zhuravska.

ISBN: 9798473818017

Contents

FOREWORD

I first heard the term "data lineage" years ago when our team had implemented a data warehouse solution. One of the consultants came with an Excel sheet and suggested documenting data lineage. The IT team's reaction was simple and direct: "No way." They argued that nobody needed this information, and in the worst-case scenario, they could check software codes. Sometime later, the topic of data lineage arose again during the implementation of a compliance-related project. One colleague of mine had unsuccessfully tried to gather requirements for data lineage. At some point, he desperately said: "Everybody needs data lineage. Nobody can explain what they mean by that." So I took over his task. Since then, data lineage has become my area of expertise and my hobby. Over the years since, I have witnessed significant changes in data lineage and observed several new trends.

DATA LINEAGE TRENDS

The situation with data lineage demonstrates several trends spanning over the course of years. The three most notable trends are:

1. The increasing pressure of regulatory and business requirements demands documentation of data lineage.
    Years ago, data lineage was a luxury. Nowadays, it has become a daily demand. Recently, different regulators have issued a substantial number of legislative documents with particular requirements for data management. To meet these requirements, companies in diverse industries have to implement data lineage. A rapidly and unpredictably changing economic environment demands corresponding developments in a business environment. Any business change touches upon data. Examples of business changes are data integration projects, digital transformation, big data, advanced data analytics initiatives, and the implementation of cloud solutions. The successful implementation of these changes requires knowledge of the location of data and the transformation that data undergoes along data chains. Data lineage serves as the source of such knowledge.
2. Both technical and business professionals have demonstrated needs and interest in data lineage.
    A while ago, only some technical professionals knew about data lineage. But even fewer had experience with it. Nowadays, data lineage has become a frequently used term among business professionals. For many of them, this concept remains abstract. It still doesn't plead with the fact that data lineage has become one of the most in-demand business needs.
3. Many different data lineage software solutions have appeared on the market.
    Until recently, the documentation of data lineage has commonly taken place in Microsoft Excel and Word. Recently, several advanced data lineage solutions have been offered on the market. Companies of different sizes and from various industries may find a solution that fits their needs and resources.

Along with these trends, I have recognized several challenges with data lineage.

CHALLENGES WITH DATA LINEAGE IMPLEMENTATION

The implementation of data lineage experiences a lot of challenges. The most critical ones are the following:

1. Data lineage remains an abstract concept for many users.
   Data lineage is a complex concept. The data management community doesn't have an aligned definition of it. Therefore, each company should start a data lineage initiative with the development of a data lineage metamodel.
2. The implementation is complex and time and resource-consuming.
   In any case, the implementation of data lineage requires much effort and many resources. The proper identification of requirements and scope is one of the key success factors.
3. Even if implemented, data management and business professionals don't use it as expected.
   At the beginning of the data lineage initiative, many stakeholders are not familiar with the concept. Their initial expectations often do not match the real outcomes. Furthermore, the use of data lineage requires some technical skills and knowledge. All of these factors lead to the situation when the results of data lineage implementation remain unclaimed.

The knowledge of trends and experience to overcome the challenges described above are what inspired me to write this book.

KEY GOALS AND TARGET AUDIENCE

This book uncovers different aspects of data lineage to data management and business professionals.

This book aims to:

- Provide the definition and model of data lineage
  Data lineage is a complex concept, and every company may define the key components of data lineage differently and in a way that best meets the company's needs.
- Demonstrate best practices in data lineage implementation
  The implementation of data lineage is time and resource-consuming. To make it successful, every company should define the appropriate scope, methods, and solutions.
- Discuss key business areas of data lineage usage
  Proper usage of data lineage should pay back the investments spent on the data lineage initiative. Different business functions may enjoy the outcomes of data lineage.

Several groups of professionals can use this book in different ways:

- Data management and business professionals can develop ideas about data lineage and its application areas.
  There are few resources about the data lineage concept. Articles on the Internet and the sites of data lineage providers are the main sources. The data lineage concept has a lack of aligned terminology. The situation causes challenges for newcomers to become familiar with the subject. This book offers a deep analysis of data lineage and also proposes a metamodel and corresponding terminology. It eases the communication regarding data lineage between different stakeholders.
- Professionals with a technical background may gain a better understanding of business needs and requirements for data lineage.

Different stakeholders have a significantly various understanding, needs, and requirements to data lineage. Technical professionals mainly focus on the implementation of metadata lineage at a physical level. Such a term says nothing to business professionals. This book DOES NOT cover the technical aspects of different data lineage solutions. Instead, it assists technical professionals in building a bridge between their viewpoints and those held by businesspeople.

- Project management professionals can become familiar with the best practices of data lineage implementation.
A proper scope and appropriate methods of implementation are the key success factors of any project. Many factors influence the choice of scope, methods, and approaches. Project management professionals can receive practical recommendations and become familiar with techniques to develop data lineage business cases. The book also provides an overview of some data lineage software solutions.

INTRODUCTION

"All theory, dear friend, is gray, but the golden tree of life springs ever green."

- Johann Wolfgang von Goethe

The famous quote by Goethe aptly expresses the core idea of this book. We need the theory of data lineage to define our goals, needs, and requirements, as the implementation of data lineage gives us insight into data behavior. However, only the active usage of data lineage allows companies to achieve their goals and satisfy their needs. The three pillars of a data lineage business case are shown in Figure 1:

- Theory
- Implementation
- Usage

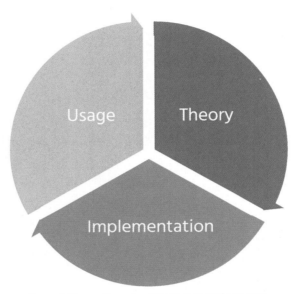

Figure 1: Three pillars of a data lineage business case.

The structure of this book follows this three-pillar idea.

THE STRUCTURE AND CONTENT OF THIS BOOK

The book consists of three parts that correspond to each pillar: theory, implementation, and usage. Each part includes several chapters that disclose the content of each pillar. A case study in Part 4 demonstrates the practical example of setting up a business case for data lineage.

Below, you will find a brief overview of parts and chapters.

Part 1: Clarifying the concept of data lineage

Data lineage is a complex concept. The complexity causes ambiguous interpretations of its meaning. Part 1 aims to resolve these challenges.

Chapter 1 provides an overview of different visions regarding data lineage. It also includes an analysis of several concepts that overlap the concept of data lineage.

Chapter 2 discusses key business drivers to document data lineage, such as legislative requirements, business changes, and data management initiatives.

Chapter 3 defines the term "metamodel" and outlines the approach to design the metamodel of data lineage.

Chapter 4 describes in-depth the key components of the data lineage metamodel. Business processes, IT systems, and data models at different levels are examples of data lineage components.

Chapter 5 discusses different types of data lineage. Various business stakeholders have different expectations and requirements for data lineage. The common understanding of data lineage remains the same. At the same time, the way to document data lineage varies depending on the stakeholders' needs.

By the end of Part 1, readers will gain comprehensive knowledge about the data lineage concept. It forms the basis for the next step: the implementation of data lineage. Different aspects of this will be discussed in Part 2.

Part 2: Implementing data lineage

Many factors influence and determine the success of data lineage implementation.

Chapter 6 describes the nine-step methodology to building a data lineage case. The subsequent chapters of Part 2 examine these steps in detail.

Chapter 7 focuses on the key parameters to scope a data lineage initiative. The correct scoping ensures the feasibility of such an initiative.

Chapter 8 provides an overview of key data lineage stakeholders. It also describes in detail the roles involved in the data lineage initiative and their accountabilities. The analysis of different factors that define the roles' design is also a part of this chapter.

Chapter 9 provides a methodology and template for defining and documenting data lineage requirements. The distinction between metadata and data value lineage requirements is explained. Clear and feasible requirements are one of the keys to implementation success.

Chapter 10 discusses different approaches to implementing data lineage. Several factors influence the various approaches. A method of data lineage documentation, scope parameters, the direction of the documentation, and project management style are examples .

Chapter 11 offers a high-level overview of data lineage solutions that exist in the market. The documentation of data lineage requires suitable software. The most important thing about the solution is to find such that meet your current requirements while leaving space for future developments.

Chapter 12 pays attention to the practical aspects of data lineage documentation. Descriptive and automated data lineage are two different methods of metadata lineage documentation. The application of each of these methods follows diverse steps and has its characteristics.

Chapter 13 shares the practical experience about the success factors of data lineage implementation.

By the end of Part 2, readers will have learned several practical insights and recommendations for the implementation of data lineage.

Active involvement of data lineage stakeholders in its usage is discussed in Part 3.

Part 3: Using data lineage

Data lineage outcomes can be used for different business purposes. Data management initiatives, critical data elements, data quality checks and controls are examples of such usage.

Chapter 14 highlights the application of data lineage for the definition of critical data. The concept of critical data is used in different contexts. Critical data assists in the scoping of different data lineage initiatives. The knowledge of data lineage is the key to discovering critical data along data chains.

Chapter 15 demonstrates the importance of data lineage for data quality. Gathering data quality requirements, designing, and building data quality checks and controls can hardly be performed without data lineage.

Chapter 16 discusses the usage of data lineage for impact and root-cause analysis. Different data management initiatives demand such analysis. Data lineage is the only means to perform it.

Chapter 17 shows a possibility to use data lineage for financial planning and analysis tasks. Driver-based modeling techniques and data lineage have a lot in common.

Chapter 18 discusses relationships between data lineage documentation and the implementation of data management frameworks. My experience brought me to the following conclusion. The setup of a data management framework follows the logic of the documentation of data lineage.

By the end of Part 3, readers will have gained a clear view of the three pillars of a data lineage business case: theory, implementation, and usage.

Part 4 consolidates the information received.

Part 4: Case study: "Build a data lineage business case"

Here we will have set the theory of data lineage aside and instead have some fun. In this section of this book, you will read a short story about a fictitious company and its journey in documenting data lineage.

Additional materials

Additional materials add value to this book and assist data lineage newcomers in proceeding with the data lineage initiative. I have added the following:

Template 1: Data lineage requirements

This template assists in gathering business requirements to scope the data lineage initiative.

The document contains general requirements and requirements to key data lineage components that a company would need to capture. The relationships between them are also a part of this template.

Template 2: The scope and progress of data lineage initiative

This template assists in communicating the scope of data lineage initiatives. It is also a good tool to demonstrate the progress of implementation.

Overview: Data lineage solutions

This overview provides an analysis of the software solutions currently available on the market. The analysis includes solutions that cover more than one data lineage component identified by the metamodel of data lineage. This overview is for informational purposes only. I don't offer any preferences regarding a solution.

Template 3: Comparing data lineage solutions

This template assists in performing a comparative analysis of different software solutions for data lineage documentation. It also includes the key software functionalities to be compared.

READING INSTRUCTIONS

Reading instructions aim to ease the reading of the text and understanding the content of diagrams.

Capitalization of industry jargon

In this book, I don't capitalize certain industry jargon, such as data management, data governance, data modeling, etc. This nomenclature is not standard throughout the industry. Quotations from an industry guide are the exception to this rule.

Diagram notations

To represent the concepts used in this book, I use the concept map technique. The set of symbols helps to demonstrate the essence of the discussed concepts. The notation used in this book is compiled from two sources: "Graph Data Modeling For NoSQL and SQL"[1] by Thomas Frisendal, and the tutorials to the MindMaster[2] software application.

The symbols in a concept map represent the following:

- Concept
  A rounded rectangle represents a concept or data element at different levels of abstraction (see Figure 2).

Figure 2: The symbol for a concept/data element.

- Linking words
  Linking words or phrases appear on the linking lines that connect concepts/data elements, as shown in Figure 3. Commonly, a linking word is a verb.

Figure 3: An example of a linking word.

- Hierarchical structure

  A hierarchical structure demonstrates the relationships between concepts at different levels of abstraction, as shown in Figure 4. Data is a term at a higher level of abstraction. Data then can be classified into different types. You read such a concept map from top to down.

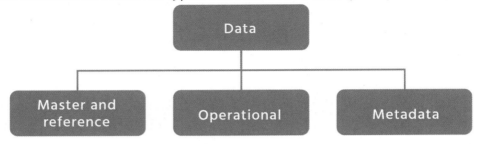

Figure 4: An example of a hierarchical structure.

The linking phrase "is a" describes the relationships between a concept and its subtypes. "Is part of" demonstrates the aggregation or composition pattern.

- Linking arrows

  Concept maps demonstrate how different concepts are interrelated. Linking arrows demonstrate the relationships between concepts, as shown in Table 1.

Type 1.

A connecting line with an arrowhead indicates the direction of the relationship. As shown in Table 1, concept A has some relation with concept B.

An example is "The organization has many employees."

Type 2.

A closed connecting line indicates that element A has a relationship to itself and takes part in a recursive relation.

"One employee manages one or more other employees" is an example of such a relationship.

Type 3.

A connecting line with two arrowheads indicates that more than one elements A are connected by one or more elements B.

An example: "Several business rules apply to several data elements."

Type 4.

A connecting line without arrowheads illustrates the relationships in hierarchical structures. The example thereof is an organizational structure.

Type No	Type	Description	Usage
1	A ⟶ B	A connecting line with an arrowhead	Indicates how the element A relates to the element B or indicates a recursive relation
2	A (closed loop with arrowhead)	A closed connecting line with an arrowhead	Indicates that element A has recursive relation
3	A ⟷ B	A connecting line with two arrowheads	Indicates that one or more elements B connect several elements A
4	A —— B	A connecting line without arrowhead	Used for hierarchical / "parent-child" structures

Table 1: Relationship symbols.

By now, you are fully equipped to start reading the book.

Part 1

CLARIFYING THE CONCEPT OF DATA LINEAGE

"If you can't explain it to a six-year-old, you don't understand it yourself."

- Albert Einstein

Data lineage is a complex concept. In a different context, it may have diverse interpretations. I once delivered a presentation on data lineage to a professional community of data architects in The Netherlands. I asked three participants to provide their definitions of data lineage, and it is easy to guess that all definitions differed from each other. The same happens throughout the entire global data management community. Since then, each time I start speaking with someone on the subject, the first question that I ask is: "What is your understanding of data lineage?" To build a common understanding, we need to clarify the data lineage concept.

Part 1 aims to clarify the concept of data lineage by:
- Providing a definition of data lineage
- Designing its metamodel
- Classifying the types of data lineage

Our first step is to study existing views and approaches to data lineage.

1 | ANALYSIS OF THE EXISTING VIEWS AND APPROACHES TO DATA LINEAGE

I have started research on data lineage with the investigation of well-known industry reference guides: the Data Management Body of Knowledge 2 (DAMA-DMBOK2) by DAMA International[1] and the TOGAF® Standard, Version 9.2[2] (later referred to as TOGAF® 9.2), a framework for Enterprise Architecture, by The Open Group. These two guides offer different views and definitions of data lineage. These guides also elaborate on other concepts similar to data lineage.

In Chapter 1, we will:

- Investigate similarities and difference between concepts comparable with data lineage
- Discover relationships between the concept of data lineage with some other fundamental data management concepts
- Demonstrate the role of data lineage for different data management capabilities
- View recommendations provided by the DAMA-DMBOK2 on data lineage

After reading this chapter, you will be able to:

- Recognize differences between different data lineage-related concepts
- Choose a data lineage concept that corresponds to your company's needs and practices
- Identify data management capabilities in your company that require data lineage

Let us start with the concepts comparable with data lineage.

1.1 DATA LINEAGE AND OTHER COMPARABLE CONCEPTS

The analysis of different sources has delivered this list of concepts comparable to data lineage:

- Data value chain
- Data chain
- Data flow
- Integration architecture
- Information value chain

For easy memorization, I put them into an infographic, as shown in Figure 5.

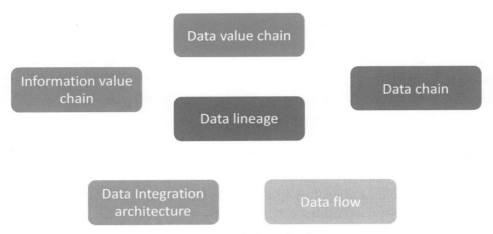

Figure 5: Concepts similar to data lineage.

Data lineage

Several DAMA publications define data lineage differently.

The DAMA Dictionary of Data Management (the DAMA Dictionary) describes data lineage as "A description of the pathway from the data source to their current location and the alterations made to the data along that pathway"[3]. The DAMA-DMBOK1, first edition, specifies "data lineage / Flows" as a deliverable of Data Integration Architecture[4]. This statement contradicts another declaration in the DAMA-DMBOK1: "Data lineage and data flows are the same names for this [Data Integration Architecture] concept"[5].

The DAMA-DMBOK2 has elaborated in-depth on the data lineage concept compared to the first edition. The DAMA-DMBOK2 comes up with a definition similar to one provided in the DAMA Dictionary. Data lineage is "...a pathway along which it [data] moves from its point of origin to its point of usage [...]"[6].

The DAMA-DMBOK2 uses the terms of data lineage and data flow interchangeably. It defines data flow as "[...] a type of data lineage documentation that depicts how data moves through business processes and systems"[7].

To summarize:
1. Data lineage is a description of the pathway between the points of data origin and the destination and transformations that data undergoes along this pathway.
2. Data lineage, data flow, and data integration architecture are the same concepts. DAMA publications consider data lineage, data flow, and data integration architecture as synonymous.

Let us now investigate the concept of the data value chain.

Data value chain

The definition of the data value chain appears only in the DAMA Dictionary.

According to the DAMA Dictionary, "Data value chain is the flow of data across processes in support of the enterprise business value chain"[8]. Data value chain analysis assumes "the identification of which functions, processes, applications, organizations, and roles create, read, update, and delete different kinds of data (subject areas, entities, attributes), expressed in CRUD matrices, particularly when the compared items are arranged in value chain sequence"[9].

The term "data value chain" has several notable features:
1. A data value chain relates to the business value chain concept.
2. A data value chain describes data flow and links it to applications and business components such as processes, functions, and roles.
3. A data value can be described at different levels of data models, such as conceptual (subject area) and logical (entities and attributes).

Data chain

The DAMA-DMBOK2 has introduced the term in the contexts of the data lifecycle and data quality. The DAMA-DMBOK2 stresses that "[...] data [...] has lineage (i.e., a pathway along which it moves from its point of origin to its point of usage, sometimes called the data chain)"[10].

From this, we can make a cursory conclusion: data chain is synonymous to data lineage.

Data flow

We have already seen that DAMA publications regard data flow as synonymous with data lineage. Let us take a deeper look into the definition of data flow.

The DAMA Dictionary specifies the concept of data flow as "the transfer of data between systems, applications, and data sets"[11]. It also introduces the definition of a data flow diagram which is "a visual representation of how data moves or is moved between logical processes or application services (i.e., how the output data from a process serves as the input data for other processes). Essentially a process model, complementary to data model"[12].

The DAMA-DMBOK2 identifies data flow design as " [...] the requirements and master blueprint for storage and processing across databases, applications, platforms, and networks (the components). The data flows map the movement of data to business processes, locations, business roles, and to technical components"[13].

The DAMA-DMBOK2 links data flow to data lineage. "Data flows are a type of data lineage documentation that depicts how data moves through business processes and systems. End-to-end data flows illustrate where the data originated, where it is stored and used, and how it is transformed as it moves inside and between diverse processes and systems."[14]

The DAMA-DMBOK2 defines the key components of data flow; "Data flow map and document relationships between data and
- Applications within a business process
- Data stores or data bases in an environment
- Network segments (useful for security mapping)

- Business roles, depicting which roles have responsibility for creating, updating, using, and deleting data (CRUD)
- Locations where local differences occur"[15].

It also determines the levels of data flow documentation. "Data flow can be documented at different levels of details: Subject Area, business entity, or even the attribute level."[16] I interpret this statement as meaning that data flow can be documented at the conceptual and logical levels of data models.

In short:

1. Data flow and data lineage are synonymous.
2. Data flow demonstrates the flow of data at the conceptual and logical levels by linking business processes, roles, and IT assets such as databases, applications, networks.

Data Integration Architecture

Different DAMA publications provide definitions of this term.

According to the DAMA Dictionary, data integration architecture identifies "how data will flow between applications and databases"[17].

The DAMA-DMBOK1 provides an even more detailed definition of integration architecture. "Data integration architecture defines how data flows through all systems from beginning to end. Data integration architecture is both data architecture and application architecture, because it includes both databases and the applications that control the data flow into the system, between databases, and back out of the system. Data lineage and data flows are also names for this concept."[18]

In the DAMA Dictionary, you can also find the classification of Data Integration Architecture.

"The data integration architecture may divide into database architecture, Master Data Management architecture, Data Warehouse/Business Intelligence architecture, and meta-data architecture. Some enterprises also include

- a) list of controlled domain values' (code sets), and
- b) the responsibility assignments of data stewards to subject areas, entities, and code sets."[19]

It is also worth noting that TOGAF® 9.2, by the Open Group, does not operate with the concept of data integration architecture.

Below is a brief summary of integration architecture:

- Data integration architecture, data flow, and data lineage are the same concept according to DAMA publications.
- Data integration architecture describes the flow of data between databases, applications, systems, business roles, and their accountabilities.

Information Value Chain

The DAMA Dictionary identifies information value chain analysis as "a process to link conceptual and logical data models to process models, applications, organizations, roles and/or goals, to provide context, relevance and timeframes"[20].

The DAMA-DMBOK1 adds that the information value chain analysis "Aligns data with business processes and other enterprise architecture components, and Related data delivery architecture: Including database architecture, data integration architecture, data warehousing/business intelligence architecture, document content architecture, and metadata architecture"[21].

It also specifies the main artifacts of this analysis: "mapping the relationships between data, process, business, systems, and technology"[22] presented in the form of matrices "Entity/Function, Entity/ Org and Role, Entity/Application"[23].

Strangely enough, the DAMA-DMBOK2 does not provide any definition of the information value chain concept and does not reference this term in its text.

Another interesting fact is that while the DAMA-DMBOK1 recognizes the information value chain as a "primary deliverable"[24] of data architecture, you can't find this term in TOGAF® 9.2, one of the leading enterprise architecture standards.

Below is a brief recap about information value chain:
1. It links conceptual and logical data models with (business) processes, roles, and different types of enterprise architecture, such as database, system and application, integration, DWH/BI, metadata.
2. The information value chain is one of the deliverables of data architecture.
3. The key artifacts are matrices that map data entities with business functions, roles, applications, etc.

As a result of analyzing the different terms, I came to the following conclusions:
1. Different reference industry guidelines have diverse viewpoints on the concept of data lineage.
2. There is no aligned unambiguous definition of data lineage. Definitions have been changed through time.
3. Several other concepts have definitions similar to data lineage. All these concepts describe data movement and transformation at different levels of abstraction.
4. The names of these concepts are often used interchangeably. Data chain is considered to be the same concept as data lineage. Data flow is defined as being a type of data lineage. Data lineage, data flow, and data integration architecture are different names for the same concept. In Figure 6, you see the graphical representation of these dependencies. It is complicated, isn't it?
5. Data movement is described in the limits of the point of data origin/source/beginning to the point of usage/current location/end/target. The words used to describe these limits demonstrate one of the important features of data lineage: the relativity of its scope or length. It means that documentation of data lineage can be limited by the relative "begin" and "end" of a data flow.
6. Data lineage maps the movement of data between systems, applications, data sets and can be documented at different levels of abstraction.
7. Data lineage maps data movement to business components such as organizations, business processes, and roles.

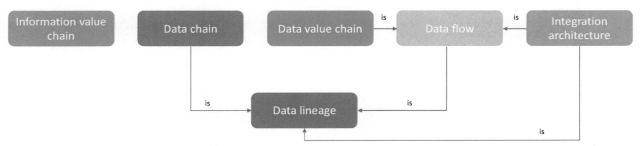

Figure 6: An overview of relationships between different concepts.

The definitions of all of these concepts have provided the list of constituent components of data lineage-related concepts.

1.2   THE CONSTITUENT COMPONENTS OF DATA LINEAGE

For analytical purposes, I combined the components related to different concepts and created a graphical overview, as shown in Figure 7. The colors of circles correspond to the colors used in Figures 5 and 6 to distinguish different concepts.

The analysis has delivered a set of components that constitute data lineage-related concepts:

- Business processes
- Business functions and roles involved in business processes
- IT assets such as a system, an application, a database, a network
- Data models at the conceptual, logical, and physical levels
- Business rules and their technical implementation in the form of ETL (Extract, Transform, Load) processes

Different data lineage-related concepts document data pathways at different levels of abstraction and use components corresponding to these levels. The analysis has resulted in the identification of the four levels of abstraction with corresponding components:

- Business level
  This level includes business processes, business functions and roles, and IT assets.
- Data model level at different levels of abstraction:
  - Conceptual level
    Subject areas, business entities, restriction rules belong to this level.
  - Logical level
    Data entities and attributes, business (transformation) rules describe the data pathway at the logical level.
  - Physical level
    At the physical level, the data lineage documents databases, tables, columns, ETL jobs, and other similar objects.

25

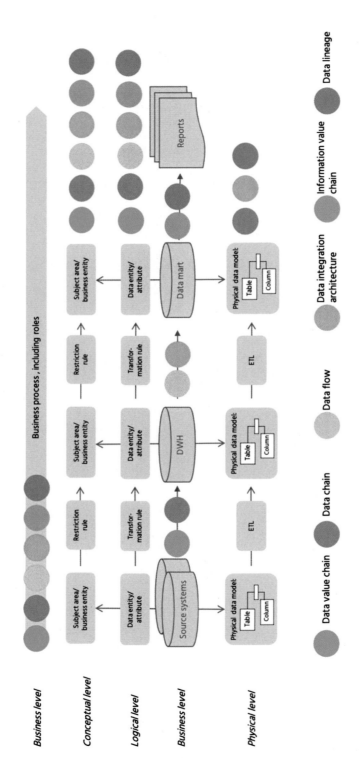

Figure 7: Comparison of the components of data lineage-related concepts.

In the final step of this analysis, we can summarize the correspondence between different data-related concepts and documentation levels. An overview is presented in Table 2.

Concept/ Level of documentation	Business level	Conceptual level	Logical level	Physical level
Data value chain				
Data chain				
Data flow				
Data integration architecture				
Information value chain				
Data lineage				

Table 2: The relationship between data lineage-related concepts and documentation levels.

The results are quite remarkable. All data lineage-related concepts include components of the business, conceptual, and logical levels. Data value chain, data integration architecture, and data lineage add components from the physical level.

We have finalized the analysis of concepts that have a lot in common with data lineage.

Some general data management concepts have some relations to data lineage. We will investigate these relations in the next sub-chapter.

1.3   RELATIONSHIPS BETWEEN DATA LINEAGE AND DATA LIFECYCLE

The concepts of data lineage and data lifecycle interrelate with each other. Let's take a look at the definition of data lifecycle given in the DAMA Dictionary. Data lifecycle is a "Conceptualization of how data is created and used which attempts to define a 'birth-to-death' value chain for data, including acquisition, storage, and maintenance, use, movement to archive, and destruction"[25]. It is interesting to see the usage of the phrase "value chain for data" in this definition. "Value chain for data" can be rephrased as "data value chain." In sub-chapter 1.2, we have seen that the "data value chain" is a concept similar to data lineage. This definition demonstrates the strong relationship between data lineage and data lifecycle.

The DAMA-DMBOK2 also stresses that "Lifecycle and lineage intersect and can be understood in relation to each other. Data not only has a lifecycle, it also has lineage [...]"[26].

The essence of this relationship can be explained as follows: The intersection point of data lineage and data lifecycle is a process. Data lifecycle describes processes that data undergoes from the moment of its creation to the moment of its archiving and/or destruction. Data lineage documents locations in which these processes take place.

One process of data lifecycle can be performed in multiple applications and databases along with data chains. Let's consider a data lifecycle process like "Transform data." You can perform data transformation in the ETL (Export Transform Load) tool, in a data warehouse, within an application. So, one data lifecycle process will be performed in different locations along data pathways.

From this, we can conclude that data lineage describes data lifecycle along different pathways.

Different data management, enterprise architecture, and information technology (IT) capabilities deal with data lifecycle and data lineage. Let us consider some of them in-depth in the following sub-chapter.

1.4   DATA LINEAGE AND THE CAPABILITIES OF DATA MANAGEMENT AND ENTERPRISE ARCHITECTURE

In this sub-chapter, we investigate the role of data lineage in different business capabilities. The relationships between data lineage and the following business capabilities are reviewed:
- Enterprise architecture, including enterprise data architecture and business architecture
- Data management capabilities

Data lineage, enterprise architecture, and enterprise data architecture

Enterprise architecture and enterprise data architecture are complex concepts. They combine the deliverables from different data management capabilities. The DAMA Dictionary provides extended definitions for both of these concepts.

Enterprise Architecture according to the DAMA Dictionary is "[...] an integrated collection of models and design approaches to align information, processes, projects, and technology with the goals of the enterprise. [...] Enterprise architecture may include:
a) an enterprise data model
b) related data integration architecture
c) a business process model
d) an application portfolio architecture
e) an application component architecture
f) an IT infrastructure technology architecture
g) an organizational business architecture, the enterprise information value chain analysis that identifies the linkage and alignment across these perspectives, and to enterprise goals"[27].

Now let's take a look at the definition of enterprise data architecture. Enterprise Data Architecture is a "master set of data models and design approaches identifying the strategic data requirements and the components of data management solutions, usually at enterprise level. Enterprise data typically consists of
a) an enterprise data model (contextual/subject area, conceptual or logical),
b) state transition diagrams depicting the lifecycle of major entities,

    c)   a robust information value chain analysis identifying data stakeholders' roles, organizations, processes and applications, and

    d)   data integration architecture identifying how data will flow between applications and data bases"[28].

These definitions are, however, a bit complicated. To simplify things, let us put them into a table format and compare them by the constituent components. Table 3 presents the results of this comparison.

Component	Data lineage and related concepts	Enterprise architecture	Enterprise data architecture
Business process			
Data model			
IT asset (system, application, etc.)			
Business functions and roles			
Data integration architecture		Synonym to data lineage	Synonym to data lineage
Information value chain			The concept comparable to data lineage
Business architecture			
IT infrastructure architecture			

Table 3: The comparison of the definitions of data lineage, enterprise architecture, and enterprise data architecture.

The observation of results leads us to the following conclusions:

1.   Enterprise architecture and enterprise data architecture are a set of components that are similar to data lineage constituent components.
Enterprise architecture and data lineage use the same components such as business processes, data models, and IT assets.
Enterprise data architecture and data lineage include data models, IT assets, and business functions and roles.

2.   Both architectures consider data lineage as a separate component. It is worth a reminder that data integration architecture and information value chains are concepts similar to data lineage. Furthermore, business processes, data models, and IT assets are components of data integration architecture and information value chains. So, the definitions of enterprise (data) architectures include duplicated components.

3.   The comparison has demonstrated an ambiguity in definitions of enterprise architecture, enterprise data architecture, and data lineage.

The relationship between data lineage and business architecture requires separate consideration.

Data lineage and business architecture

TOGAF® 9.2 gives the following definition of business architecture: "A representation of holistic, multi-dimensional business views of: capabilities, end-to-end value delivery, information, and organizational structure; and the relationships among these business views and strategies, products, policies, initiatives, and stakeholders"[29].

For the purpose of this book, we need to investigate the concept of a "business capability."

A business capability is "a particular ability that a business may possess or exchange to achieve a specific purpose"[30]. For example, data management is a business capability that enables a company to be in control of and get value from data.

A business capability at any level of abstraction can be realized by a process, role, information/data, and tool, as shown in Figure 8.

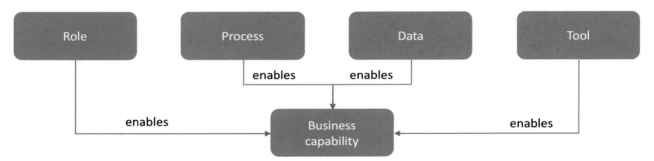

Figure 8: The model of a business capability.

These four dimensions enable a business capability. Let us define each of these dimensions.

Process

A process is a set of activities to achieve desired goals and/or produce outcomes. A process can be described at different levels of abstraction.

Role

A role is responsible for the delivery of business capabilities. Stakeholders, business units, partners may perform one or more roles.

Data

In "Business Capabilities," a publication by The Open Group, data is "information and knowledge required or consumed by the business capability [...]. There may also be information that the capability exchanges with other capabilities to support the execution of value streams"[31]. In the context of this book, I regard "data" as a "data element," which is a "single unit of data that in a certain context is considered indivisible"[32]. The lower level of a business capability, the lower level of data elements that should be used.

Tool

In the older version of The Open Group publication "Business capabilities,"[33] they specified that tools might include IT information technology systems and other tangible and intangible assets. In the new version of this paper[34], they renamed "Tools" into "Resources." The specification of a tool as an IT asset such as a system or application matches the need of data lineage. Therefore, in this book, I still use the "Tool" as the fourth dimension of a business capability.

If we compare the key components of data lineage and a business capability, we will see that they match, as shown in Table 4:

Data lineage component	Business capability component
Business process	Process
Business functions and roles	Role
IT assets, including system, application, data base	Tool
Data model at conceptual, logical, physical levels	Data
Business rules	Data

Table 4: The comparison of data lineage and business capability components.

This comparison leads to the following conclusion: Data lineage describes not only the data pathway but documents business capabilities along these pathways.

To better understand the concept of data lineage, it is important to realize its role in the different data management capabilities.

Data lineage and data management capabilities

I use the generally accepted model of the data management framework "The DAMA Wheel"[35] provided by the DAMA International. The Data Wheel defines eleven data management Knowledge Areas:

- Data Governance
- Data Architecture
- Data Modeling and Design
- Data Storage & Operations

- Data Security
- Data Integration & Interoperability
- Document & Content Management
- Reference & Master Data
- Data Warehousing and Business Intelligence
- Metadata Management
- Data Quality

In the course of this book, I use the term "data management capability" instead of Knowledge Area.

Data management capabilities can treat data lineage as output or input.

I have analyzed the DAMA-DMBOK2[36] and discovered the following usage of data lineage by different capabilities. I have also combined the analysis results in Figure 9.

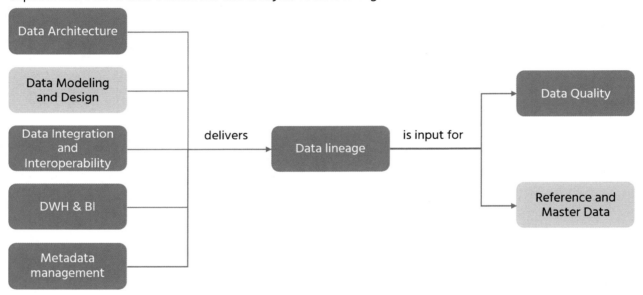

Figure 9: The role of data lineage in different data management capabilities.

Data lineage is the deliverable of such capabilities as Data Architecture[37], Data Integration and Interoperability[38], Data Warehousing and Business Intelligence (DWH&BI)[39], and Metadata[40].

A data model is an important component of data lineage. Data models are the deliverables of Data Modeling and Design capability. Therefore, I have added this capability to the list.

The DAMA-DMBOK2 has only taken Data Quality as a capability that requires data lineage as an input. Based on my experience, Reference and Master Data is also the area of data management in which data lineage is a highly demanded pre-requisite.

All capabilities that have been mentioned in the DAMA-DMBOK2 are colored blue in Figure 9. Those that I have added myself have a light-grey color.

The DAMA-DMBOK2 has also provided other guidance on data lineage. We elaborate on this topic in the next chapter.

1.5 DAMA-DMBOK2 RECOMMENDATIONS ON DATA LINEAGE DOCUMENTATION

As the result of my DAMA-DMBOK2 analysis, I have discovered two challenges with the guidance regarding data lineage:

- The DAMA-DMBOK2 provides guidance not only for data lineage but also for related concepts.
  I have already demonstrated in sub-chapter 1.1 that several other concepts are similar to data lineage. There are no clearly distinguished differences between them. These concepts are often used interchangeably. Data lineage and data flow are examples of the most common interchangeable terms. Therefore, the reader of the DAMA-DMBOK2 should take into account recommendations applicable not only for data lineage but also for synonymous concepts.
- The DAMA-DMBOK2 provides guidance in different chapters associated with various Knowledge Areas.
  Each chapter of the DAMA-DMBOK2 describes different Knowledge Areas. The information about data lineage spreads out through chapters. In combination with the first challenge, it creates difficulties for readers to get a complete picture of data lineage.

Below, you will find a summary of the DAMA-DMBOK2 recommendations regarding data lineage. I found these recommendations in chapters devoted to the following knowledge areas:

- Data Architecture
- Data Modeling and Design
- Data Integration and Operability

Recommendation 1: Data lineage can be documented at the conceptual, logical, and physical level.

In different chapters, the DAMA-DMBOK2 provides different recommendations regarding the level of documentation.

For example, in the Data Integration and Interoperability chapter, the DAMA-DMBOK2 speaks only about the high-level of data lineage: "[...] to document high-level data lineage: how the data under analysis is acquired or created by the organization, where it moves and is changed within the organization, and how the data is used by the organization for analytics, decision-making, or event triggering"[41].

In the chapter devoted to Data Architecture, the DAMA-DMBOK2 makes the following important statement: "Data flows can be documented at different levels of details: Subject Area, business entity, or even the attribute level"[42]. In other words, data flow can be documented at the conceptual or logical level of the data model.

In the section dedicated to Data Modeling and Design, the DAMA-DMBOK2 stresses the necessity to document data lineage at the physical level as well. "Often lineage takes the form of a source/target mapping, where one can capture the source system attributes and how they populate the target system attributes."[43] Data lineage is able to "trace the data modeling components from conceptual to logical to physical [...]"[44] levels.

Recommendation 2: Data lineage should include the documentation of business rules.

The DAMA-DMBOK2 makes a clear statement that data lineage "[...] ensures that business rules in the applications along data flow are consistent and traceable"[45].

In the chapter dedicated to Data Integration and Interoperability, the DAMA-DMBOK2 provides the recommendation to document business rules. "Detailed lineage can include the rules according to which data is changed, and the frequency of changes."[46]

Recommendation 3: Data lineage can be documented by using different tools.

The DAMA-DMBOK2 defines a data lineage tool as "[...] software that allows capture and maintenance of the source structures for each attribute on the data model"[47]. In my opinion, this definition is not complete. It omits the documentation of business rules that explain data transformations.

The DAMA-DMBOK2 indicates that "[...] Microsoft Excel® is a frequently used lineage tool"[48]. "Lineage is also frequently captured in a data modeling tool, Metadata repository, or data integration tool."[49]

Data lineage solutions and tools are discussed more in-depth in Chapter 11.

In the previous sections, we have discussed several different concepts, but we need to agree on the terminology used in this book before we go any further.

1.6 CONCEPTS USED IN THIS BOOK

To ease the reading and understanding of this book, let us agree on the following terms and definitions:

Data lifecycle is the set of processes that move and transform data from the moment of its creation to the moment of its archiving and/or destruction.

Data chain is the physical realization of data lifecycle.

Data lineage is the description of a data chain at different levels of abstractions.

In Chapters 3 and 4, we will enrich the definition of "data lineage." The relationship between these terms is shown in Figure 10.

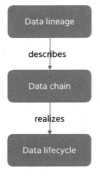

Figure 10: Relationship between data lineage, data chain, and data lifecycle..

By now, we have finalized the analysis of existing views and approaches to data lineage. Below you will find a short summary of Chapter 1.

SUMMARY OF CHAPTER 1

- Several concepts have definitions similar to data lineage. These are data value chain, data chain, data flow, integration architecture, and information value chain.
- These concepts are often considered synonymous with data lineage. They are used interchangeably.
- Data lineage includes the following components:
  - Business process
  - Business function and role involved in business process
  - IT asset such as a system, an application, a database, a network
  - Data model at the conceptual, logical, and physical level
  - Business rule
- The concept of data lineage and data lifecycle interrelate with each other. Data lineage describes data lifecycle along different data chains.
- Data lineage, enterprise architecture, and enterprise data architecture have commonalities. They share similar constituent components.
- Enterprise architecture and enterprise data architecture consider data lineage as one of the constituent components.
- Data lineage and business capability concepts comprise identical components. Data lineage describes not only a data pathway. It also documents business capabilities along data chains.
- Several data management capabilities have relationships to data lineage:
  - Data architecture, data modeling and design, data integration and interoperability, data warehouse and business intelligence, metadata management deliver data lineage.
  - Data quality and reference and master data require data lineage as an input for their processes.
- DAMA-DMBOK2 provides several recommendations regarding data lineage:
  - Data lineage can be documented at the conceptual, logical, and physical level.
  - Data lineage should include the documentation of business rules.
  - Data lineage can be documented by using different tools.
- In this book, we use three interrelated concepts: data lifecycle, data chain, and data lineage.

2 | KEY BUSINESS DRIVERS TO DOCUMENT DATA LINEAGE

A company should have strong drivers to start the data management, particularly data lineage, initiative. These initiatives may bring many challenges associated with the resources required. Such drivers usually play the roles of "carrot and stick" simultaneously. So, the company should find a balance between the needs of implementing data lineage and the benefits that such an implementation could deliver.

In Chapter 2, we will:

- Analyze different types of business drivers for a data lineage initiative
- Demonstrate the benefits these drivers bring to a company

After reading this chapter, you will be able to:

- Define groups of data lineage business drivers that are relevant to your company
- Translate legislative requirements into a data lineage model

There are at least four key types of business drivers for data lineage that we will study one by one:

- Compliance with legislative requirements
- Business change
- Data management initiatives
- Audit requirements

2.1 COMPLIANCE WITH LEGISLATIVE REQUIREMENTS

Multiple legislative documents put requirements that can be met by knowing data lineage. The most well-known legislative acts are the Basel Committee on Banking Supervision's standard number 239 "Principles for effective risk data aggregation and risk reporting" (BCBS 239 or PERDARR)[1], the EU General Data Protection Regulation (GDPR)[2], European Central Bank (ECB) Guide to internal models[3] issued by ECB Banking Supervision, IFRS17 Insurance Contracts[4], and many others. Legislative requirements vary per industry. For example, BCBS 239 is only applicable for financial institutions, while GDPR is industry-agnostic.

The strangest thing is that, so far, I have not seen the term "data lineage" being literally mentioned in any regulatory documents.

So, how do data management professionals recognize that data lineage is a means to meet legislative requirements? They investigate legislative requirements and translate them into the data management language, in particular, into a data lineage model.

Below you will find an example of such a translation of two legislative documents mentioned above: BCBS 239 and GDPR. To map legislative requirements, I use the model of data lineage discussed in sub-chapter 1.2 (Figure 7). The results of such a mapping can be seen in Figure 11.

So far, we have identified the following components when mapping requirements to a particular data lineage component:

- Business processes
- Business functions and roles involved in business processes
- IT assets such as a system, an application, a database, a network
- Data models at the conceptual, logical, and physical level
- Business rules and their technical implementation in the form of ETL (Extract, Transform, Load) processes

Business process and roles

BCBS 239 specifies that "Supervisors expect banks to document and explain all of their risk data aggregation processes whether automated or manual (judgement based or otherwise)"[5]. This requirement matches the component "business process" specified as being a part of data lineage.

BCBS 239 stresses the necessity to record business metadata, i.e., in the form of "ownership of risk data and information for both the Business and IT function"[6]. In the context of the data lineage model, you map it to business roles.

IT assets

IT assets include IT systems, applications, databases, networks, ETL tools, etc.

The second principle of BCBS 239, "Data architecture and IT infrastructure," states that "a bank should design, build and maintain data architecture and IT infrastructure which fully supports its risk data aggregation capabilities and risk reporting practices [...]"[7].

GDPR requires that a company should "implement appropriate technical and organizational measures to ensure and to be able to demonstrate that processing is performed in accordance with this Regulation"[8]. There are several articles in GDPR, i.e., 24, 25, 32, that focus on the necessity of the appropriate technical and organizational measures to ensure proper processing of personal data.

Even if there is no direct requirement to document data flow through applications, every data management professional still "translates" these requirements as such.

Now we can move to the following data lineage element: data models.

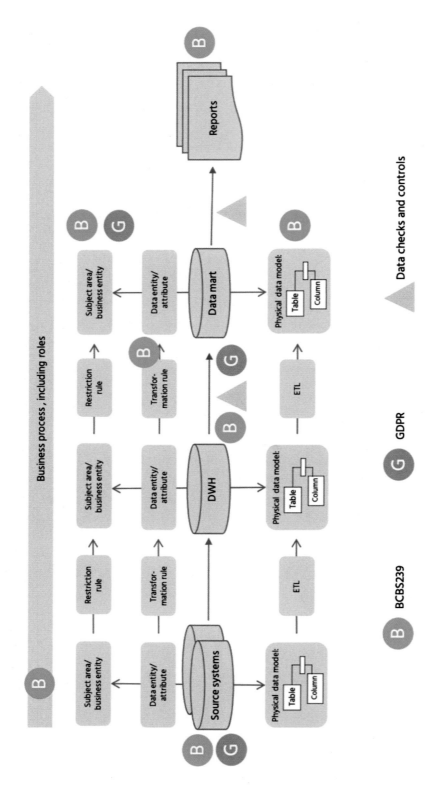

Figure 11: The mapping of legislative requirements to the data lineage model.

Data model at the conceptual, logical, and physical levels

We usually recognize data models at three levels of abstraction: conceptual, logical, and physical. Let us consider requirements level by level.

Conceptual level

BCBS 239 draws the attention of organizations to a business dictionary, which is "the concepts used in a report such that data is defined consistently across the organization"[9]. In this context, a business dictionary is a set of business terms. From the data lineage perspective, a business dictionary corresponds to the conceptual level of data models.

Logical level

BCBS 239 points out the requirement to maintain "inventory and classification of risk data items"[10] that can be recognized as data elements at the logical level of data models. In addition to that, "automated and manual edit and reasonableness checks, including an inventory of the validation rules that are applied to quantitative information"[11] are also required. "The inventory should include explanations of the conventions used to describe any mathematical or logical relationships that should be verified through these validations or checks."[12] In the language of data management, we interpret it as a repository of business rules.

BCBS 239 recommends documenting "integrated data taxonomies and architecture [...], which includes information on the characteristics of the data (metadata) as well as use of single identifiers and / or unified naming conventions for data including legal entities, counterparties, customers and accounts"[13]. I also recognize this as a requirement for the documentation at the logical level.

Among other requirements for recording personal information, GDPR demands the documentation of "[...] c) a description of the categories of data subjects and of the categories of personal data [...]"[14]. Such categories might be translated as data taxonomies and relate to logical data models.

Physical level

GDPR lists the rights of the data subject. Some examples of them are:
- "Right to obtain from the controller the erasure of personal data concerning him or her"[15]
- "Right to obtain from the controller restriction of processing"[16]
- "The right to receive the personal data [...] in a structured, commonly used and machine-readable format and [...] the right to transmit those data to another controller"[17]

To ensure the exercise of these rights, a company needs to know how data flows through applications at the physical level.

Besides requirements to the initially identified components of data lineage, both legislative documents, BCBS 239 and GDPR, stress the necessity to control the quality of data.

Data quality controls

BCBS 239 is rather direct about the necessity to "measure and monitor accuracy of data"[18]. It stresses that "Banks must produce aggregated risk data that is complete and measure and monitor the completeness of their risk data"[19] and "controls surrounding risk data should be as robust as those applicable to accounting data"[20]. "Integrated procedures for identifying, reporting and explaining data errors or weaknesses in data integrity via exceptions reports"[21] are to be in place.

GDPR focuses on "technical and organizational measures to ensure a level of security appropriate to the risk"[22] related to the processing of personal data.

The mapping of data quality requirements is the last example of our mapping between legislative requirements and the data lineage model.

You can apply this approach to map requirements to a data lineage model for other legislative documents and data management concepts.

Legislative requirements are the key drivers for many companies in the commencement of data lineage initiatives. The second group of business reasons to document data lineage is business changes. These reasons may even be more vital for the performance of daily tasks of lots of business and IT professionals.

2.2   BUSINESS CHANGES

A company often deals with different types of business changes; changes in information needs and requirements, changes in application landscape, organizational changes are examples. Impact and root-cause analysis is a tool required to perform these changes. Documented data lineage can be of great help to perform such analysis. Let us take a look at each type of analysis that is graphically represented in Figure 12.

Impact analysis

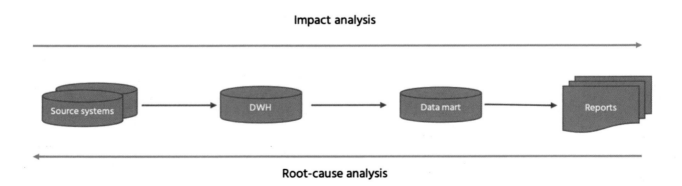

Root-cause analysis

Figure 12: The essence of impact and root-cause analysis.

Impact analysis

Impact analysis allows tracking down the changes in data chains from their beginning to their end. Changes in databases require the performance of impact analysis. Such changes affect the databases subsequent in the data chain and final reports. Data lineage helps to foresee the necessary changes along the whole data chain.

Root-cause analysis

New information requirements need the performance of the root-cause analysis. Nowadays, it happens very often. Examples are new regulatory and management information requirements.

Root-cause analysis helps to track data origins back from the point of data usage. Such an analysis allows for:
- Specifying data needs
- Assessing the availability of required data
- Evaluating potential data sources

Data lineage eases the performance of the root-cause analysis.

The next group of drivers is various data management initiatives.

2.3   DATA MANAGEMENT INITIATIVES

Data quality, reference and master data management, data warehouse and business intelligence (DWH & BI), and data integration are key data management capabilities that require data lineage as an input to perform their activities. The implementation of these capabilities is on the agenda of a lot of companies around the globe.

Let us briefly analyze the usage of data lineage for these capabilities.

Data quality

There are two key activities in data quality that can hardly be performed without data lineage.

The first type of activity is the resolution of data quality issues. Usually, issues with information are discovered at the end of the data and information chain. In most cases, the inconsistencies in reports highlight   issues. To find the causes of the issues, a thorough and detailed backward analysis of data transformation is required.

The second type of activity focuses on the prevention of issues with data. It is achieved by gathering data and information quality requirements and building data checks and controls along the data and information chain.

Reference and master data

Reference and master data are the most shared and used within the organization. To manage this data rightly, you need to coordinate and align data sources. Data lineage allows tracing sources of reference and master data. It also assists in the optimization of data chains that use this data.

DWH &BI, data integration

From the DWH and BI perspective, optimized data integration is key to effective use of IT resources. Documented data lineage and business rules assist in making information about data transformation transparent.

The last group of business drivers for data lineage is audit requirements.

2.4   TRANSPARENCY AND AUDIT REQUIREMENTS

Finance and risk professionals spend a tremendous amount of time meeting audit requirements. These requirements focus on the explanation of reports' figures. This task requires knowledge about data transformations along data chains. Properly documented data lineage assists in providing data traceability and transparency.

By now, we have identified the key groups of business drivers that motivate companies to initiate a data lineage initiative. To start such an initiative, a company should have a model of data lineage that corresponds to the business drivers.

Our next step is the alignment of the metamodel of data lineage.

SUMMARY OF CHAPTER 2

- A company should have strong business drivers to perform data lineage initiatives. Such an initiative is time and resource-intensive.
- There are four key types of business drivers that require the implementation of data lineage:
    - Compliance with legislative requirements
    - Business changes
    - Data management initiatives
    - Audit requirements
- The mapping of legislative requirements to the data lineage model is a way to recognize legislative requirements for data lineage.
- Legislative requirements for data lineage affect all data lineage components such as:
    - Business processes and roles
    - IT assets such as a system, an application, a database, a network
    - Data models at the conceptual, logical, and physical level
    - Business rules
- Data quality controls are also part of these requirements.
- Business changes require the performance of impact and root-cause analysis. Data lineage is a means to perform these types of analyses.
- Different data management capabilities require documented data lineage. Data quality, reference and master data management, data warehouse and business intelligence (DWH & BI) implementation are examples of these capabilities.
- Data lineage assists in meeting transparency and auditability requirements.

3 THE CONCEPT OF A METAMODEL

A metamodel of data lineage serves two purposes. It should first assist in specifying the needs and requirements for data lineage. It should then optimize its implementation.

The quote "A model should be as simple as it can be but no simpler"[1] by Albert Einstein expresses my attempt to build the data lineage metamodel. It should be generic enough to cover different needs. It should also be simple enough for implementation.

In Chapter 3, we will:

- Align the terminology required to design the metamodel of data lineage
- Investigate the concept of metamodel and metadata
- Agree on the structure of the data lineage metamodel

After reading this chapter, you will be able to:

- Identify the definitions of data, information, metadata that meets your company practices
- Comprehend the way to design the metamodel of data lineage

To succeed in our goals, we need to be on the same page regarding terminology.

Let us start with the basic concepts of data and information.

3.1 THE CONCEPTS OF DATA AND INFORMATION

I once received a good lesson from one of my clients. We have discussed the scope of the data management framework already for several weeks. At some point, one of the top managers asked me a simple question: "What does 'data' mean. What are we talking about?" Then, it took us several weeks to agree on the definitions of "data" and "information" that suited the company's business practices.

So, to begin, let us align our understanding of these two basic concepts.

I have used industry guides and ISO standards to find out definitions.

According to the DAMA Dictionary, data is "facts represented as text, numbers, graphics, images, sound, or video"[2]. The DAMA Dictionary also indicates that data is "individual facts that are out of context, and have no meaning by themselves"[3]. ISO/IEC Standard No. 11179-1:2015. "Information technology — Metadata registries (MDR) — Part 1: Framework." specifies data as "reinterpretable representation of information in a formalized manner suitable for communication, interpretation or processing"[4]. TOGAF® 9.2 by The Open Group defines information as "Any communication or representation of facts, data, or opinions, in any medium or form, including textual, numerical, graphic, cartographic, narrative, or audio-visual forms"[5]. In the Merriam-Webster Dictionary, you will find that data is "information in digital form that can be transmitted or processed"[6].

As you can see, there are a lot of confusing and mismatched definitions. I combined all these definitions in the form of a concept map shown in Figure 13.

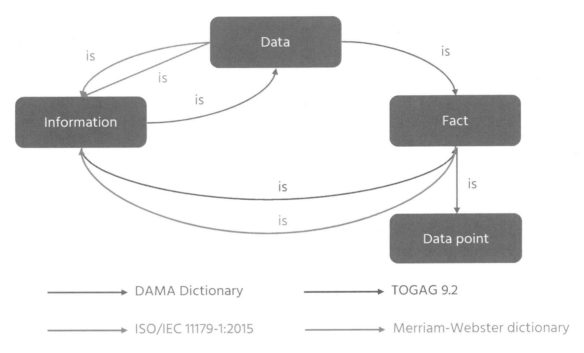

Figure 13: The concept map of "data" and "information" definitions.

At first glance, you can understand that there is no clear and aligned definition of data and information in this model, even in the leading guides and standards applicable in the same field of expertise.

If you want to become confused even more with definitions, you should look at the definitions of a "fact." In the DAMA Dictionary, it is a "verifiable true data point"[7]. By the way, the DAMA Dictionary does not provide any definition for a "data point." So without having it, the definition of the "fact" has no value. The Merriam-Webster Dictionary defines the "fact" as "a piece of information presented as having objective reality"[8]. After adding these two additional definitions, we have ended in the closed loop, as shown in Figure 13.

This challenge with the definitions of "data" and "information" evoked in my memory the famous "chicken and the egg" dilemma. While writing this book, I decided to dig into the concept of data and information deeper and use clear and logical definitions. Unsurprisingly, I have found a substantial number of definitions for data and information that have been proposed in widely different contexts. In most cases, these definitions have little applicability beyond the specified context.

For this book, I decided to apply the approach outlined in the "data-information-knowledge-wisdom" hierarchy by Russell L. Ackoff [9], as shown in Figure 14.

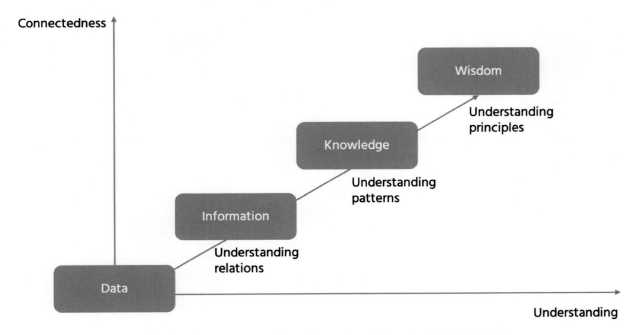

Figure 14: The "data-information-knowledge-wisdom" hierarchy by Russell L. Ackoff.

"Data" is a basic concept. When you understand relationships between data elements, you proceed with "information". By discovering patterns in "information", you gain "knowledge". When you understand principles, hidden in knowledge, you reach "wisdom."

In the context of data lineage, we are interested in definitions for "data", "information" and related terms. For this book, I apply the following definitions:

Data is the physical or electronic representation of signals "in a manner suitable for communication, interpretation, or processing by human beings or by automatic means"[10].

Some examples of data representations are files, text, numbers, graphics, sound, video, and audio records.

"**Signal** is something that shows that something else exists or might happen or exists in the future."[11]

"**Data element** is the smallest identifiable unit of data within a certain context for which the definition, identification, permissible values and other information is specified by means of a set of attributes."[12]

Data instance is a particular value of a data element valid at a point in time.

Context is a set of conditions that identifies boundaries for a particular physical object, concept, process, phenomenon, etc.

Information is data in a context that permits the explanation of its meaning and specification of relational connections.

Metadata is data that defines and describes other data in a particular context.

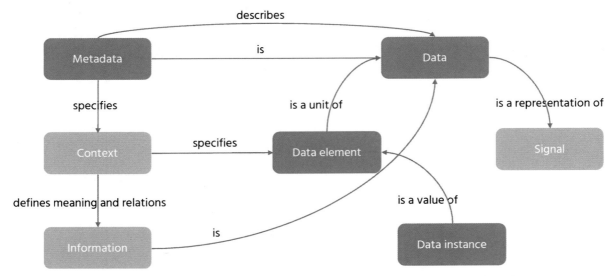

Figure 15: Relationships between terms of data, information, metadata, data element, and data instance.

The concept map in Figure 15 demonstrates the relationships between these terms.

Data is a representation of signals. A data element is a unit of data in a particular context. A data instance is a value of a data element at a specific point in time. Metadata is data that in a particular context can describe another data. Data in a specific content turns to be information. Content identifies the meaning and relations of data.

The terms "data," "metadata," "data element," and "data instance," marked in dark blue in Figure 15, are used intensively further in this book.

3.2   DATA LINEAGE IN THE METADATA CONTEXT

As we have just defined, metadata is data. This fact means that the same data depending on the context, can either be data or metadata. Remember that specific data is not always metadata. To understand the role metadata plays in the data lineage concept, we need to dive deeper into the metadata classification.

Through different sources, I discovered totally different metadata classifications. Even in DAMA publications, they have drastically changed the approach in classifying metadata.

The DAMA Dictionary[13] described eight metadata categories. The DAMA-DMBOK2 identifies categories and classifies metadata as the following:

- Business metadata
  "Business metadata focuses largely on the content and condition of the data and includes details related to data governance."[14]

- Technical metadata
  "Technical Metadata provides information about technical details of data, the systems that store data, and the processes that move it within and between systems."[15]
- Operational metadata
  "Operational Metadata describes details of the processing and accessing of data."[16]

One of the key challenges with metadata classification is to understand the underlying principles for metadata categories. The DAMA-DMBOK2 classification is based on the viewpoints of different data stakeholders involved in data lifecycle processes. However, such an assumption does not fully explain the distinction between different metadata types described in the DAMA-DMBOK2.

Let us move forward and check what the DAMA-DMBOK2 says about data lineage in the metadata context. Unfortunately, there is no clear view of it. First, "Data provenance and data lineage"[17] is classified as business metadata. Then, I have found "Data lineage documentation, including upstream and downstream change impact information"[18] in the list of technical metadata. So, data lineage seems to be business and technical metadata at the same time. Such a categorization initially seems ambiguous. It can be explained, however. Data lineage can be documented at different levels of data models. The documentation of data lineage at the conceptual and logical data model level can be considered as being business data lineage. Business stakeholders will have needs in business data lineage. The documentation of data lineage at the physical level may belong to technical metadata and be a concern of technical staff.

I would like to draw your attention to one challenge. This challenge is the relationship between metadata and data lineage concepts. Data lineage by itself is metadata. To describe and document data lineage, other metadata should be used. It results in a complex metamodel of data lineage. I made a comparison between data lineage components we discussed in sub-chapter 1.2 and metadata related to data lineage described in the DAMA-DMBOK2[19]. The results I put in Table 5.

In the first column, you find the key components of data lineage identified in sub-chapter 1.2. The second column contains metadata components retrieved from the DAMA-DMBOK2. In columns 3,4,5 you find the DAMA-DMBOK2 classification of specific metadata components and metadata that describe these components.

The analysis confirms that data lineage as a metadata object must be described by other metadata objects. These metadata objects form a hierarchical structure with multiple layers. To illustrate this structure, in the consequent sub-chapters, we discuss the metamodel of data lineage.

Data lineage component	Metadata from DAMA-DMBOK2	Business	Technical	Operational
Data lineage as the whole object	Data provenance and lineage			
	Data lineage, including upstream and downstream change impact information		documentation	
Business process				
Business functions and roles				
Systems and applications	Programs and applications		names and descriptions	
	Database		object properties	
Data model	Data set	definition and description		
	Data model:			
	-conceptual			
	-logical			
	-physical		table names, keys, indexes	
	Vertical linkage between models and physical assets			
	Table	definition and description	physical name	
	Column	definition and description	physical name, properties	
	File format schema		definition	
	Business rule			
	Transformation rule			
Business (transformation rule)	Calculation			
	Derivation			
	ETL job		details	logs of execution for batch programs
Data quality rules	Data quality	rules and measurement results		

Table 5: The comparison between components of data lineage and metadata types.

3.3 THE CONCEPT OF A METAMODEL

To build the metamodel of data lineage, we should agree with the definition of a metamodel.

Different industry guides and standards take different viewpoints on the concept of a metamodel. Definitions they provide indicate these differences.

The DAMA Dictionary provides the following definition of a metamodel: "[...] a model that specifies one or more other models"[20]. In the context of TOGAF® 9.2 standard by The Open Group, a metamodel is "a model that describes how and with what the architecture will be described in a structured way"[21].

The ISO standard, ISO/IEC 11179 "Information Technology – Metadata registries (MDR) – Part 1: Framework", also delivers a definition of a metamodel. The definition has evolved over time. The ISO/IEC 11179:2004 specified metamodels as "Models that describe metadata"[22]. The new version, ISO/IEC 11179-1:2015 defines a metamodel as a "data model that specifies one or more other models, such as data models, process models, ontologies, etc."[23].

It is rather challenging to read all these definitions, is not it? To make it understandable, let us put all these definitions in the form of a concept map, as shown in Figure 16.

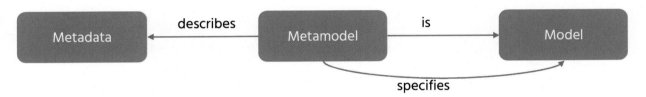

Figure 16: The concept map of the term "metamodel".

I have pulled out several statements from the concept map and definitions:
- Metamodel is a model
- Metamodel describes metadata
- Metamodel specifies other models

I have summarized my understanding into the following definitions:

Model is an abstract representation of something, such as a physical object, process, phenomenon, etc.

Metamodel is a model that describes the metadata needed to specify other models.

Now it is time to summarize all investigations and create a metamodel of data lineage.

SUMMARY OF CHAPTER 3

- A metamodel of data lineage serves two purposes:
    - Specify data lineage needs and requirements
    - Scope and optimize the implementation of data lineage
- The terms "data" and "information" have different definitions depending on the context.
- In this book, we use the following terminology:
    - Data is the physical or electronic representation of signals "in a manner suitable for communication, interpretation, or processing by human beings or by automatic means"[24].
    - Information is data in a context that permit the explanation of its meaning and specification of relational connections.
    - Metadata is data that in a particular context defines and describes other data.
- Metadata has different classifications. In this book, we use the classification proposed by the DAMA-DMBOK2.
- Metadata can be split into the following categories:
    - Business
    - Technical
    - Operational
- According to the DAMA-DMBOK2, data lineage is metadata and belongs to business and technical metadata.
- Model is an abstract representation of something such as a physical object, process, phenomenon, etc.
- Metamodel is a model that describes metadata needed to specify other models.

4 | THE METAMODEL OF DATA LINEAGE

By now, we have already investigated several topics related to the metamodel of data lineage. Based on the analysis of industry guides, legislative documents, and different data management concepts, we have made the following conclusions:

- The concepts of data lineage, data chain, and data lifecycle relate to each other. Data lifecycle is a set of processes that move and transform data from the moment of its creation to the moment of its archiving and/or destruction. Data chain is the physical realization of a data lifecycle. Data lineage documents data chains.
- Data lineage can be documented at four levels of abstraction:
  - Business layer
  - Data model at different levels of abstraction:
    - Conceptual level
    - Logical level
    - Physical level

Throughout this book, I will use "level" of abstraction and "layer" of abstraction interchangeably.

- The key components of data lineage are:
  - Business processes and roles
  - IT assets such as a system, an application, a database, a network
  - Data models at the conceptual, logical, and physical level
  - Business rules and their technical implementation in the form of ETL (Extract, Transform, Load) processes
- Data lineage documents business capabilities along data chains.

Now we need to assemble all of these findings together.

In Chapter 4, we will:

- Finalize the design of the metamodel of data lineage
- Provide the list of metadata components, metadata elements, and relationships for each level of abstraction
- Design the concept map and logical model of the data lineage metamodel

After reading this chapter, you will be able to:

- Design the metamodel of data lineage that suits your company's requirements
- Identify key data lineage components and metadata elements to be documented

We discuss in-depth key metadata components, objects, and elements for each of the data lineage layers.

4.1   THE STRUCTURE OF THE DATA LINEAGE METAMODEL

In sub-chapter 3.3, we provided definitions of "model" and "metamodel." Now we can design the corresponding definitions for data lineage.

Data lineage is a model that describes a data chain at different levels of abstraction.

The metamodel of data lineage is a metamodel that describes metadata needed to document the data lineage model.

The proposed structure of the data lineage metamodel can be seen in Figure 17. The data lineage metamodel includes one or more data lineage layers. Business, conceptual, logical, and physical layers are examples. One or more components belong to a particular layer. For example, data lineage at the logical level is described by data entities, attributes, business rules, and relationships between them. Metadata elements describe both data lineage layers and components. For example, a business process should have such metadata as an identification number (ID), name, owner, etc.

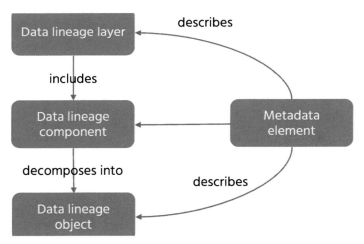

Figure 17: Structure the data lineage metamodel.

Below we will discuss each layer, corresponding components, and metadata elements in-depth.

4.2   BUSINESS LAYER

Data lineage at the business layer serves the needs of business stakeholders. It includes and maps the following components:

- Business capability
- Process
- Business role
- Business subject area

- IT assets

I hope you realize that the last four components represent dimensions that enable a business capability: process, role, business subject area (data), IT assets (tool).

The graphical representation of the model can be seen in Figure 18.

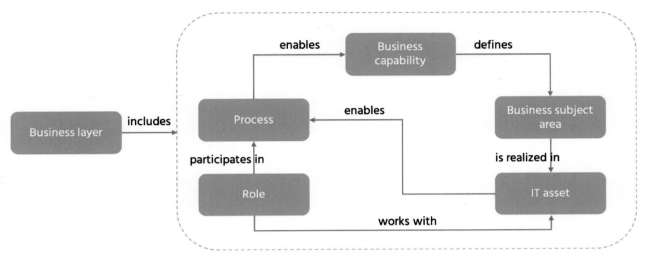

Figure 18: The concept map of the business layer.

Data lineage at the business layer includes a set of components; the leading one is the business capability. The process enables one or more business capabilities. Roles and IT assets enable the performance of processes. Roles work with IT assets. The business capability defines the business subject area.

4.2.1 BUSINESS CAPABILITY

Each company deals with data that corresponds to its business model. According to TOGAF® 9.2, a business model is "a model describing the rationale for how an enterprise creates, delivers, and captures value"[1]. Business architecture describes a business model using business capabilities and business processes.

"Business Capabilities"[2], by The Open Group, presents the concept of business capability:

"A business capability is a particular ability or capacity that a business may possess or exchange to achieve a specific purpose or outcome."[3]

Two key metadata elements describe a business capability:

- The level of the business capability
- Enabling dimensions

Let us investigate each of these metadata elements.

The level of a business capability

According to "Business Capabilities"[4], there are three categories of business capability:

- Strategic
  Strategic capability is a business capability that "[...]relates to the strategy- and direction setting"[5] of a company.
  Examples of strategic capabilities are business planning, policy management, etc.
- Core
  Core capability is a business capability representing "[...] the core, customer-facing elements of the business"[6].
  Customer and product management are examples of the core business capabilities.
- Supporting
  Supporting capability is a business capability that is "[...] essential for the business to function [...]"[7].
  Financial management and data management represent supporting business capabilities.

Business capabilities can be decomposed into lower levels to communicate more details.

Now let us take a look at the second metadata element: the enabling dimension.

Enabling dimension

Process, role, tool, and data enable a business capability. The definitions of these dimensions have already been discussed in sub-chapter 1.4.

The concept map of a business capability shown in Figure 19 demonstrates two metadata elements discussed above: the level of business capability and the enabling dimension.

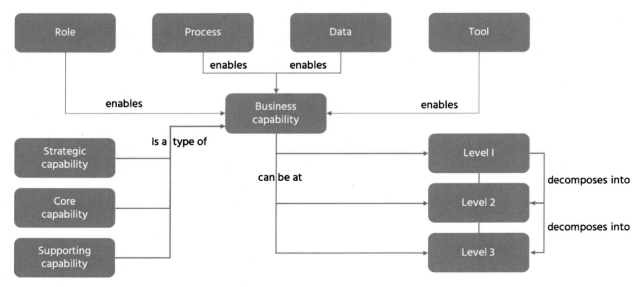

Figure 19: The concept map of a "business capability" component.

Next to these two metadata elements, a company should also document other metadata elements, such as an identification number and the name of a business capability.

The name of a business capability is typically a compound noun. The reason for this is because a business capability describes what a business does. It does not try to explain how, why, and where the business needs this capability.

4.2.2 PROCESS

A process is a set of activities to achieve desired goals and/or produce outcomes. A process of a higher level can be decomposed into processes of lower levels. So, a set of processes form a hierarchical structure. Processes can also be linked horizontally, forming a chain of processes. Processes can be of different types depending on the goal of classification.

At the lower level of abstraction, a process can be broken down into activities. Within one process, activities should be linked horizontally to form a logical order. All of these relationships can be seen in Figure 20.

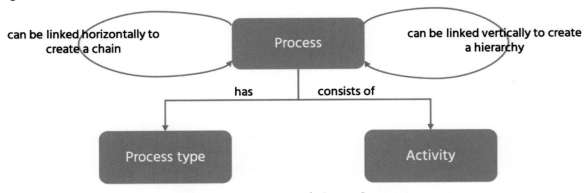

Figure 20: The concept map of a "process" component.

Business process management is a business capability that specifies requirements regarding documentation of processes.

Process and activity are both metadata components. Metadata elements describe these components. For the process, you can document business, technical, and operational metadata. Below, you will find several examples:

Business metadata elements

- ID and name
  Each company should maintain the catalog of existing processes. Therefore, the process and/or activity should have an ID and a name.
- Business process type
  Several options to classify processes exist. Such a classification depends on the company's needs and is business-specific. For example, a process can be classified by the method of

its performance: automated, manual, or semi-automated. In the context of data lineage, it means a process may be performed either by people or by an IT system.

- Business process owner
  This metadata element is highly recommended for documentation. Companies pay much attention to their assets and ownership.
- Business process status
  The status specifies a stage in process development and documentation. The values of this element are company-specific. "Designed" and "implemented" are examples of values. The choice depends on the purpose and the context of the classification.

Technical metadata elements

Technical metadata elements should be used for IT system processes. The example there of is an ETL process name and description.

Operational metadata elements

Operational metadata elements may describe both business and IT system process:

- Time required to perform a process and/or activity
- Logs of jobs performance
- Error logs

4.2.3 ROLE

The role in the data lineage context can be assigned to different categories of objects. An organization, a particular person, and an IT system/application are examples. This definition specifies the key business metadata elements that may be applied to the role:

Business metadata elements:

- ID and name
  The name depends on the object to which the role is assigned.
- Role object
  A business role can be assigned to an organization, person, or IT system/application. The specification of roles will be dependent on the business context. Let us take the data management context as an example. An organization can get a role of a data supplier or data consumer. A person may get a functional role of a data manager or data analyst. To a system, the role of a data consumer or producer may be assigned.

The remaining business data elements depend on the context in which a role is specified.

4.2.4 BUSINESS SUBJECT AREA (DATA)

A business subject area represents data that is required by a business capability. For example, the customer management capability deals with customer data. The **business subject area** is a data element that describes data at the highest level of abstraction.

We will discuss the business subject area in detail in sub-chapter 4.3.

4.2.5 IT ASSET (TOOL)

The next metadata object is an IT asset. For data lineage purposes, "IT asset" means an IT system, application, database, and ETL tool.

Frequently, the terms "system" and "application" are used interchangeably. However, these terms have different definitions. In this book, I use the following definitions:

"**System** is a combination of interacting elements organized to achieve one or more stated purposes."[8]

Information Technology (IT) system is a system composed from "[...] one or more computers, associated software, databases, peripherals, terminals, human operations, physical processes, information transfer means, that form an autonomous whole, capable of performing information processing and/or information transfer"[9].

IT Application is software that supports one or more related business capabilities.

Database is the "collection of interrelated data stored together in one or more computerized files"[10].

The relationships between the above-listed terms can be found in Figure 21.

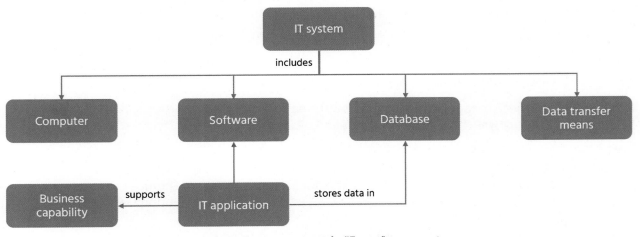

Figure 21: The concept map of a "IT asset" component.

An IT system, application, databases, and data transfer means should be considered as the components of the data lineage metamodel. The following business and technical metadata elements serve as examples to describe these components of data lineage at the business layer:

Business metadata elements

- ID, name, and description of an IT asset
- IT asset owner

Technical metadata elements

- ID, name, and description of an application and/or database
- Database type
- ETL type
- Database schema

By now, we have described the key components of data lineage at the business layer. We can move on to the next layers: conceptual, logical, and physical. All of these layers correspond to data models at different levels of abstraction. Before diving into details, I discuss some challenges associated with the structure of data models in the next sub-chapter.

4.3   CHALLENGES ASSOCIATED WITH DATA MODELS

In the previous chapters, we have provided the definitions of two terms: "data" and "model".

Data is the physical or electronic representation of signals "in a manner suitable for communication, interpretation, or processing by human beings or by automatic means"[11].

Model is an abstract representation of something such as a physical object, process, phenomenon, etc.

Data model is a model that represents data at different levels of abstraction.

There are several challenges associated with data models. We take a deeper look at some of these challenges:

Challenge 1. There are different approaches to structure a data model.

The classical approach recognizes data models at three levels of abstraction: conceptual, logical, and physical. The DAMA-DMBOK2[12] provides a detailed description of such an approach.

Two other approaches are also worth mentioning:

- The method by Thomas Frisendal, a recognized consultant in the area of data modeling
  In one of his books, "Graph data modeling for NoSQL and SQL"[13], Thomas Frisendal recommends three levels of models: Business Concept Model, Solution Data Model, Physical Data Model.
- The "Domain-driven design"[14] approach initially developed by Eric Evans
  This approach offers to split a business into different sub-domains at different levels of abstraction

There is no "good" or "bad" approach. The use of each of these methods is justified in certain conditions. It depends on the purpose of usage and the information systems architecture. Now let us take a look at the second challenge.

Challenge 2. Diverse data models have different purposes of usage.

Data models can be used for different purposes. Data description, solution design are examples. For the purpose of data description, data models are usually system-agnostic. For the purpose of solution design, data is system-dependent. Sometimes, the same model can serve two purposes.

You can find a brief analysis of the usage of data models in Table 6 below.

Approach to data models	The abstraction level of a data model	Purpose of usage	
		System-agnostic	System-dependent
Classical	Conceptual		
	Logical		
	Physical		
The method of Thomas Frisendal	Business Concept Model		
	Solution Data Model		
	Physical data model		
Domain-driven design			

Table 6: The comparison of the purpose of usage of different data models.

For example, we can see that the logical data model can be either system-agnostic or system-dependent. Physical data models are always system-dependent and serve the purpose of solution design.

Let us move to the third challenge with data models.

Challenge 3. Different data modeling schemes require specific diagramming notations.

The DAMA-DMBOK2[15] mentions six common schemes with diagramming notations, specific for each scheme. The usage of these schemes depends on the choice of databases. A company with numerous types of databases can be forced to apply different methods to document data models. In its turn, it may complicate the documentation of data lineage. Data lineage demonstrates the movement of data elements between different data models. If data models have been created using different notations, data lineage documentation becomes a challenging exercise. The fourth challenge focuses on the relationship between business and data models.

Challenge 4. The method to link business models and data models is not clearly defined.

The existing data modeling approaches do not provide clear rules on linking business models with data models.

In Chapter 12, I provide recommendations on mapping business capabilities and data models.

The fifth challenge relates to a logical level of a data model.

Challenge 5. One logical model can be realized in multiple software applications.

Logical data models are being considered independent from the software. It means that a logical model can have multiple physical implementations. Data lineage is a movement of data at different levels of data models. For example, a company decides to document data lineage at both logical and physical levels. The same logical model can be implemented by different software applications in different locations across the company. Furthermore, one data element or attribute of the logical data model can be transformed across different physical locations and different systems. In such a situation, a company faces two challenges with the documentation of data lineage:

- Maintenance of the vertical linkage between logical and physical data models
- Documentation of the horizontal lineage with one logical model and multiple underlying physical data models

The dependency between database schemes and data modeling creates a doubt about the above-mentioned independency of the logical model from software.

We have discussed five challenges with data models that I came across in my practice. You may add some others to this list.

Now, we move on with the definition of data lineage components at different levels of data models.

In this book, I use the classical names for data model layers:

- Conceptual
- Logical
- Physical

We continue with the conceptual layer.

4.4 CONCEPTUAL LAYER

To derive the key metadata components at the conceptual layer, we must first investigate two different approaches:

- Classical conceptual model
- Semantic model

Let's examine them in detail one by one.

4.4.1 CLASSICAL CONCEPTUAL MODEL

DAMA-DMBOK publications summarize the essence of the conceptual data model.

Interestingly enough, the DAMA-DMBOK1 and the DAMA-DMBOK2 have different approaches to specify a conceptual model.

In the first edition, the DAMA-DMBOK1[16] states that an organization should first define the Subject Area Model (Figure 22). The model includes 12-20 business subjects. Each business subject is decomposed into a set of business entities. The conceptual view contains 15-300 business entities and relationships between them.

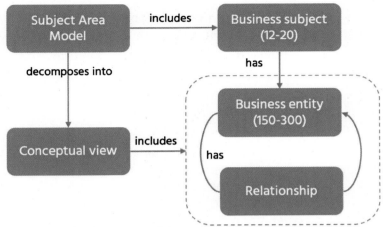

Figure 22: The concept map of the conceptual level as per DAMA-DMBOK1.

The second edition of DAMA-DMBOK2[17] has changed the structure and subordination between the Subject Area Model and Conceptual models contrariwise, as shown in Figure 23.

A conceptual model is a set of key business subject areas and relationships. Business subject areas should be connected to the business model of an organization. The definition of the business subject area has not been specified.

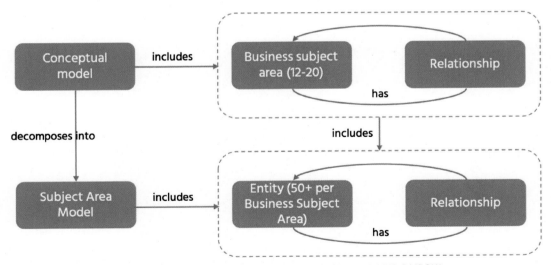

Figure 23: The concept map of the conceptual level as per DAMA-DMBOK2.

The Conceptual model should include 12-20 Business Subject Areas. Then, the Conceptual model decomposes into the set of Subject Area Models. Each Subject Area Model corresponds to one Business Subject area and includes 50+ business entities.

The good news is that a business subject area, business entities, and relationships between entities remain the key metadata objects at this level of abstraction.

The classical approach lacks semantic components such as a business term and a definition. Challenges with business terms and definitions can be overcome using semantic models instead of the classical conceptual models.

Now let us take a look at the semantic model, which is another form of a data model, at the conceptual level.

4.4.2 SEMANTIC MODEL

The DAMA Dictionary defines a semantic data model as a "conceptual data model that provides structure and defines meaning for non-tabular data, making that meaning explicit enough that a human or software agent can reason it"[18]. Technopedia also describes the semantic model as "a conceptual data model that includes semantic information that adds a basic meaning to the data and the relationships that lie between them"[19].

I could not find the agreed structure and metadata objects of a semantic model. Thomas Frisendal describes his approach to semantic modeling in his book "Graph Data Modeling for NoSQL and SQL"[20]. He has developed the concept of a Business Concept Model. The model describes the key metadata objects shown in Figure 24.

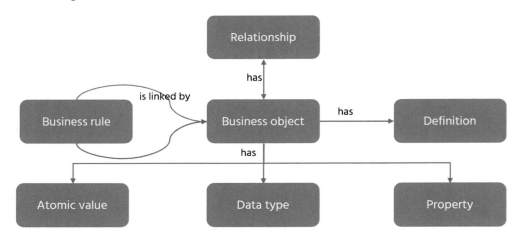

Figure 24: Key objects of Business Concept Model by Thomas Friesendal[21].

A business object has properties, data type, atomic values, and a business definition. Business objects have relationships with each other. Business rules specify constraints for business objects.

The comparison of the classical conceptual model and the semantic model brings the following conclusion. Both models have similar metadata objects as business objects and entities. However, the semantic model includes more objects and is worked out in more detail than the classical conceptual model.

In this book, we continue with the metamodel of the conceptual layer of data lineage that is described below.

4.4.3   THE MODEL OF THE CONCEPTUAL LAYER USED IN THIS BOOK

This model combines the best features of the two models discussed above: classical conceptual and semantic model. You find the graphical representation of the model in Figure 25.

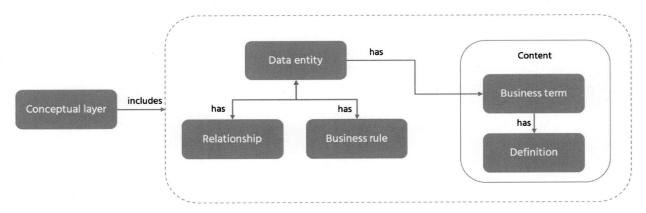

Figure 25: The concept map of the model of the conceptual layer.

The conceptual layer includes data entities and relationships between them. Business rules identify constraints between different data entities. A data entity has a unique business term and corresponding definition. The conceptual layer provides the content in which a business term and definition remain unique.

At the conceptual layer, business metadata elements describe the components of data lineage. Below, you find several examples.

Business metadata elements:

- Owner
  Owner is the role that is accountable for the description and maintenance of the component.
- Dates of creation, modification, deletion
- A status that indicates the stage in the lifecycle of the object
- Type of a relationship
  For example, relations can have different types. The relations used in this book is an example.

Components at the conceptual level of data lineage can be decomposed into the logical level and mapped correspondingly. The logical layer is the topic of our next sub-chapter.

4.5   LOGICAL LAYER

To derive the key metadata components at the logical layer, we first compare two different approaches:

- Classical logical model
- Solution model

Let us start with the classical approach.

4.5.1 CLASSICAL LOGICAL MODEL

DAMA publications provide an overview of the approaches to the classical logical models. The DAMA-DMBOK2 defines the logical model as "an entity-relationship data model including data attributes that represent inherent properties of the data, including names, definitions, structure, and integrity rules, independent of software, hardware, volumetrics, frequency of use, or performance consideration"[22]. The approach and terminology used by DAMA-DMBOK2 mainly focus on relational databases.

Data entity, data attribute, and relations are the key metadata components of the classical logical model. Let us check the definitions of these terms provided in DAMA publications.

Data entity

The DAMA Dictionary and DAMA-DMBOK2 provide quite different definitions of a data entity. In the DAMA Dictionary, you find that data entity is "a classification of objects found in the real world described by the Noun part of speech –persons, places, things, concepts, and events – of interest to the enterprise"[23]. The definition provided by the DAMA-DMBOK2 specifies a data entity within a data modeling context as a "thing about which an organization collects information"[24]. In my opinion, the definition has some vague references. First of all, what is a "thing"? Secondly, the DAMA-DMBOK2 mentioned that data and information are used interchangeably. So, is the data element a thing about which data is collected? It sounds strange, isn't it?

The ISO 21961:2003 "Space data and information transfer systems — Data entity dictionary specification language (DEDSL) — Abstract syntax" provides the following definition: "A data entity is a concept that can, or does, take on one or more values. Semantics of a data entity, such as a text definition of its meaning, are defined by attributes"[25].

Now let us check the definition of the data attribute.

Data attribute

The DAMA Dictionary[26] comes up with three different definitions for a data attribute without clearly identifiable contexts for each definition. The DAMA-DMBOK2 narrows the definition in the context of logical data models to the following statement: "An attribute is a property that identifies, describes, or measures an entity"[27]. The ISO /TS 21089:20189 "Health informatics — Trusted end-to-end information flows" defines a data attribute as a "single unit of data that in a certain context is considered indivisible"[28]. Strangely enough, data attributes and data elements are considered either by the DAMA Dictionary or by the ISO standards to be synonymous.

I compiled the definitions provided by DAMA publications into a concept map shown in Figure 26.

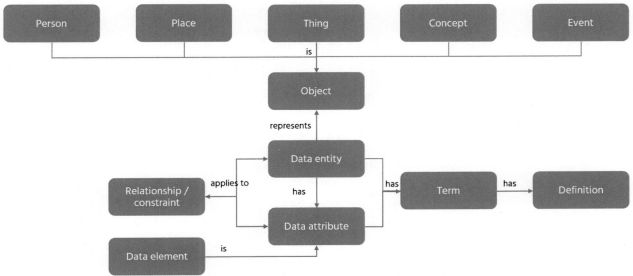

Figure 26: The concept map of the classical logical model.

Person, place, thing, concept, event are objects. A data entity represents an object. Data attributes describe different features of the data entity. A data entity has relationships with other data entities. Some constraints restrict these relationships. The same applies to data attributes. Both data entities and data attributes have a corresponding term and definition. A data element is synonymous with a data attribute.

One of the key challenges with the classical data model is that it relates to relational databases. Thomas Friesendal, in his book "Graph data modeling NoSQL and SQL"[29], overcomes this challenge. He introduces a "solution" model for the model at the logical layer. Let us take a brief look into his approach.

4.5.2 SOLUTION MODEL

This approach demonstrates the application of graph data modeling for both relational and graphical databases. The metadata objects of the solution data model have different names compared to the classical logical model. Data entity, for example, the name of a "business object" and a data attribute turns to be a "property" of a business object. The requirements for these components are comparable to those of the classical approach.

Now it is time to discuss the model of the logical layer applied in this book.

4.5.3 THE MODEL OF THE LOGICAL LAYER USED IN THIS BOOK

The concept map of the logical layer is shown in Figure 27.

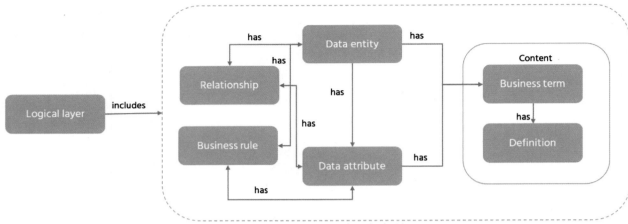

Figure 27: The concept map of the logical layer.

Let us discuss the definitions that I apply to the key components of the logical layer.

Data entity is a metadata object in a logical data model that identifies, describes, or measures a business subject area.

Data attribute is a metadata component in a logical data model that identifies, describes, or measures a data entity.

Data element is a "unit of data that is considered in context to be indivisible"[30]. It means that both data entity and data attribute can be a data element in different contexts. Data entity is a data element in a conceptual business model, while a data attribute is a data element in a logical model.

The first component at the logical layer of data lineage is a data entity. Data entity has one or more data attributes. Both data entities and data attributes have relationships with each other at the same level of abstraction correspondingly. Business rules define conditions and restrictions that apply to the combination of data elements or data attributes. Both data entities and data attributes have a unique business term and definition in specific content.

Business and technical metadata describe the components at the logical layer. Below are some examples thereof.

Business metadata

A logical model by itself is a metadata object. So, for a logical model and its constituent metadata objects such as data entity and data attribute require the documentation of owners.

Technical metadata

According to the DAMA-DMBOK2[31], the following metadata element should be identified for a data attribute:

- ID and name (identifier) of data entity or attribute
- Data value domain
  This is a list of all permissible values for a data element.

- Data type
  Numeric date and time are the examples of data types.

For relationships you should think about:

- Uniqueness constraints for data attribute
  It defines the restrictions put on a data attribute. For example, the value of a data attribute cannot be null.
- Relationship cardinalities between data elements
  Relationship cardinalities demonstrate the relationship between two entities. The example "one writer has written three books" demonstrates the one-to-many relationship. In this case, "one" writer can have "zero or more" books.

In practice, professionals use much more metadata elements for the components at the logical level.

For physical implementation, logical data models should be transformed into or linked with physical data models. Let us consider the data lineage components at a physical level.

4.6   PHYSICAL LAYER

A physical model usually derives from a logical model.   A physical data model has a strong dependency on database structure. One of the key requirements to the physical model is the ability to link metadata objects in the logical and physical data models. If we take, for example, a relational database, a data entity should correspond to one or more tables and a data attribute to one or more columns, as shown in Figure 28.

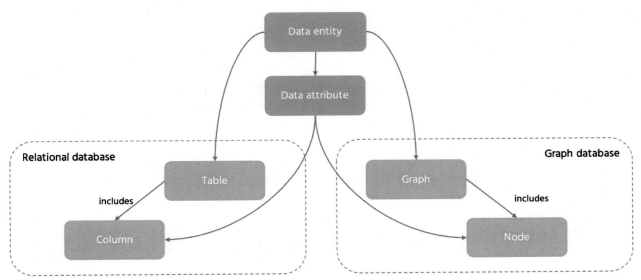

Figure 28: The concept map of the physical layer.

For graph databases, a data entity corresponds to a graph, and the data attribute relates to a node.

Depending on the database types, different metadata components and corresponding metadata elements should be documented.

Different automated data lineage solutions may document a great variety of metadata components at the physical layer. For example, the SAS data lineage application can document more than 400 metadata objects used in SAS applications. Therefore, metadata components, relationship types between them, and metadata elements that describe them vary depending on the company's practices and choices made to document data lineage at the physical level.

By now, we have examined four key layers to document data lineage. There is one special component that resides at each level. This component is a business rule. The documentation of business rules is a challenging task. Furthermore, the term "business rule" has different definitions and interpretations. Therefore, I have decided to discuss this component in a separate sub-chapter.

4.7   BUSINESS RULE

A business rule is one of the most challenging components of data lineage because:

- The term "business rule" has different meaning and definition in different contexts.
- The taxonomy of the term has a poly hierarchical relationship and depends on various factors.
- Business rules have diverse representation and terminology depending on the level of a data model.

Let us first dive into the existing definitions of business rules.

The DAMA Dictionary defines a business rule as a "[…] formally stated constraint governing the characteristics of an object or entity, or the relationship between objects or entities, used to control the complexity of an enterprise"[32]. The DAMA Dictionary puts the term "business rule" at a high level of abstraction. This definition associates with the conceptual or logical layers of a data model. To better understand this definition, let us check the definition of "constraint."

According to the DAMA Dictionary, the term "constraint" has two definitions depending on the context. In a general context, a constraint is a "restriction on a business action and the resulting data"[33]. The example of a restriction is "only a customer who paid in advance can get a discount of 10%." This definition corresponds to the conceptual level of data models, right?

In the data management context, the DAMA Dictionary provides another definition. A constraint is a "specification of what may be contained in a data or metadata set in terms of the content or, for data only, in terms of the set of key combinations to which specific attributes (defined by the data structure) may be attached; and how. Examples of how include dependency (must have at least one), exclusivity (at most one; non-overlapping, subset, or equality"[34]. This rather complex definition relates to the logical or physical levels of the data model.

The definition proposed by the ISO/TR 25102:2008 "Intelligent transport systems — System architecture — 'Use Case' pro-forma template" is more relevant to the physical level of data model: "Business rule is a 'rigorous statement of policy, sometimes expressed in the format IF…THEN…ELSE…, that must be followed when the stated conditions are satisfied"[35].

There are plenty of other definitions of the term "business rules" that you can find, for example, in the article by Ronald G. Ross, "What is a 'Business Rule?'"[36] or the "Semantic of Business Vocabulary and Business Rules"[37] by the Object Management Group, Inc.

In this book, for each data model level, business rules have different terms and definitions. Let us consider in detail for each level. The concept map of business rules can be seen in Figure 29.

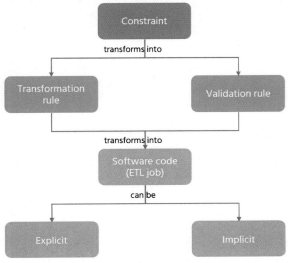

Figure 29: The concept map of a "business rule".

- Conceptual layer
  A constraint is a specification that defines the characteristics of a particular data entity or describes relationships between different data entities.
  Example: A birthday cannot be before the date of death.

- Logical layer
  Depending on the purpose of business rules, they can be classified at least into two types: transformation and validation.
  A transformation rule is a specification that defines the way a data attribute or a set of data attributesshould be transformed to create a new data attribute. Usually, the created data has a value that differs from the values of the original attributes. Examples of transformation rules are calculations, aggregations, etc.
  A validation rule is a specification that controls the correspondence of values of data attributes to predetermined data quality requirements. Validation rules can be applied to a singular data attribute or a set of data attributes.

- Physical level
  Transformation or validation rules specified at the logical level are written in programming language at the physical level. For example, ETL (Extract, Transform, Load) jobs perform transformation and validation rules.
  At the physical level, business rules can be performed at different locations. We recognize explicit and implicit rules.
  Implicit business rules are those that are embedded in the logic of programs. Explicit business rules are stored in a database. From a data lineage perspective, the latter approach allows:

    ◦   Making business rules transparent for end-users
    ◦   Analyzing the set of business rules across data chains
    ◦   Changing the way an application performs transformations

Implicit business rules can hardly be documented and remain a "black box" for data lineage users.

Below, you can find some examples of metadata elements to document business rules:

Business metadata

- Business rule ID
- Business rule name
- Business rule description
  Business rule description should be written by using business language and terms.
- Business rule owner

Technical metadata

- Business rule statement in a programming language
  The business rule description should be turned into the statement by using a programming language.

The explanation of business rules closes the description of the data lineage metamodel. In the next sub-chapter, we assemble all layers and components in a graphical format.

4.8   GRAPHICAL REPRESENTATION OF THE DATA LINEAGE METAMODEL

In this chapter, we combine and link all data lineage layers and components in a graphical format. In my practice, I usually use different schemas depending on a stakeholder group. These schemas are similar by content. They vary by visualization approach to make it understandable for a target group.

The way you explain the concept to a business audience varies from the audience of data management professionals or data architects. In this sub-chapter, I share different versions. You can use them depending on the audience you communicate with:

- The schema in Figure 30 is intended for communication with inexperienced business users.
- The format of the Figure is a simple free format to explain key concepts.
  Figure 31 can be used for communication with advanced business users as well as data management professionals.
  The format is a concept map.
- Figure 32 is only for advanced data management professionals who are fond of the Chen data model notation.

The logic behind each of these schemas remains the same.

Data lineage can be documented at different abstraction levels. We speak about four layers: business and three levels of a data model.

Let's start at the business level. All components of the business layer are marked blue. At this level, we document all dimensions of a business capability. A process enables a business capability. Role participates in the performance of the process and works with IT assets. IT assets enable a process.

IT assets generate reports. A business capability defines the set of business subject areas. A business subject area defines data entities. At this point, the conceptual level begins.

All components at the conceptual level are colored purple. A set of data entities is linked by constraints. Data entity is also a component at the logical layer. That is why the shape of the data entity is double-colored.

Components at the logical layer have a green color. Data entities are linked by relationships and business rules. Data attributes describe data entities. Data attributes are also linked by relationships and business rules.

The components at the physical level are colored orange. The physical level includes IT assets such as databases and ETL tools. Databases include tables and columns. Software codes perform data transformations.

All components of the metadata model are linked in two directions: vertical and horizontal.

In the vertical direction, we link IT assets, for example, systems, applications, databases. Databases include tables and columns. The tables and columns of a particular database should be linked to the corresponding data entities and attributes. Data entities lead to business subject areas. Such a link, is called "vertical data lineage."

In the horizontal direction, at each layer, we link the components of this layer. For example, at the business layer, we connect all IT assets into the data chain to demonstrate how data entities move from one asset to another. Such linking we call "horizontal data lineage." We discuss these types of data lineage in detail in the next chapter.

By now, we have finalized the design of the data lineage metamodel.

The model that I described is the generic one. It demonstrates the key components of data lineage. This metamodel should assist a company in designing its metamodel. A company can reduce the number of layers and components depending on the scope of data lineage initiatives.

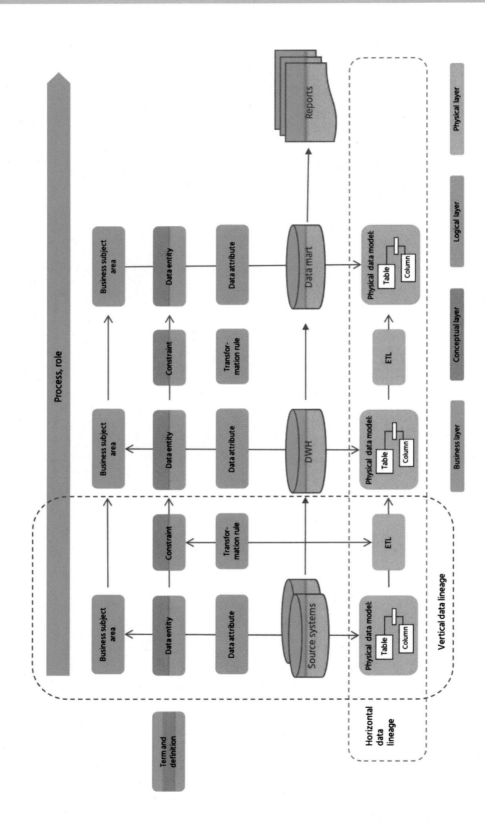

Figure 30: The data lineage metamodel in a free format.

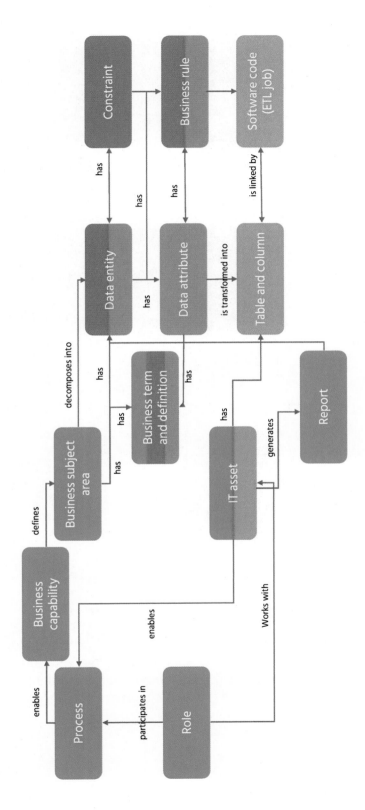

Figure 31: The concept map of the data lineage metamodel.

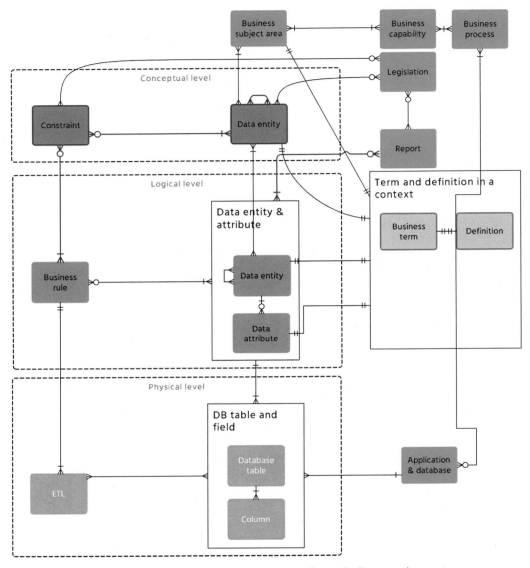

Figure 32: The metamodel of data lineage in Chen notation.

Some companies may add extra components such as legislative documents, for example.

The customization of the metamodel takes place during the implementation of data lineage. We discuss it in Part 2. But before thinking about the implementation, we still need to examine which types of data lineage exist, which is outlined in the next chapter.

SUMMARY OF CHAPTER 4

- The metamodel of data lineage has the following structure:
    - Data lineage layer
      We recognize four layers: business layer and data model layers such as conceptual, logical, and physical.
    - Data lineage component
      Each layer has a set of corresponding components.
    - Metadata element
      Metadata elements describe both the data lineage layer and components.
- The business layer includes the following components:
    - Business capability
    - Process
    - Role
    - Business subject area
    - IT asset
- Following challenges with data models influence data lineage documentation:
    - Different approaches to structure a data model exist.
    - Diverse data models have different purposes of usage.
    - Different data modeling schemes require specific diagram notations.
    - The method to link business models and data models is not clearly defined.
    - One logical model can be realized in multiple software applications.
  These challenges have been taken into account in the design of data model-related layers.
- The conceptual layer consists of the following components:
    - Data entity
    - Relationship
    - Business rule
    - Business term and definition
- The following components constitute the logical layer:
    - Data entity
    - Data attribute
    - Relationship
    - Business rule
    - Business term and definition
- The set of components at the physical level depends on the database structure and the functionality of tools for automated lineage recording.
  The common components in relational databases are:
    - Table
    - Column
    - Software codes to realize ETL processes

- A business rule is a component of data lineage that at different layers have different names:
    - Conceptual level – constraint
    - Logical level –business rule (transformation or validation)
    - Physical level – a business rule is realized by software code (i.e., ETL job)
      Depending on the location, business rules can be either implicit or explicit.
- Different graphical representations of the data lineage metamodel serve the needs of diverse stakeholders' groups.

5 | DATA LINEAGE TYPES

Different business stakeholders have quite different expectations and requirements for data lineage. The common understanding of data lineage remains the same and describes the movement and transformation of data from its source to its destination. At the same time, a method to document data lineage varies depending on the stakeholders' expectations and needs.

In Chapter 5, we will:
- Outline different types of data lineage
- Demonstrate the dependencies between them

After reading this chapter, you will be able to:
- Perform interviews with data lineage stakeholders
- Understand their needs and expectations
- Identify the types of data lineage that your company needs

Based on my experience, I propose the following classification of data lineage that can be seen in Figure 33.

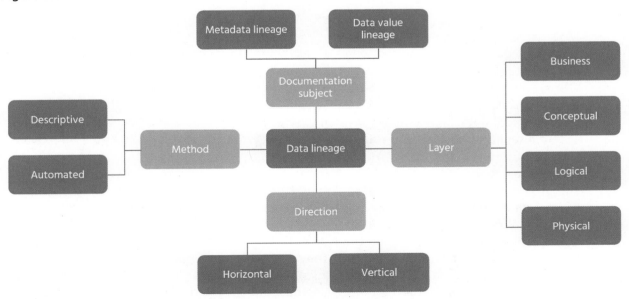

Figure 33: The concept map of data lineage classification.

Four factors define different types of data lineage:

1. The subject of documentation

   Metadata and data value lineage are two quite different types of data lineage.

2. The layer of documentation

   In Chapter 4, we have already discussed the layers to document data lineage. These are business, conceptual, logical, and physical.

3. Direction of documentation

   Depending on the direction, we recognize vertical and horizontal data lineage.

4. A method of documentation

   Depending on the method, we talk about descriptive or automated data lineage.

Below, we examine in detail each of these methods of classification.

5.1   METADATA AND DATA VALUE LINEAGE

Various stakeholders have quite different expectations and understanding regarding data lineage. I want to share with you my experience. We have just started a metadata lineage implementation project. I gathered requirements from business stakeholders, data architects, IT professionals. I delivered many presentations with a summary of requirements and demonstrations of the solution's functionality. I started every presentation with the definition of metadata lineage. I stressed that users would be able to see only the design of data transformation, not data values. At every meeting, the first question I got during the Q&A session was: "Will we see the changes in data values?" Believe it or not, but this situation has continued throughout the whole project.

Let us consider differences between these two types of data lineage. Each of this type has its own stakeholders.

- Metadata lineage
  Data management and IT professionals usually understand data lineage as the documentation of the data processing and transformation made by means of metadata. Often, some professionals use the term "metadata lineage" only in the context of the automated data lineage on a physical level. Such an approach is not entirely correct. The description of data lineage at any level of abstraction is also metadata lineage. Simply, at different levels of abstraction, you use different metadata. We have discussed it already in Chapter 4.

- Data value lineage
  The business stakeholders' understanding of data lineage differs from the understanding of their data management and IT colleagues. Business stakeholders want to see the transformation of data at a data instance level. Business stakeholders need to trace the changes in values of data through the whole data chain. For example, if the total revenue in the management report is EUR 1 million, they want to trace it back to the value of a singular contract. They also want to know the transformations applied to contract values to derive the EUR 1 million value. I use the term "value data lineage" to describe such requirements.

So, the difference between metadata and value data lineage should be taken into account during communication with different groups of stakeholders.

We discuss requirements for these two types of data lineage in-depth in Chapter 9, "Data lineage requirements."

The next factor of the classification is the layer of documentation.

5.2   DATA LINEAGE AT DIFFERENT DOCUMENTATION LAYERS

We have discussed this topic in-depth in Chapter 4. I want to stress the following. Different companies use the various number of layers and constituent components to describe data lineage. They also use different terminology to describe these layers.

In this book, I propose the classification that is based on common practice and is the result of my practical experience. Every company should make a choice regarding the number, names, and content of layers.

In this book, I recognize the documentation of data lineage at four levels:
- Business
- Conceptual
- Logical
- Physical

The next factor in classifying data lineage depends on the direction of documentation.

5.3   HORIZONTAL AND VERTICAL DATA LINEAGE

Depending on the direction of documentation, professionals recognize horizontal and vertical data lineage. I demonstrated these two types of data lineage in Figure 30.

The conventional definition of data lineage specifies the horizontal type of data lineage. It demonstrates the path that data flows from the origination point to the point of usage. The horizontal data lineage can be documented at each of the four layers.

Vertical data lineage links data lineage components between different layers. The example is the link between business subject area, data entity, data attribute, and then a table and a column in a database.

"Vertical data linkage" and "vertical data architecture" are synonymous with "vertical data lineage."

Data lineage can also be classified by the means of documentation.

5.4   DESCRIPTIVE AND AUTOMATED DATA LINEAGE

The method to capture data lineage is the fourth factor to classify data lineage.

Descriptive data lineage is a method to record metadata data lineage manually in a repository.

Automated data lineage is the method to record metadata data lineage by implementing automated processes to scan and ingest metadata into a repository.

Each of these methods has its area of application, corresponding advantages, and disadvantages.

The following aspects allows choosing the method of documentation:

- Level of data model
  Descriptive data lineage is feasible to document metadata lineage at the business, conceptual, and logical level. It will be hardly possible to record data lineage at the physical level manually. It is worth mentioning that I have experience in practicing such initiatives. It resulted in thousands of rows in Excel and cost hundreds of man-hours.
  Automated data lineage is suitable for capturing data lineage at the physical level. It is worth mentioning that in the case of mapping logic to the physical level, such a mapping should be done manually.
- Required resources
  Data lineage is time- and resource-intensive at any stage of documentation, either creation or maintenance. Should changes occur, you would always need to keep an eye out for these changes and adjust the documentation.

Furthermore, if the documentation is done in a collaborative environment, a central team should perform:

- Linking between data lineage from different parts of the application landscape
- Consistency check
- Update control

Descriptive and automated data lineage require resources at different stages.

Automated data lineage initially requires many resources to create the automated process of reading and uploading metadata. Then, with new releases, the data lineage information should be updated automatically. Yet, should some new applications be included in the process, manual efforts for coding would be required.

Descriptive data lineage needs resources at the design as well as at the maintenance stage.

In detail, we consider these two approaches of data lineage documentation in Chapter 12, "Document data lineage and build analytics."

All data lineage types described above have some interdependencies.

5.5 INTERDEPENDENCIES BETWEEN DIFFERENT DATA LINEAGE TYPES

In this sub-chapter, we analyze dependencies between different data lineage types. There is one reason for such analysis. In my practice, I often come across communication challenges on the data lineage subject. For example, a metadata architect said: "We develop a future state architecture (FSA) for horizontal lineage." My first question back was: "At which level? Horizontal data lineage can be documented at all four levels." For him, it was obvious that he spoke about physical metadata lineage. He simply shortened it to the horizontal data lineage.

So, let us investigate possible combinations and dependencies. The results of the analysis one can see in Table 7 and Table 8.

Let us analyze the content of Table 7.

	Data lineage by the level of documentation				Data lineage by direction		Data lineage by the method of documentation	
	Business	Conceptual	Logical	Physical	Horizontal	Vertical	Descriptive	Automated
Data lineage by subject — Metadata lineage								
Data lineage by subject — Value data lineage								

Table 7: The dependencies between data lineage by subject with the rest of data lineage

- Data lineage by subject vs. the level of documentation
  Metadata lineage can be documented at each level of abstraction. Metadata components and elements differ. In any case, metadata lineage describes the process of data flow and transformation.
  Value data lineage can only be documented at the physical level. In this case, we talk about data instances that exist only at the physical level.
- Data lineage by subject vs. by direction
  Metadata lineage can be documented in both directions. Horizontal data lineage demonstrates how data flows along with a data chain. Vertical data lineage links components at a different level of abstraction.
  Value data lineage can be documented only in the horizontal direction. The reason is that data instances reside only at the physical level.
- Data lineage by subject vs. the method of documentation
  Both descriptive and automated methods can be used to document metadata lineage.
  Data value lineage can be recorded by using automated methods. The reason is the same as explained above. Data values resign in the physical layer.
  Now it is time to examine the content of Table 8.

		Data lineage by the level of documentation			
		Business	Conceptual	Logical	Physical
Data lineage by method	Descriptive				
	Automated				

Table 8: The dependencies between data lineage by the method and by the level of documentation.

- Data lineage by method vs. the level of documentation
  The descriptive method to document data lineage can be applied at all layers. I have seen in my practice physical lineage documented in MS Excel or Word. But this is the last thing that I recommend. The descriptive method can be applied for the documentation at the business and conceptual level. There is no option to apply the automated method here. For the physical level, I strongly recommend using only automated data lineage. The logical level is a delimited zone. Logical schemas can be reverse-engineered from the physical ones. They also can be created manually in data modeling tools.

We have finalized the consideration of data lineage types. It may happen that in your practice, you come across some other factors of classification.

This chapter is also the last chapter of Part 1. We have concluded our theoretical investigations, and now it is time to move to the implementation practices.

SUMMARY OF CHAPTER 5

- Different stakeholders have diverse expectations and needs for data lineage. To ease the communication, we should specify different types of data lineage requested by various stakeholders.
- In this book, we consider four factors of data lineage classification:
    1. By the subject of documentation

       We recognize metadata and data value lineage.

    2. By the layer of documentation

       In this book, we propose four layers:

         - Business
         - Conceptual
         - Logical
         - Physical

    3. By the direction of documentation

       Data lineage that describes the data pathway between two locations along the data chain is a horizontal data lineage.

       The lineage that links components at different layers is the vertical lineage.

    4. The method of documentation
       Depending on the level of automation, descriptive (manual) and automated data lineage are recognized.
- Different types of data lineage have dependencies and interconnections.

SUMMARY OF PART 1

In Part 1, we have investigated different theoretical aspects of data lineage and made the following conclusions:

- Several concepts have definitions similar to data lineage. Some of these concepts are considered being synonymous with data lineage and are used interchangeably. These concepts are data value chain, data chain, data flow, integration architecture, information value chain.
- Data lineage interrelates and has commonalities with the concepts of data lifecycle, enterprise (data) architecture, business capability.
- Several data management capabilities either deliver data lineage as an outcome or use it as an input.
- A company should have strong business drivers to perform data lineage initiatives. The key group of drivers are:
  - Compliance with legislative requirements
  - Business change
  - Data management initiatives
  - Audit requirements

We have also designed the metamodel of data lineage:

- A metamodel of data lineage is a metamodel that describes metadata needed to document data lineage models.
- A metamodel of data lineage serves two purposes:
  - Specify data lineage needs and requirements
  - Scope and optimize the implementation
- The metamodel of data lineage includes four different layers with corresponding data lineage components:
  - Business
    The key components are business capability, process, role, IT asset, business subject area.
  - Conceptual
    Data entity, relationship, business rule, business term and definition constitute this layer.
  - Logical
    Data entity, data attribute, relationship, business rule, business term, and definition belong to the logical layer.
  - Physical
    The components of the physical layer depend on the database or ETL tool type.

We came to the conclusion that depends on stakeholders' needs and expectation, we can classify data lineage by different factors:

- By the subject of the documentation: metadata and data value lineage
- By the layer of documentation: business, conceptual, logical, physical
- By the direction of documentation: horizontal and vertical
- By the method of documentation: descriptive and automated

Part 2

IMPLEMENTING
DATA LINEAGE

*"In theory, theory and practice are the same.
In practice, they are not."*

- Albert Einstein

To prove the trueness of Einstein's quote, I want to share with you an important lesson learned. In the beginning of my first data lineage implementation project, I have spent three months investigating data lineage topics, examining legislative requirements, and performing interviews with stakeholders. It resulted in a thorough document called "Business requirements for data lineage." It covered all requirements and included all imaginable components and relationships. When we started a proof of concept, we realized that only 30% of the requirements put in this document were feasible. We have also understood that the requirements document remained our "blueprint," and some of these dreams would never be realized. The implementation of this feasible scope lasted for several years.

This story leads to a simple but very serious conclusion: to be successful, the scope of data lineage should be "just enough" and feasible.

Part 2 aims to provide guidance to data management and project management practitioners to:
- Scope data lineage initiative
- Choose the right methods of implementation
- Select a proper software solution

We start with the overview of the nine-step methodology to scope and implement your data lineage business case.

6 | BUILD YOUR DATA LINEAGE CASE WITH THE NINE-STEP METHODOLOGY

The documentation of data lineage is a long-time project that involves many stakeholders and demands a lot of resources. To make it successful, it requires thorough preparation and efficient execution.

To succeed, a company should follow certain steps to implement data lineage.

In Chapter 6, we will:

- Highlight the key steps to build a data lineage business case

After reading this chapter, you will be able to:

- Define a strategy to build a data lineage business case
- Design a road-map for your business case
- Communicate with decision-makers on this topic

I have put the nine-step methodology in a graphical format presented in Figure 34. In this chapter, we highlight the content of each step. Some of these steps I explain in-depth in the consequent chapters.

Step 1: Identify key business drivers

Each data lineage initiative should start with the definition of key business drivers for this initiative. The chosen business drivers determine the feasible scope, deadlines, and resources needed.

In Chapter 2, we have discussed the key four groups of business drivers:

- Compliance with legislative requirements
- Business change
- Data management initiatives
- Audit requirements

It may happen that several drivers simultaneously call for data lineage. In this case, a company should set up priorities. For example, a company defines that compliance with regulations belongs to the highest business priorities. The challenge is that different legislations relate to different business areas. For example, the compliance to SOX or BCBS 239 regulations impact risk- and finance-related capabilities, organizational units, data sets, etc. At the same time, the GDPR or PII requirements focus on personal data and related business capabilities.

Depending on the choices made, the scope of and approach to the project vary significantly.

To specify the key drivers, a company should perform the following steps[1]:
- Create a list of possible business drivers
- Involve key sponsors and decision-makers, usually members of the C-suite group, to choose the most critical ones
- Limit the number of key drivers to 1 or 2

After the identification of key business drivers, the next step is the analysis of key stakeholders.

Step 2: Buy-in support and involvement of key stakeholders

The chosen drivers determine the key stakeholders of the data lineage initiative. A **stakeholder** is an individual or a group of individuals with particular concerns and interests in the outcomes of the data lineage initiative. Data lineage stakeholders reside at all levels of authority within an organization.

C-suite members have various concerns regarding data lineage. The key one relates to the compliance with regulations that data lineage can ensure.

Stakeholders at the C-suite level should act as sponsors of the data lineage initiative. Following reasons support this proposal:
- Data lineage documentation is a time- and resource-consuming initiative.
  Even if the scope of the project is feasible, its implementation may last months and even years. Such an initiative requires a strategic approach and a sufficient budget to make it done. Therefore, the sponsorship from C-suite managers is one of the key success factors.
- Data lineage documentation is a cross-organizational unit initiative.
  Data flows through different organizational units and requires joint efforts to document it. Long and complex data chains make this task even more challenging. Business units involved in such chains may have different priorities and concerns. In this case, the support of top management to coordinate these joint efforts is critically important.

Business and data analysts need data lineage to analyze data quality issues and build data quality checks and controls. Data and application architects require data lineage to assess the impact of changes in applications and/or databases on data delivery.

In my book "Data management toolkit"[2], I provided advanced techniques to perform data stakeholders' analysis.

We discuss in detail data lineage stakeholders, their roles, and accountabilities in Chapter 8.

After the identification of sponsors and stakeholders, the next step is to scope the initiative.

Step 3: Scope data lineage initiative

The correct scope of the data lineage initiative is very important for its success. I recommend always starting with a pilot project and limiting the scope to the feasible minimum.

Techniques to identify the scope we examine in detail in Chapter 7.

When the scope has been identified, the next step is to involve stakeholders in the process.

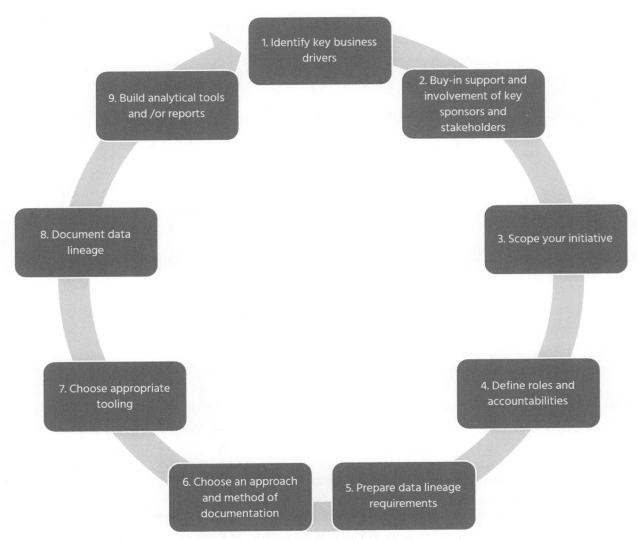

Figure 34: The nine-step methodology to building a data lineage business case.

Step 4: Define roles and accountabilities

Data lineage documentation project as every data and IT-related project has several standard steps. For examples, as those that are listed below:

1. Gather and analyze requirements
2. Develop plans
3. Choose a solution
4. Implement the solution
5. Test

Multiple stakeholders get different roles, accountabilities, and responsibilities to accomplish these complex tasks. We discuss these roles in depth in Chapter 8.

When the roles have been assigned, the dedicated stakeholders proceed with the specification of requirements.

Step 5: Prepare data lineage requirements

Stakeholders have different concerns and requirements. We recognize functional and non-functional requirements. The most important feature of a requirement is its measurability. In Chapter 9, we examine the requirements for data lineage. Different types of data lineage have diverse requirements. For example, requirements for metadata lineage and data value lineage differ to a great extent.

The finalized requirements provide input to make decisions about the approach and method of data lineage documentation.

Step 6: Choose an approach and methodology to document data lineage

The right decision about the approach and methods to document data lineage ensures the initiative's success.

Decisions depend on the size of your organization and the scope of the project. We discuss the process to derive the correct decision in Chapter 10.

As soon as the decision has been made, a company can proceed with finding the appropriate solution.

Step 7: Choose an appropriate data lineage solution

Technologies have been developing rapidly over the last several years. The number of data lineage solutions has grown. This tendency will continue. Data lineage is a complex concept that requires different functionalities. Therefore, data lineage solutions, especially integrated ones, are sophisticated. Such software products can be quite costly. Therefore, a company should base its choice of a solution on clear requirements. The choice should also cover a strategic perspective. I provide some advice on how to choose an appropriate application in Chapter 11.

After a solution has been chosen, it is time to proceed with the documentation of data lineage. As discussed in Chapter 5, descriptive and automated methods are two key methods to document data lineage. These two methods have their own techniques and areas of applicability.

Step 8: Document data lineage

Data lineage can be documented differently. The choice of methods depends on many factors. But even the same method of documentation may explore different techniques. In chapter 12, I highlight some techniques to document descriptive data lineage at the different levels of abstraction. I also provide a high-level overview of automated data lineage technologies. This overview focuses on business professionals. As stated in Foreword, this book does not aim to dive into technical details of the automated data lineage technologies.

Documented data lineage may not satisfy the needs of business stakeholders. To ease the usage of data lineage, analytics should be built above metadata repositories.

Step 9: Build analytical tools

Those who believe that implemented data lineage, especially automated one, is the end of the story are totally wrong. Only at this point, the real challenge starts. Data lineage should form a part of the daily life of business stakeholders. To make data lineage user-friendly and let business stakeholders use it, you should build analytical reports above metadata repositories.

By now, you got a vision about the steps to build a data lineage case.

SUMMARY OF CHAPTER 6

The successful implementation of a data lineage business cases includes the following steps:
1. Identify key business drivers
2. Buy-in support and involvement of key stakeholders
3. Scope your data lineage initiative
4. Define roles and accountabilities
5. Prepare data lineage requirements
6. Choose an approach and methods to implement data lineage
7. Choose an appropriate data lineage solution
8. Document data lineage
9. Build analytical tools

7 | SCOPE YOUR DATA LINEAGE INITIATIVE

Step 3 of the nine-step methodology focuses on the definition of a feasible scope.

The documentation of data lineage is a time- and resource-consuming exercise. The thoroughly identified scope is the first step to success. The scope should meet the following criteria:

- Match the company's resources
  Regardless of the chosen method, the documentation of data lineage remains a resource-intensive exercise. A company should carefully estimate the resources required to deliver results.
- Manage time expectations
  Data lineage is also a time-consuming exercise. Timing plays an important role when data lineage is needed to comply with regulations. Therefore, the scope should carefully assess deadline requirements.
- Deliver quick results and meet expectations of end users
  It might happen that the results of data lineage implementation don't match expectations or can't cover the needs of ordinary business users. Therefore, the sooner the data lineage initiative delivers results, the sooner business users can evaluate its usability.

In this chapter, we will:

- Specify key parameters that define the scope of data lineage
- Discuss each of these parameters in detail

After reading this chapter, you will be able to:

- Define parameters to identify the scope
- Outline the scope for the data lineage initiative
- Start a discussion about the scope with key stakeholders

We have discussed the metamodel of data lineage in Chapter 4. This metamodel assists us in establishing key parameters of a data lineage scope. These parameters are:

- The scope of an "enterprise"
- The "length" of data lineage
- The "depth" of data lineage
- The set of critical data
- Data lineage components

Let's use the metamodel of data lineage to explain one by one the key parameters of the scope, as shown in Figure 35.

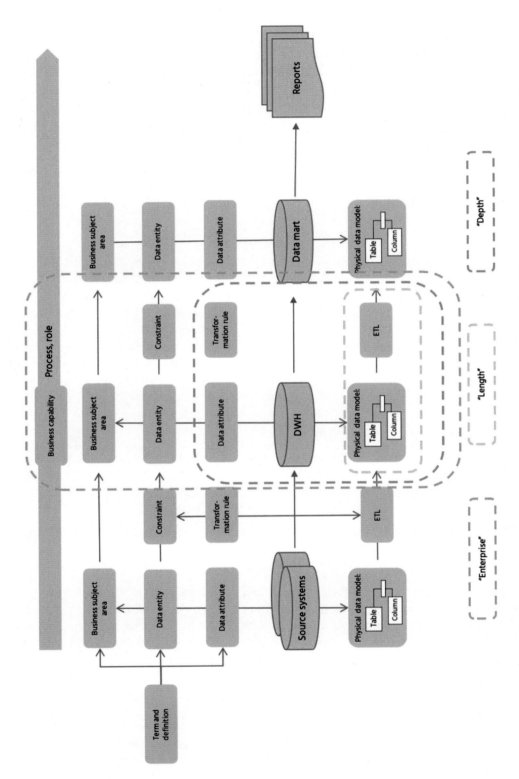

Figure 35: Key parameters to scope a data lineage initiative.

93

7.1 THE SCOPE OF AN "ENTERPRISE"

Enterprise architects should be familiar with the term "enterprise." According to TOGAF® 9.2, an enterprise is "The highest level (typically) of description of an organization and typically covers all missions and functions"[1].

You identify the "enterprise" in the limits of the agreed business drives. For example, the driver is compliance with GDPR regulation. Yet, you may need to limit the organizational units to be involved at the first stage.

In the context of data lineage, an "enterprise" includes the set of interrelated business capabilities, organizational units, business processes. In Figure 35, the example of "enterprise" has been marked with a blue dash line. The next factor is "length."

7.2 THE "LENGTH" OF DATA LINEAGE

Horizontal data lineage describes the movement of data from its origin to its destination. Often, companies declare the necessity to document data lineage from a "golden" source to the final reports and/or dashboards. Such a claim has a challenge. Large companies with extended the "enterprise" scope have long data chains. It is difficult to document data lineage for such a scope at once. To make the initiative feasible, you should cut data chains into segments. The points of data "origin" and data "destination" become relative. The "length" is the size of such segments. In Figure 35, "length" has been marked with a yellow dashed line. The "length" is limited to the scope of the one data chain with the "enterprise" limit. In practice, one or more data chain segments can be included in the initiative. After the definition of "length," you can proceed to evaluate the "depth".

7.3 THE "DEPTH" OF DATA LINEAGE

The "depth" specifies the number of data lineage layers. This factor relates to the concept of vertical lineage. Usually, a company starts the documentation at one level and then extends the scope. Different approaches to document data lineage at multiple levels we discuss in chapter 10. In Figure 35, the "depth" of data lineage has been highlighted with the lilac dash line.

The scope limited by "enterprise," "length," and "depth" still include multiple sets of data lineage.

7.4 THE SETS OF CRITICAL DATA

Every business capability and every data chain deal with several sets of data elements. Some of these data elements are more critical for business than others. For example, a company proceeds with documentation of data lineage for compliance with GDPR. In this case, only the set of personal data confines the scope of data lineage. This set is critical for business. In Chapter 14, we discuss the concept of critical data in depth.

The last factor is the number of components.

7.5 THE NUMBER OF DATA LINEAGE COMPONENTS

In chapter 4, we have analyzed in-depth each layer of data lineage and corresponding components. A company can still limit the scope by identifying the partial set of components. Let us take, for example, a physical level. The SAS data lineage solution includes more than 400 components. In the project I have participated in, we chose only 15 to proceed. Even then, the number of documented components reached hundreds of thousands with a couple of millions of related relationships. When choosing a scope, you should be careful with defining the number and type of data lineage objects; otherwise, your metadata repository may blow up.

We have finalized the consideration of Step 3 and are ready to move on to Step 4. Our focus is now on roles that are involved in data lineage initiative and their accountabilities.

SUMMARY OF CHAPTER 7

- The following factors allow to limit the data lineage initiative to the feasible level:
  - The scope of an "enterprise"
  - The "length" of data lineage
  - The "depth" of data lineage
  - The sets of critical data elements
  - The number of data lineage components

8 | DEFINE DATA LINEAGE-RELATED ROLES

The identification of data lineage-related roles is the content of Step 4 of the nine-step data lineage business-case methodology.

Data lineage is a deliverable of several data management (DM) capabilities. I have experience in implementing data management frameworks. In my opinion, the design of data management roles is one of the most challenging tasks since many different factors influence the roles' design.

In Chapter 8, we will:
- Examine factors that influence the data management roles' design
- Discuss the key types of data management roles
- Identify data management roles required for the data lineage initiative

After reading this chapter, you will be able to:
- Recognize factors that influence the DM roles' design in your company
- Identify roles needed to implement data lineage
- Assign accountabilities for the chosen roles

To identify the roles involved in the data lineage initiative, we first need to agree on the definitions of roles. We also have to investigate the main factors that influence the role design.

8.1 KEY FACTORS THAT INFLUENCE ROLE DESIGN

In this book, I apply the following definitions of roles. The relationships between them can be seen in Figure 36.

Role is "the position or purpose that someone or something has in a situation, organization, society, or relationship"[1].

Business role is a role that contributes to organizational performance through the application of skills, knowledge, experience, or abilities. An organization, a person, or a software system may perform different roles to achieve the business goals of the organization.

Data management role is a business role that performs data management-related tasks and delivers intended data management outcomes.

Data management roles can be functional and virtual. **Functional role** is a data management role that is defined by the organizational structure of an organization. **Virtual role** is a data management role that is not defined by the organizational structure of an organization and can be assigned to a

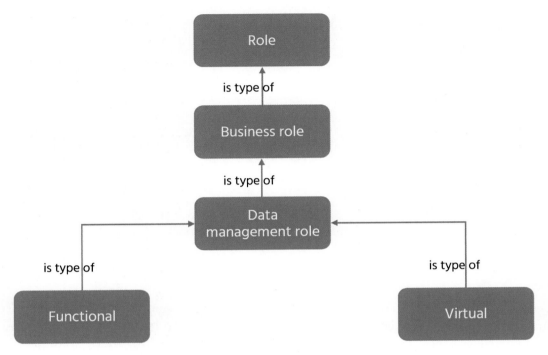

Figure 36: The concept map of role-related definitions.

functional role. For example, the head of the financial department is a functional role. The role of a data owner or a data user can be assigned to the functional role, the head of the financial department. Some companies have created a functional role of data steward, which is taken into the organizational structure.

Multiple factors influence the design of data management roles:

- The type of data stewards
- The dimensions of a business capability
- The location of roles along with data chains
- Data management sub-capabilities
- Data architecture styles
- The approach to the IT solution design
- Data domain definition
- The scope of the "enterprise"

The concept map of these factors can be seen in Figure 37.

In the consequent sub-chapters, we briefly discuss each of these factors. We start with the concept of data stewardship and the types of data stewards.

8.1.1 THE TYPES OF DATA STEWARDS

During the last few years, the concept of stewardship role has been widely used in the data management community.

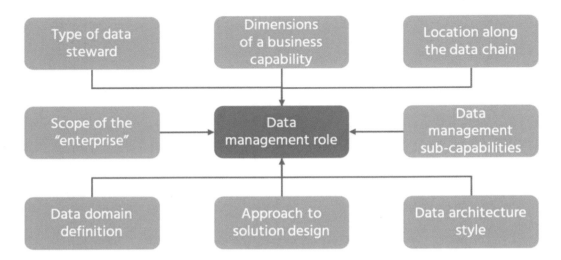

Figure 37: Main factors that influence roles' design.

The concept of stewardship is based on the idea that an organization owns assets and resources. The organization delegates accountabilities and responsibilities to manage assets on its behalf to its employees. Data is one of the organization's assets. Therefore, data stewardship requires a set of data steward roles.

In this book, I use the following terms and definitions:

Steward is a business role assigned to an employee that manages the organization's assets on behalf of the organization.

Data steward is a steward that manages data assets.

Professional background splits data stewards into three categories: business data stewards, data management stewards, technical data stewards.

Business data steward is a data steward with significant knowledge, skills, and experience in one or more business domains.

Data management steward is a data steward with knowledge, skills, and experience in one or more data management domains.

Technical data steward is a data steward with knowledge, skills, and experience in one or more information technology (IT) and/or security domains.

The concept map of these roles is presented in Figure 38.

Data steward roles can be either functional or virtual. If a data steward role is virtual, it should be linked to a functional role. In practice, each company has its approach and roles' structure. Below, you find several examples of the mapping between data steward roles and regular functional roles.

The role of a business data steward can be assigned to:

- Subject matter experts from business units such as commercial, risk, compliance, finance, marketing and sales, legal, production

- Business analysts

Data management stewardship is associated with such groups of professionals as:

- Enterprise architects with specialization in business, data, and application architecture
- Data modelers
- Data analysts
- Data scientists

Technical data stewardship roles can be given to:

- Technical and IT security architects
- Data engineers
- Database specialists
- IT security professionals

Each organization should analyze the existing functional roles and their professional profiles and map them accordingly to the data steward type.

In this book, I use these three groups of data stewards to demonstrate the assignment of roles to data lineage-related tasks.

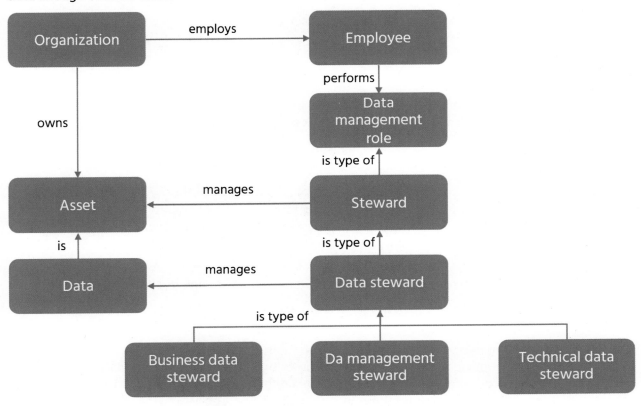

Figure 38: The concept map of data stewardship roles.

The next factor that influences the design of roles is the dimensions of a business capability.

8.1.2 THE DIMENSIONS OF A BUSINESS CAPABILITY

The second factor is the dimensions that enable a business capability. In sub-chapter 1.4, we have discussed the model of a business capability. We have identified four dimensions that enable a business capability: process, role, data, and tool. Data management is also a business capability. Each of these dimensions requires associated data management-related roles. The roles per each dimension you can see in Figure 39.

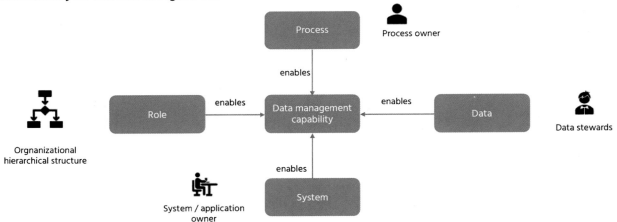

Figure 39: The concept map of the roles per dimension of a business capability.

Process owners manage processes. I specify a **process owner** as a business role that defines and maintains a process as well as manages the process's performance and change.

System or application owner is a business role that is accountable for a system lifecycle.

Data stewards manage data.

All these roles should split into different levels of authority. This authority structure reflects the organizational hierarchical structure. Usually, the structure of data management-related roles mirrors an organizational hierarchy. For example, an executive business data steward has the ultimate accountability. Then his accountabilities could be downsized to responsible data stewards at the lower levels of authorities.

All of the above-mentioned roles get some tasks related to data lineage documentation.

The location of roles along data chains influences the roles' design as well.

8.1.3 THE LOCATION OF ROLES ALONG DATA CHAINS

In sub-chapter 1.6, we concluded that data lineage describes data chains. In turn, data chains realize a data lifecycle. The accountabilities of the same roles depend on the location of these roles along data chains. Let us take, for example, the role of a business data steward. This role, depending on the location along the chain, performs the role of data owner or data user. These roles have quite different accountabilities.

Each company has its approach to describe the data lifecycle. Such an approach is industry-specific.

In this book, I use the simplified schema of a data lifecycle demonstrated in Figure 40.

This schema includes several high-level stages.

Stage 1: Specify information and data requirements

This step identifies the information needs of end-users. To create the required information, you need to obtain and transform needful data.

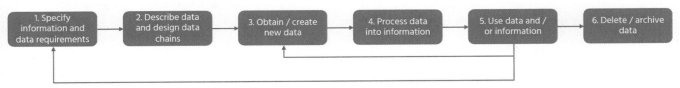

Figure 40: A simplified data lifecycle schema.

Stage 2: Describe data and design data chains

To identify data needs, you need to describe both information and data. The consequent step is to design data chains.

Stage 3: Obtain/create new data

The next step is to identify sources of needful data. Data can be either created within an organization or obtained from a source outside the organization.

Stage 4: Process data into information

The implementation of the designed data chains is the next step in the data lifecycle.

Stage 5: Use data and/or information

Two options to use data exist. Data can be used to produce new data along the chain. In this case, Step 5 has a back loop to Stage 3. Data can also be used to produce information at the end of the chain. End users consume this information. In this case, new information requirements appear, Step 5 has a back loop to Stage 1.

Stage 6: Delete / archive data.

Data is either deleted or archived according to the retention requirements at this final stage of the data lifecycle.

All roles described in sub-chapters 8.1.1 and 8.1.2 are involved in the Stages of the data lifecycle.

Different data management sub-capabilities enable the execution of the data lifecycle.

The next factor that influences the roles' design is the set of data management sub-capabilities.

8.1.4 DATA MANAGEMENT SUB-CAPABILITIES

Different definitions and approaches to describe data management exist. In my practice, I use the "Orange" model of data management[2].

I identify **data management** as a business capability that safeguards data assets and delivers business value from them. This value is delivered via optimized data chains. The data management capability can be decomposed in the set of capabilities at a lower level. The set of these data management capabilities enables data chains. Three types of data management capabilities exist: core, supporting IT capabilities, and other capabilities. The concept map of this model is presented in Figure 41.

The core data management capabilities are:

- **Data management framework**
  Data mangement framework is a business capability that delivers the structure in which other data management capabilities operate.
- **Data modeling**
  Data modeling is a business capability that delivers data models "[...] a) to define and analyze data requirements; b) design logical and physical structures that support these requirements; and c) define business and technical meta-data"[3].
- **Information systems architecture**
  Information systems architecture is a business capability that enables the delivery of data and application architecture required for designing data and information value chains.
- **Data quality**
  Data qualityis a business capability that enables the delivery of data and information of required quality.

Different stages of the data chain require various data management sub-capabilities.

For example, a data management framework governs all data lifecycle processes. Data modeling is only required to specify requirements, describe and design data chains. Information systems architecture enables every process with the exception of the specification of requirements. Data quality tasks should be performed at every stage, except for deleting and/or archiving data.

Data management capabilities require different sets of roles to perform related tasks. Therefore, the accountabilities of the roles within one capability may change along data chains.

Schematically, I demonstrate these dependencies in Figure 42.

For example, systems (application) owners perform tasks at stages 3, 4, and 5, where IT applications perform data processing.

The factors that we examined in sub-chapters 8.1.1 – 8.1.4 significantly impact the accountabilities of roles involved in data lineage documentation. Therefore, I provided detailed explanations of the nature of such an impact. Factors described in the consequent sub-chapters 8.1.5-8.1.8 have lesser influence. Thus, I only briefly explain these factors. The next factor to investigate is the data architecture styles.

8.1.5   DATA ARCHITECTURE STYLES

Organizations use different data architecture styles. The examples thereof are canonical architecture and big data architecture. Canonical data architecture assumes multiple and complex relationships between different sourcing and consuming applications. In big data architecture, data from different source systems enter the central big data platform. Data integration and data distribution are key processes. The location of data transformation processes along with data chains influences the accountabilities of roles. If data is transformed before entering the big data platform or at the

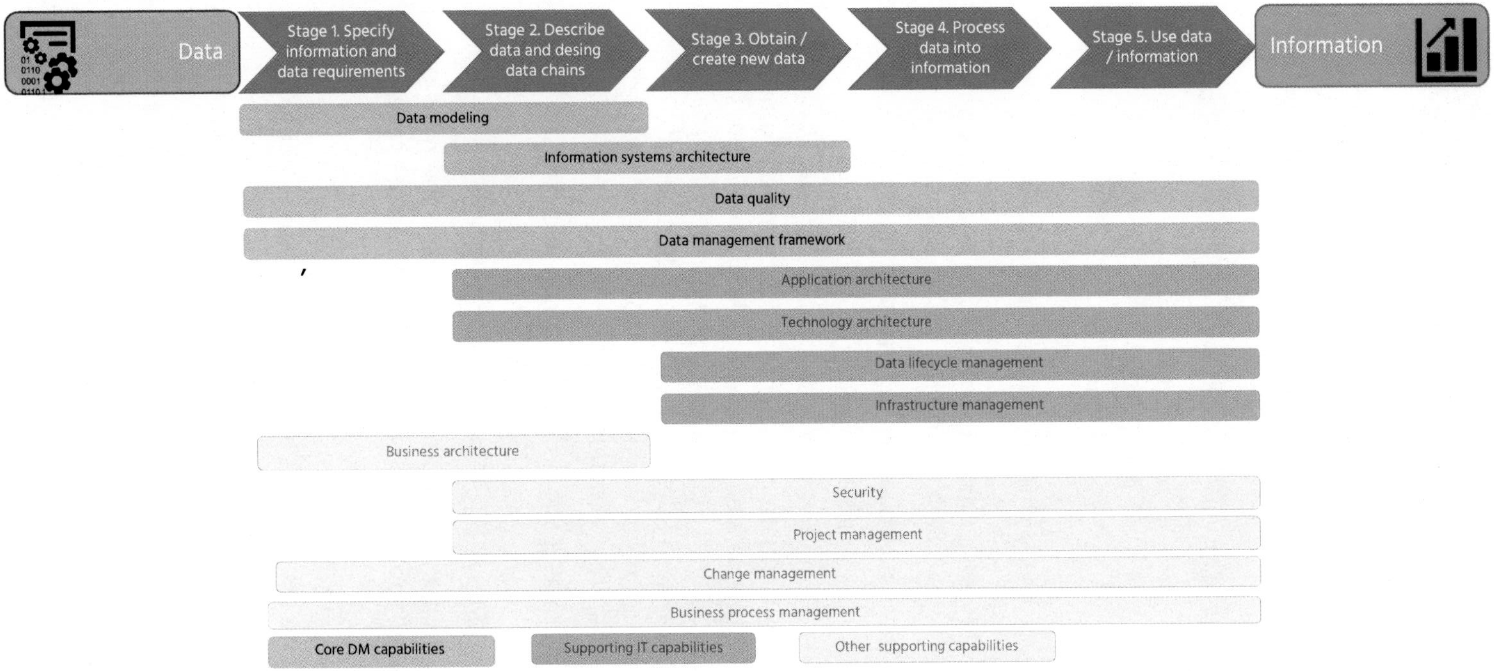

Figure 41: An example of data management capabilities that enable data lifecycle and data chains.

103

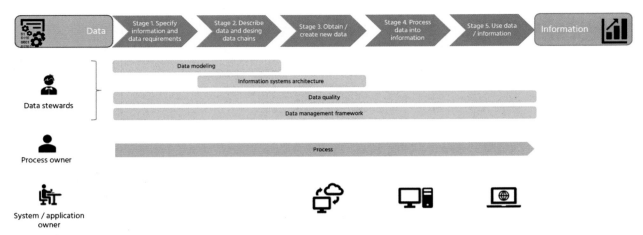

Figure 42: Dependencies between data management sub-capabilities and roles along data chains.

platform, data owners probably take this responsibility. If the transformation occurs when data leaves the platform, data users could be accountable for this process.

The approach to IT solutions' design also influences the roles' design.

8.1.6   AN APPROACH TO THE IT SOLUTIONS' DESIGN

In the canonical approach, different data management functions perform a data model design and solution design. Data architecture delivers conceptual, logical, and physical data models. Solution architecture implements physical data models into practice. New approaches to IT solution design, on the contrary, unites the data model design and the solution design. One process looks after the design of semantic (logical) and solution data models. Depending on the approach, data management technical data stewards have different accountabilities.

The next factor that influences roles' design is the approach to define data domains.

8.1.7   AN APPROACH TO DEFINING A BUSINESS DOMAIN

The definition of a business domain is important to distinguish the roles of data owners and data users. Unfortunately, no agreed approach exists. I have come across several approaches to define a business domain based on:

1. The moment of new data creation
    This approach takes into account the following. Data flows along data chains. On its way, data can either change or not. If data is being changed, new data is being created. New data owners take over the accountabilities for newly created data. Usually, master and reference data mainly stay unchanged. Transactional data tends to change more often. This approach is difficult to apply for long data chains. Along data chains, new data is being created in multiple data points. Numerous data owners and users should distribute and align their accountabilities accordingly. Oftentimes, such a task is not feasible. Another approach offers to define a business domain based on a business subject area.
2. Business subject area

The second approach focuses on the identification of business subject areas. For example, a customer is a business subject area. A particular business function takes ownership accountability about customer data. This ownership remains unchanged along with data chains.

3. Organizational structure
   This approach is less common. It allows for data ownership based on organizational structures.

One organization may apply different approaches simultaneously in diverse business units.

The last factor that influences the roles' design is the size of the "enterprise."

8.1.8   THE SIZE OF AN "ENTERPRISE"

As we discussed in sub-chapter 7.1, the definition of "enterprise" is the way to scope data lineage initiative. Such an approach makes sense if an organization has different types of business lines and business models. The size of the "enterprise" influences the complexity of the data management roles' design. The number of levels of authorities is an example of such complexity.

So far, we have analyzed the key factors that influence the design of data management roles. We have realized the complexity of this topic. Now it is time to assemble this knowledge and apply it to the data lineage initiative.

8.2   DATA MANAGEMENT ROLES INVOLVED IN DATA LINEAGE DOCUMENTATION

In this sub-chapter, we define accountabilities of key data management roles needed for data lineage documentation. The high-level mapping you find in Table 9. We map the following:

- Data lineage layer
  In the first column, you see the four levels of data lineage documentation: business level, and three levels of data models (conceptual, logical, and physical).
- Key metadata components of data lineage per each layer
  At each level, a set of metadata components define data lineage. We discussed the metamodel of data lineage in detail in Chapter 4.
- Data management capabilities required to deliver data lineage outcomes. To document data lineage components, an organization needs to have in place different data management capabilities. Some of them we discussed in sub-chapter 8.1.4.
- Key data management roles

In this table, I demonstrate only several roles such as business process owner, system owner, and data steward discussed earlier in this chapter.

Each company should have a company-specific set of roles. These roles then should be mapped to the data lineage metadata used in the company.

To specify the accountabilities of each role, I use the RACI (Responsible, Accountable, Consulted, Informed) matrix[4]. In the context of this book:

- Responsible: a data management role that performs a process to perform the task and/or deliver an outcome
- Accountable: a data management role that is accountable for the correct execution of the process and/or the delivery of the intended outcome

In this chapter, we have now identified roles accountable for the documentation of data lineage. Now we can proceed with the requirements for data lineage. All identified roles have their own concerns and requirements for data lineage.

Data lineage layer	Data lineage component	Data management capability	Data management roles*				
			Process owner	System owner	Business data steward	Data management steward	Technical data steward
Business	Business capability map	Business architecture			A	R	
Business	Business subject area	Business architecture			A	R	
Business	Process	Process management	A				
Business	IT asset / data set catalog / Data lineage at the business layer	Information systems (data and application) architecture		A		R	R
Conceptual	Data entity, relationships, constraints	Data modeling			R	A	
Logical	Data entity, data attribute, relationships, business rules	Data modeling, Information systems architecture			R	A	
Physical	Database structure, table, column, relation, ETL job, etc.	Data modeling, application and technology architecture, IT capabilities				R	A

*RACI matrix; A – accountable; R – responsible.

Table 9: Roles and their accountabilities concerning data lineage documentation.

SUMMARY OF CHAPTER 8

- Multiple data management roles perform the documentation of data lineage.
- Data management role is a business role that performs data management-related tasks and delivers intended data management outcomes.
- Data management roles can be functional and virtual.
- Each organization should analyze the existing functional roles and their professional profiles and map them accordingly to the data steward type and role.
- Data steward is a steward that manages data assets on behalf of the organization that owns data.
- Professional background splits data stewards into three categories: business data stewards, data management stewards, technical data stewards.
- Multiple factors influence the design of data management roles:
    - The type of data stewards
    - The dimensions of a business capability
    - The location of roles along with data chains
    - Data management sub-capabilities
    - Data architecture styles
    - An approach to IT solution design
    - Data domain definition
    - The scope of the "enterprise"
- The set of roles needed to document data lineage depends on the following characteristics of data lineage:
    - Data lineage layer
    - Data lineage components
    - Data management capabilities required to deliver data lineage outcomes

9 DEFINE DATA LINEAGE REQUIREMENTS

To define data lineage requirements, a company should have already completed the following:

- Define an applicable data lineage metamodel
  We discussed the metamodel of data lineage in-depth in Chapter 4. The metamodel proposed in this book includes four layers, corresponding components, and metadata elements. Each company should specify the metamodel that suits its needs and requirements.
- Identify data lineage types
  We examined data lineage types in Chapter 5. Data lineage types correspond to the chosen business driver for the data lineage initiative and the selected metamodel. Data lineage types relate to the selected metamodel. Assume, a company has chosen a metamodel with a physical layer only. Two types of data lineage, horizontal and automated, correspond to such a metamodel.

Knowledge of these two factors allows a company to proceed with data lineage requirements.

Data lineage requirements aim to communicate the needs and expectations of stakeholders and fine-tune the scope of the initiative. Data lineage requirements do not depend on the solution. The data lineage requirements can be later used to choose an appropriate IT solution.

In Chapter 9, we will:

- Discuss general requirements
- Examine functional requirements for:
    - metadata and data value lineage
    - vertical and horizontal data lineage

After reading this chapter, you will be able to:

- Organize the gathering of data lineage requirements
- Summarize requirements in a final document

Before we dive into data lineage requirements, we need to agree on the terminology and methodology.

9.1 TYPES OF REQUIREMENTS

Every software implementation recognizes two types of requirements: functional and non-functional. **Functional requirement** is a requirement that specifies what the system should do. Functional requirements define the expected behavior of a system between inputs and outputs. **Non-functional requirement** is a requirement that identifies how the system should do it. In this book, we describe functional requirements only. Non-functional requirements depend on architecture and technology architecture that is unique for each company.

We have identified the relationships between different data lineage types in sub-chapter 5.5. In this chapter, we take the full scope of the data lineage metamodel into consideration. First, we draft requirements for metadata lineage. We start with general requirements. Then proceed with requirements for horizontal and vertical data lineage types.

For data value lineage, we can only identify general requirements and requirements for horizontal data lineage type.

The scope of requirements that we discuss in this chapter has been presented graphically in Figure 43.

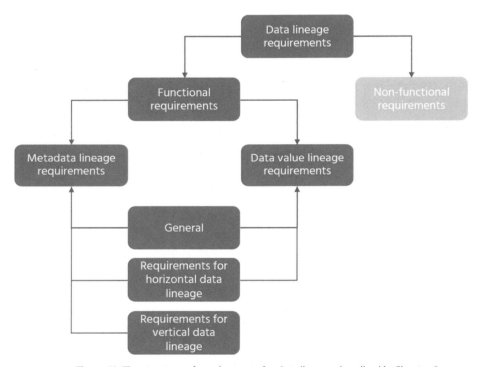

Figure 43: The structure of requirements for data lineage described in Chapter 9.

We start with the consideration of metadata lineage requirements.

9.2 METADATA LINEAGE REQUIREMENTS

I recommend splitting data lineage requirements into general requirements and requirements per data lineage layer:

- General requirements
  General requirements are requirements that apply to every layer of data lineage

documentation. For example, requirements for visualization can be similar to any level of documentation.

- Requirements for horizontal data lineage per each level of abstraction
Commonly, a company starts with the horizontal data lineage at one or more levels of abstraction.
Metadata components, metadata elements, and relationships differ per layer, as demonstrated in sub-chapter 4. Therefore, the requirements per layer vary. Below you find some examples of metadata components per data model level:
  - The business level includes business capabilities, processes, roles, IT assets, and business subject areas (data sets).
  - The conceptual data model level is described with the help of data entities, constraints, and relationships.
  - The logical data model level includes data entities, attributes, business rules, and relationships between them.
  - The physical level description differs per database type. For relational databases, tables, columns, ETL jobs, and other metadata objects are in use.
- Requirements for vertical data lineage
If horizontal data lineage has been documented at more than one layer, then these layers could be linked using vertical data lineage. In the requirements document, you should indicate the required mapping between components at different levels.

Let us elaborate on the example of such requirements in detail. In the additional materials section, you find Template 1, "Data lineage requirements." This template assists in gathering business requirements to scope the data lineage initiative.

9.2.1   GENERAL REQUIREMENTS

General requirements are applicable to every layer of the data lineage metamodel.

You may think about the following:

1. Graphical representation of data lineage as a chain of linked metadata objects and relationships between them
For example, if you document the flow of data between applications, the applications should be linked with each other to demonstrate the direction of data flows along with applications.
2. The visualization of metadata elements for the metadata component
3. Seeing not only the physical name of a column but also its business name
4. The ability to trace the link between metadata objects in two directions: from source to destination and vice versa
It assists you in performing impact and root-cause analysis.
5. Zoom in (drill up and drill down) capability to move between different levels of abstractions
If you investigate data lineage at the table level, you need to drill it down to the column level.
6. A "print document" function in order to get printed evidence about data lineage.
7. Ability to maintain versioning control and archive data lineage for auditability purposes

Now we discuss the requirements for the horizontal data lineage.

9.2.2 HORIZONTAL DATA LINEAGE REQUIREMENTS

We examine requirements for each layer. Let us start with the business layer.

Business layer

1. Maintain the map of business capabilities and related metadata.
2. Maintain the catalog of business processes, roles, and related metadata.
3. Maintain the IT asset catalog and related metadata.
4. Maintain the catalog and business subject areas and corresponding data sets.
5. Catalogs should be centrally maintained.
6. Employees across the company should get access to the information within catalogs.
7. Visualize the following metadata objects and links between them:
   - Business capabilities
   - Business processes
   - IT assets
   - Business subject areas and data sets
8. Visualize metadata elements that describe each of the above-mentioned objects.
9. Maintain data lineage for historical periods.

Conceptual layer

1. Maintain conceptual models with the set of key subject business areas.
2. One central tool should maintain the conceptual models.
3. Each business subject area and data entity should have an unambiguous term and definition.
4. A central tool should maintain business terms and definitions.
5. Maintain the relationships between subject business areas, data entities, and constraints.
6. Visualize the following metadata objects and relationships between them:
   - Business subject areas
   - Data entities
   - Constraints
   - Terms and definitions
7. Visualize metadata elements that describe each of the above-mentioned components.

Logical layer

1. Maintain multiple logical data models with different notations.
2. Link multiple logical data models with each other.
3. Maintain logical data models in one or more central tools to make them accessible throughout the enterprise.
4. Data entities and data attributes should be linked by specified relationships.
5. A central repository should maintain documented business rules.
6. Visualize the following metadata objects and relationships between them:

     ○   Data entities and data attributes
     ○   Business rules
     ○   Terms and definitions

7. Visualize metadata elements that describe each of the above-mentioned components.

Physical level

1. Maintain a central repository of ETL processes.
2. Visualize relationships between physical metadata components.
   For example, for a relational database, visualize links between tables, columns, views, ETL mapping, and ETL content within one database.
   ETL mapping only indicates the location of ETL jobs in data chains. ETL content includes the description of ETL processes.
3. Visualize relationships between metadata objects between different databases.

Requirements at the physical level mainly relate to the automated method to data lineage documentation. Therefore, the following additional requirements should be taken into account:

4. Database type
   Depending on the database type, different methods to record automated data lineage can be realized. Furthermore, scanners to read metadata vary per database type.
5. ETL tool type
   Data moves between different databases and is being transformed by using different ETL tools. Therefore, scanners should be able to read metadata within ETL tools.
6. Level of automation
   In some cases, metadata can be read automatically from databases and ETLs. In some cases, scripts should be provided to upload metadata into a metadata repository and data lineage tool.
7. Response time
   Working with data lineage tooling, you should think about the response time when data lineage diagrams become available. Data lineage can include hundreds of thousands of metadata objects and millions of relationships. Therefore, the capacity of metadata and relationship repositories should meet the expected volumes of metadata objects and relationships.

We have investigated the examples of horizontal data lineage requirements, so now it is time to see the examples of requirements for vertical data lineage.

9.2.3   VERTICAL DATA LINEAGE REQUIREMENTS

You can set up the requirements for vertical data lineage when horizontal data lineage has been documented at more than one layer. The examples of such requirements are:

1. Map the following components between the business and conceptual layer:
        ○   Business capability with subject business area
2. Map the following components between conceptual and logical layers:

      ◦   Subject business area with data entities

      ◦   Constraints with business rules

3. Map the following components between logical and physical layers, for example, for a relational database:

      ◦   Data entity with table

      ◦   Data attribute with column

      ◦   Business rule with ETL job

By now, we have discussed examples for metadata lineage. Now we can focus our attention on the requirements for data value lineage.

9.3   DATA VALUE LINEAGE REQUIREMENTS

Data value lineage explains the path that an individual data record (instance) travels from its origin to its destination and transformations that this record undergoes on its way.

Data value lineage assists in:

- Performing data reconciliation:
  - ◦ Between the same data record in different locations along with a data chain
  - ◦ Between source data records and targeted data records. Targeted data records are the result of aggregation or transformation of the source data record
- Explaining transformations that particular data records are undergone

The identification of business goals should precede the requirements for data value lineage. You may find a less costly solution to meet these requirements. Building reconciliation reports in defined data points, thoroughly document business rules are examples of such workaround solutions. Some applications possess drill-back and audit capabilities that can substitute data value lineage.

If the data value lineage remains in the agenda, you should think about such requirements as, for example:

1. Visualize and track information in a run environment at the level of a data record for executed data processing.
2. For each data record, visualize metadata it has been processed with (i.e., data owner). The properly documented requirements play a great role when a company should choose a tool or set of tools to document data lineage. If the requirements are organized in the form of a checklist, then the comparison of functionality of different solutions becomes much easier.

We have finalized the preparation of data lineage requirements. The next step of the nine-step methodology focuses on choosing appropriate approaches and methods to document data lineage.

SUMMARY OF CHAPTER 9

- To proceed with data lineage requirements, a company should first agree on the required metamodel of data lineage and the types of data lineage.
- Data lineage requirements aim to communicate the needs and expectations of stakeholders and fine-tune the scope of the initiative.
- In this chapter, we have discussed functional requirements for metadata and data value lineage.
- Metadata lineage requirements split into general requirements, requirements for horizontal and vertical data lineage.
- Data value lineage requirements can include only general requirements and requirements for horizontal lineage.
- General requirements are requirements that apply to every layer of data lineage documentation.
- Requirements for horizontal data lineage differ per layer. The reason is that each layer has a corresponding set of components.
- If a horizontal data lineage has been documented at more than one layer, then the requirements for vertical data lineage can be identified.
- Data value lineage requirements should be carefully assessed prior to taking the decision of its implementation. Several workaround solutions exist.

10 | IDENTIFY APPROACHES TO DATA LINEAGE IMPLEMENTATION

Each company should choose its approach for a data lineage business case. Such an approach has to fit the company's goals and resources. The correctly chosen approach enables the feasible and successful implementation of data lineage.

Different factors influence the choice of an approach, as demonstrated in Figure 44:

1. The "enterprise" coverage
2. The method of data lineage documentation
3. The scope parameters of data lineage
4. The direction of documentation
5. The project management style
6. The maturity of metadata architecture

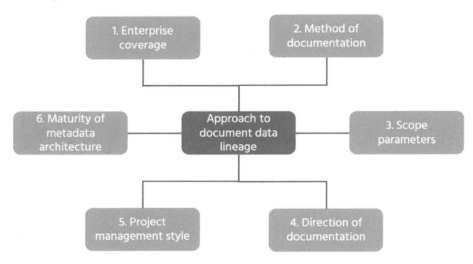

Figure 44: Different factors that influence the choice of an approach to document data lineage.

When you choose an approach, all factors should be analyzed and taken into account.

In Chapter 10, we will:

- Discuss different factors that influence the choice of an approach
- Design a Template to document the progress of the data lineage initiative

After reading this chapter, you will be able to:

- Design the data lineage documentation approach that is applicablea nd feasible for your company
- Analyze the pros and contras of different approaches
- Adjust the Template for progress control for your data lineage initiative

Let us consider one by one each of the factors that influence the choice of the approach.

10.1 FACTORS THAT INFLUENCE THE CHOICE OF AN APPROACH.

The first factor is the "enterprise" coverage.

The "enterprise" coverage

Each company has a choice. It can start an extensive campaign to document data lineage in full scope. It can also bind the initiative to some reasonable and feasible limits.

The concept of business criticality assists in identifying the enterprise scope. Within the data lineage initiative, you should evaluate the criticality of the following:

- Key business drivers
  As we have discussed in Chapter 2, a company may have different drivers to document data lineage. Compliance with legislative and audit requirements, data quality initiatives, and business changes are examples thereof. Among these drivers, a company should choose the most critical one. This driver limits the scope of the "enterprise." The "enterprise" includes a limited group of business units and related data chains. For example, a business change for customer experience is the key business driver. Consequently, only business stakeholders, business units, and data chains involved in the processing and using of customer-related data will be involved in the initiative.
- Business information
  Usually, business users get information in the form of reports and/or dashboards. The specification of the critical reports and critical information that reside there is the next step of the scoping exercise. In our case, only reports and/dashboards that include critical customer data will be taken into the scope.
- Data chains
  Data chains deliver critical business information. Therefore, only data chains that deliver and transform critical business information fall into the scope.
- Data sets and data elements
  To produce critical business information, you need a corresponding set of data. These sets also limit the scope of a data lineage initiative.

The criteria of criticality may vary depending on the business drivers of the data lineage initiative. The common criteria are reputation damage, financial loss, operational risk, sensitive information disclosure, personal safety, and legal violation, etc. More about the concept of criticality, critical business information, data sets, and data elements you find in Chapter 15.

A company may have more than one critical business driver for data lineage. In this case, two or more "enterprises" can be identified. In other words, a company may perform several initiatives on data lineage implementation. Every initiative forms a separate project with its own scope and approaches.

The next factor that impacts the choice of an approach is the scope and types of data lineage.

The method of data lineage documentation

We discussed the key methods of data lineage documentation in sub-chapter 5.4. Descriptive and automated data lineage are two key methods. For different "enterprise" initiatives, you could choose diverse methods of documentation. For one business driver and corresponding "enterprise" scope, you select the descriptive method. For example, many companies to comply with the GDPR (The General Data Protection Regulation) have chosen the descriptive method of data lineage documentation. They mainly focused on the documentation of business processes related to personal data. To comply with such regulation as PERDARR ("Principles for effective risk data aggregation and risk reporting" by the Basel Committee on Banking Supervision's standard number 239), banking institutions have opted for the automated data lineage.

Descriptive and automated methods can be combined within the scope of one "enterprise" initiative. A company could start with the descriptive data lineage and later proceed with the automated one.

The parameters to scope a data lineage initiative represent the next factor that impacts the approach to implement data lineage.

Parameters to scope data lineage

We have discussed in-depth the parameters that help to scope data lineage in Chapter 7. The parameters that influence the choice of the approach are:

- The "length" of data lineage
  The "length" limits the data lineage by identifying the start and endpoints of the documentation along with data chains.
- The "depth" of data lineage
  The "depth" restricts the number of layers for data lineage documentation. You may document data lineage, for example, only at the physical level. You may also extend your initiative by documenting horizontal data lineage at conceptual, logical, and physical levels, and then linking them using vertical lineage.
- Data lineage components
  Each layer has a specific set of components. The number of chosen components will also influence the approach. For example, data lineage at the physical level can document the flow of data between tables and columns and omit ETL mapping and translations.

I want to stress again that for different "enterprise" initiatives, you can choose various scoping parameters.

The next factor that impacts the choice of the implementation approach is the direction of data lineage documentation.

The direction of documentation

This factor is in effect when you are planning to document data lineage at more than one layer. You can perform documentation using one of three approaches: top-down, bottom-up, or hybrid. Let us investigate them one by one.

Top-down approach

The top-down approach assumes that documentation starts at the upper level and then goes down. For example, you start at the business level, then go down to the conceptual level, and so on. In the end, you link all levels using vertical data lineage techniques. It means that you start with the descriptive data lineage and, at the latter stage, implement automated data lineage.

This approach has the following advantages:

- Ability to analyze and optimize business models and data chains
  The business model and key data value chains are the starting points in this approach. The analysis from the top-level highlights the areas of improvement for the whole business.
- Ability to optimize data management capability
  This method stimulates the development of such capabilities as business and data modeling, information systems architecture.
- Ability to link and optimize business and data models
  Using this approach, a company can optimize and link its business and data models as it links the business model level with three levels of data models.
- Ability to optimize application landscape
  The optimization of business and data models may lead to the optimization of the underlying application landscape. In turn, it potentially can reduce IT maintenance costs.

The key disadvantage of this approach is its time- and resource intensity.

It may take a long time until a company gets practical results from the documented data lineage. This approach also requires that such business capabilities as business architecture, data modeling, information systems architecture are in place. Not many companies possess all these capabilities.

Usually, companies prefer the more pragmatic bottom-up approach.

Bottom-up approach

This approach assumes that a company starts with automated data lineage at the physical level.

The key advantage of this method is that a company can start the data lineage initiative and get results in a short time. It is very important for data quality initiatives, for example.

The following disadvantages accompany the bottom-up approach:

- High initial investments
  Automated data lineage requires initial investments to cover the costs of software licenses and implementation.
- Limited scope
  Several factors may limit the scope of automated data lineage. The first factor is the type of databases. For legacy software, automated data lineage can become a challenge. The second is the number of applications. The more applications with different databases, the longer the duration of implementation.
- Limited business usability
  Usually, the deliverables of automated data lineage do not meet the needs and requirements of business users.

If a company has enough resources, it may use the hybrid approach to combine the advantages and overcome the disadvantages of both methods.

Hybrid approach

The hybrid approach assumes the simultaneous documentation of data lineage at two levels:
1. Business level combined with the conceptual and logical levels of data models using descriptive data lineage
2. Physical level of data models by implementing automated data lineage

One of the challenges of this method is the link between data lineage at logical and physical levels. The reason is that one logical model can be realized in multiple physical models. The implementation of data catalogs is an unavoidable condition to succeed.

The last decision about the approach to implementing data lineage goes about the method of the implementation.

The project management style

Many companies face the situation when they need to implement data lineage simultaneously in different parts of the company or across the whole company at once.

From the project management perspective, they can use one of the following approaches:
- Centralized
- Decentralized
- Hybrid

Let us consider in depth each of these approaches.

Centralized approach

The centralized approach usually assumes a standard approach to the data lineage documentation across a company. This approach can be used when a company has the ambition to document data lineage across the whole company. The standard approach includes:
- A common metadata model of data lineage
  Common metadata includes a set of components and metadata elements recommended for the documentation. For example, metadata models may include the combination of the data lineage at the physical levels and business processes.
- A common approach to scope data lineage and corresponding methods of documentation
  The common approach to scope and methods predefine the standard set of approaches discussed above in sub-chapters 10.1 - 10.4.
- Data lineage tooling
  The same set of tools should be used across the company.

This method has significant advantages:
- Provide control and optimization of company's resources
  The documentation of data lineage is a resource-intensive exercise. The usage of the

same approach and tooling allows a company to save resources on the development of a methodology, gain benefits from the learning curve, and re-usage of building blocks.

- Link data lineage documented in different parts of the company
One of the key challenges in data lineage implementation is to cover the whole company landscape. If a company has long and complex data chains, data lineage will be documented in parts. Therefore, the task of combining deliverables of different data lineage initiatives is crucial.

Several disadvantages accompany this approach:

- Difficulties in designing the common approach
To design the common approach, the requirements from different parts of a company should be gathered and analyzed. It may take months and years to design the common approach and implement recommended tooling.
- Dependency on a vendor provider for data lineage tooling
If a company has a large-scale application landscape, the dependency on one vendor may have a tremendous financial impact due to the license costs. It also causes risks for the success of the implementation if the functionality not fully matches all requirements.
- The necessity to have a well-established data management function across the company
The centralized approach does not always mean that the same team will implement data lineage across the whole company. Teams of data management professionals in diverse organizational units should be capable of performing the implementation.

If the disadvantages of this approach override the advantages, a company can opt for a decentralized approach.

Decentralized approach

A decentralized approach can be useful when only some parts of the company's application landscape require the knowledge of data lineage. In this case, data lineage can be documented by individual teams in diverse parts of a company. In this case, to speed up the initiative, each team takes the responsibility to:

- Gather requirements and define the metamodel of data lineage
- Specify the scope and approaches
- Choose a tool that meets the specified requirements

The advantages and disadvantages of the centralized approach become the opposites for the decentralized approach.

The advantages of this approach are that a company could:

- Spare time on the design of the common approach
- Reduce the dependency on one vendor

The biggest disadvantage is the challenge of getting a complete overview of data lineage across the company. This challenge results from the differences in metamodels of data lineage, different scope, and tools.

To use the advantages of both approaches and diminish disadvantages, a company should develop a hybrid approach.

Hybrid approach

Each company should develop its approach for data lineage implementation by analyzing and thinking through all approaches discussed in this chapter. It should put at the forefront the following factors:

- Required scope of data lineage
- Expected deadlines
- Resources available

The last but not least factor that impacts the approach for data lineage is metadata architecture.

The maturity of metadata architecture

Metadata management is one of the data management capabilities that delivers data lineage. I mentioned it in sub-chapter 1.4. Metadata architecture is one of the capabilities of metadata management. The relationship between data lineage and metadata management is much more profound. Metadata lineage has many dependencies with metadata architecture. I am convinced that a lot of topics that we have already discussed about data lineage intercect the area of metadata architecture.

It is generally accepted to think that metadata architecture focuses on gathering metadata at the physical level. In reality, the challenge is much broader. All data that describes other data is metadata. Metadata forms complex structures. As I pointed out in sub-chapter 3.2, data lineage is also metadata. It is difficult for companies to develop and implement metadata architecture due to the complexity of the metadata concept. Even metadata architecture at the physical level is considerable progress.

If metadata architecture at any scope is being implemented, it impacts the approach to implement data lineage. Metadata repositories contain metadata that creates the basis for data lineage. The approach to implementing a metadata repository forms the basis to approach data lineage documentation.

By now, we have finalized the consideration of different factors that influence the approach to data lineage implementation.

Each data lineage business case should take into consideration these and some other factors to define the proper approach. Approaches will differ per company. Even within one company, approaches for different data lineage initiatives can vary.

When the scope and approach to document data lineage have been identified, you need to communicate your approach.

10.2 COMMUNICATE THE SCOPE AND APPROACHES

I have found a simple way to communicate the scope of data lineage initiative and demonstrate progress in my practice.

Template 2 "The scope and progress of a data lineage initiative" you can find in the Additional materials of this book.

The approach is simple. You create a matrix, as shown in Table 10. Horizontally, you demonstrate different data lineage initiatives and IT assets that form data chains. Vertically, you indicate data lineage layers and components. In the matrix body, you show the correspondence between layers and components, from one side, and initiatives and IT assets, from another side. Such a matrix can also be used to demonstrate plans and progress follow-up.

DL layer	DL component	DL Initiative 1		DL Initiative 2	
		IT asset 1	IT asset 2	IT asset 3	IT asset 4
Business	Process	Q2 2022	Q2 2022		
Conceptual	Data entity	Q3 2022	Q3 2022		
Logical	Data attribute				
Physical	Table			Q4 2021	Q1 2021

Table 10: An example to demonstrate the scope, planning, and progress follow-up for data lineage initiatives.

The next step in our nine-step methodology is choosing a solution.

SUMMARY OF CHAPTER 10

- Each company should choose its approach for the implementation of data lineage.
- Such an approach should fit the company's goals and resources.
- Different factors influence the choice of an approach:
    1. The "enterprise" coverage
       The "enterprise" coverage factor requires the evaluation of criticality of the following:
        a) Key business drivers
        b) Business information
        c) Data chains
        d) Data sets and data elements
    2. The method of data lineage documentation
       Descriptive and automated methods of data lineage form the second factor.
    3. The scope parameters of data lineage
       The parameters that influence the choice of the approach are:
        a) The "length" of data lineage
        b) The "depth" of data lineage
        c) Data lineage components
    4. The direction of documentation
       Three approaches characterize the direction of data lineage documentation:
        a) Top-down approach
        b) Bottom-up approach
        c) Hybrid approach
    5. The project management style
       From the project management perspective, a company can use the following approaches:
        a) Centralized
        b) Decentralized
        c) Hybrid
    6. The maturity of metadata architecture

       The approach to design metadata architecture and implement a metadata repository forms the basis to approach data lineage documentation.

11 | CHOOSE A SUITABLE DATA LINEAGE SOLUTION

Years ago, I was a project manager for the implementation of an advanced ERP solution at a big machinery plant. Until then, they used an internally built Access-based database. My first task was to gather business requirements. I would never forget one conversation with a top stakeholder. He dreamed that once the ERP is installed, he should never do something manually with the system. One press on button...and the system would perform all operations.

Years later, dealing with data lineage, I see back situations similar to those that I have just described.

The documentation of data lineage requires suitable software. For the last several years, a significant number of data lineage applications with different technologies have appeared on the market. This tendency would continue. The most important thing about the software is to find such that meets your current requirements. It also should leave some space for future developments. There is no bad or good solution. A solution either meets or does not meet your requirements and resources.

In this chapter, we will:

- Speak about the relationships between software needs, requirements, solutions, products, and functionality
- Discuss key software functionalities required to document data lineage
- Present the key sources of information about software providers
- Discuss the challenges associated with the software choice
- Provide an overview of the types of software and products that can be used to record data lineage

After reading this chapter, you will be able to:

- Identify requirements to choose a software solution
- Investigate sources of information about solutions
- Compare different solutions and products

11.1 TERMINOLOGY RELATED TO A SOFTWARE SOLUTION

Once I spoke to a newly appointed chief data officer of a large American company. He proudly said: "We have not had so far a data governance and data management function. We have just bought a data governance tool. We hope it will help us to implement these functions." This statement is the "best" example of what companies SHOULD NOT do to implement any kind of software.

In this sub-chapter, I would like to reach a common understanding of the logical way to find the software you need. For that, let me outline the provided definitions and specify relationships between needs, requirements, solutions, products, and functionality, as shown in Figure 45.

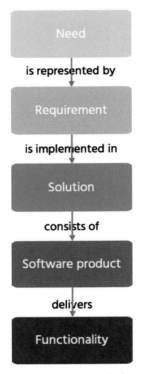

Figure 45. The relationships between need, requirement, solution, software product, and functionality.

The Guide to the Business Analysis Body of Knowledge (BABOK® Guide) specifies a need as a "problem or opportunity to be addressed"[1]. To meet the needs, they have to be translated into requirements. According to the BABOK® Guide, "requirements is a usable representation of a need"[2]. To meet requirements, a company should implement a solution. A solution is "a specific way of satisfying one or more needs in a context"[3]. A solution may require several products. According to the ISO/IEC/IEEE 24748-5:2017 "Systems and software engineering – Life Cycle Management – Part 5: Software development planning", a software product is a "set of computer programs, procedures, and possibly associated documentation and data"[4]. The software possesses one or more functionalities. As per ISO/TR 17427-4:2015 "Intelligent transport systems — Cooperative ITS — Part 4: Minimum system requirements and behavior for core systems" a functionality is "capabilities of the various computational, user interfaces, input, output, data management, and other features provided by a product"[5].

In my opinion, the model in Figure 45 demonstrates an order in which each company should proceed with looking for any software:

1. Define business needs
   Let us take as an example the search for the data lineage product. One of the key needs of

business stakeholders is to comply with regulations. Compliance means the following. Data business users should know the origin of data, the path that data flows across different systems, and the transformations that data undergoes. Other examples of business need we discussed in Chapter 2.

2.   Translate business needs into requirements
     Needs should be translated into requirements. Requirements should be specific, measurable, assignable, realistic, and time-related (SMART[6]) to be implemented. Let us continue the above-mentioned example. The needs of business users have been translated into the requirements to document data lineage at a physical level.
     The full list of requirements for data lineage we have overseen in Chapter 9.

3.   Find out solutions, products, and functionality that meet the specified requirements
     In this chapter, we discuss how to discover and evaluate software products, and their functionality to meet the company's requirements in data lineage. For our example, a company should search for a provider that delivers a solution for automated data lineage. This solution should have a functionality compatible with the company's IT assets.

11.2 TYPES OF SOFTWARE SOLUTIONS FOR DOCUMENTING DATA LINEAGE

For this book, I have analyzed 145 different software solutions mentioned in 13 different sources. During this exercise, I came across several challenges. I address all challenges in sub-chapter 11.3. One challenge I want to discuss now. The challenge is about the terminology. I have seen that different providers use different approaches to demonstrate their "solutions" and "products." "Functionality" is a term that is hardly used. Therefore, I use only the terms "solution" and "product."

For analysis purposes, I split solutions into the following categories:

- Business process management
- Enterprise architecture
- Data governance
- Data modeling
- Metadata management
- Data quality
- Data management/data fabric

I aligned these categories with the metamodel of data lineage, discussed in Chapter 4.

Examples of software solutions and their mapping to the key components of data lineage you can see in Figure 46.

In Chapter 4, we have identified the following components of data lineage:

- Business capability
  To document business capabilities, an enterprise architecture solution is required.
- Business process, role, IT assets
  A business process modeling solution usually assists in documenting business processes. Often, IT assets are linked to business processes. Therefore, business process modeling solutions also document these components.

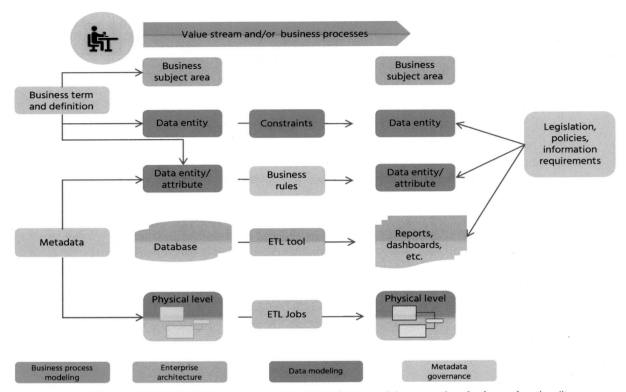

Figure 46. The relationship between key components of data lineage and the categories of software functionality.

- Data models at different levels of abstraction
  A data modeling solution ensures the documentation of conceptual, logical, and physical data models. Metadata solutions document actual components involved in data transformations at the physical level.
- IT asset
  Different solutions can document this component of data lineage. Enterprise architecture, business process modeling, and metadata management solutions use this component in their repositories.
- Business rule and/or ETL
  Metadata solutions usually document business rules. Sometimes, business data modeling software maintains the documentation of such components.

Additionally, to the key components of data lineage, a company may need to document the following:

- Business term and definition
  Business subject areas, data entities, and probably, data attributes should have unambiguous business terms and definitions. Data governance solutions or metadata solutions could assist in documenting these components.
- Legislation, policy, requirements
  Data governance solutions can offer the functionality for documentation.

Every solution includes a set of products and/or functionalities. In-depth, we discuss this topic in sub-chapter 11.4. Now we proceed with the description of sources where you can find information about data lineage-related software.

11.3 KEY SOURCES FOR DATA LINEAGE SOLUTIONS

The Internet is the first place and Google search is the first engine that you probably use for searching. You get a lot of information, and you need to know how to proceed. I recommend performing the search following three steps. Graphically, you find these steps in Figure 47.

Figure 47. Key steps to investigate software solutions.

Step 1. Research well-known and trustworthy sources.

Gartner's reviews are the first source I take a look at. The second option is to use Google Search. Using Google Search, you come across multiple reviews having a headline like "the best ...software" in the field. Some of these sources already have brief information about vendors and products, and solutions they offer. When you have gathered enough reliable sources, you can proceed with the next step.

Step 2. Create a list of vendors and solutions.

In step 2, you focus on the creation of the list of potential solutions. You will come across overlapping information. So, clean up the list and proceed with further investigation.

Step 3. Visit vendors' sites and map their solutions and products to your requirements.

Before performing this step, you should already have requirements for data lineage. We discussed requirements in Chapter 9. This step is the most time-consuming. It would help if you tried to map your requirements with offered solutions and products.

These steps seem to be simple and straightforward, but you should be prepared for some unexpected challenges. During my investigation, I experienced some challenges. I list some of them to ease your task. So, be prepared.

Challenge 1 - *The classification terminology of solutions often does not match the generally accepted terminology. It is also not in sync at different sites.*

As an example, let us take "data governance" tools. The DAMA-DMBOK2 defines data governance as "Exercise of authority and control (planning, monitoring, and enforcement) over the management of data assets"[7]. According to the DAMA-DMBOK2[8], the examples of data governance deliverables are:

- Data Strategy
- Data Principles
- Data Governance Policies, Processes
- Operating Framework
- Business Glossary
- Etc.

In short, data governance develops and maintains the framework that consists of rules and roles. This framework enables the operation of data management processes. Data management organizes and coordinates the activities to conduct data lifecycle operations. In-depth investigation on the subject you can read in the series of articles "Data Management & Data Governance 101: The Yin and Yang Duality"[9].

I compared four sites that provided an overview of data governance-related solutions. I collected their definitions of data governance in Table 11.

So, even from a first glance, you can see that different companies explore the diverse understanding of data governance and related solutions. These definitions and goals of the data governance software solutions do not match each other. They also do not always correspond to the generally accepted definition of data governance provided by the DAMA-DMBOK2.

For example, the definition provided by Capterra includes "availability, usability, security, and storage of enterprise level data." In my opinion, these characteristics relate to operational data management, not to data governance.

The difference in the definitions causes the next challenge related to the unclearness about the functionality of particular software.

Challenge 2 - *Even if the classification of solutions is similar, very often, the lists of software providers and/or products differ greatly.*

Let's return to Table 11 and check the column "The name of a solution classification." It is noticeable that the names differ slightly, even if everything goes about data governance. But the key question is whether the vendors and tools advertised at these sites are the same?

In Table 12, I demonstrate how often different sites mention the same tool.

Finally, I found only three software solutions referenced twice at different sites: A.K.A, Collibra, and Informatica. It means that the criteria to reference solutions at different sites differ greatly.

Source	The name of the solution classification	Definition
Software Testing Help[10]	Data governance tool	"Data Governance is a centralized control mechanism to manage data availability, security, usability, and integrity."[14]
Capterra[11]	Data governance software	"Data Governance software employs modern tools and visualization techniques to manage the availability, usability, security, and storage of enterprise level data."[15]
Towards Data Science[12]	Data governance framework tools	"[…] a system of data governance[…]is essentially a methodical approach of dealing with a company's data. It provides a structure of policies, protocols, procedures, and metrics to help companies dodge risks and liabilities, as well as a set of tools to mine data[…]."[16]
Datamation[13]	Data governance tool and software	"Gartner defines master data management, its term for data governance, as 'a technology-enabled discipline in which business and IT work together to ensure the uniformity, accuracy, stewardship, semantic consistency, and accountability of the enterprise's official shared master data assets.'"[17]

Table 11: The definition of "data governance" at Internet sites that provide the overview of data governance solutions.

	Software Testing Help[18]	Capterra[19]	Towards Data Science[20]	Datamation[21]
The total number of referenced software solutions	10	103	5	10
The same tool, referenced at 2 sites:	3	1	2	
A.K.A.	1	1		
Collibra	1		1	
Informatica	1		1	

Table 12: The number of software solutions with repeated references.

It brings me to the following striking conclusion. Depending on the site you visit, you may get quite a different list of recommended software. But it is not the end of the story. The different choices at the diverse sites lead to the following confusion. The tools of the same category recommended at different sites have different functionality.

Challenge 3 - *Software products with similar solutions have quite different functionalities.*

To demonstrate this challenge, I still elaborate the examples with data governance software and use some examples of software recommended by Capterra.[22] I have randomly chosen three software providers from the list of 103. I went to the sites of these providers and checked the content of their solutions. The results you find in Table 13.

Software provider	Product / functionality
A.K.A.[23]	• Information assets register • Information architecture • Taxonomy, thesauri and ontology • Glossaries • Metadata repository • Etc.
Alfresso Content Services[24]	• Document management • Document scanning and Capture • Information governance • Etc.
ArcTitam[25]	• Email archiving product

Table 13: Examples of the functionality of different "data governance" software solutions.

I hope you get the point. The functionalities of these software products differ greatly. So, if you are looking for a metadata repository, you don't need to spend your time searching for email archiving solutions. Furthermore, the metadata repository product belongs to the metadata management solution, in my opinion. Of course, the classification of software solutions is subjective. You simply need to be aware of the differences in understanding of terms used at the sites with the "best" software. The word "best" brings us to the next challenge.

Challenge 4 - *The criteria to define software as "the best" is unclear. Furthermore, the criteria used by different sources may differ greatly.*

I went through several sites that promote "the best" software. For example, Software Testing Help[26] says that the software is "the most popular"[27]. My question is: "What are the criteria of "popularity?"

Capterra[28] uses reviews, but some of the software has no reviews at all. In any case, the question about the criteria to mark a software as "the best" remains. In my opinion, the definition of "the best" is relative. Something can be "the best" when it meets some criteria and fits some requirements.

For example, Gartner provides clear evaluation criteria for "Magic Quadrants." These criteria include not only the evaluation of products but also the company's market strategy, performance, etc. Of course, the question is whether the vendor's strategy would assist you in choosing software that meets your requirements. It is wise to keep in mind that you first need to specify your requirements and only then start investigating "the best" products and solutions. I want to mention the last challenge associated with the software classification that I found.

Challenge 5 - *The same product can be classified differently at different sources.*

To explain my point, let us take Informatica as an example. Informatica appears in Gartner's "Magic Quadrant" 2020 for Data Quality Tools[29] and Metadata Management Solutions[30]. At the same time, Informatica has been classified as "Data governance tools" by Software Testing Help[31], as "Data Governance Framework tools" by Toward Data Science[32], and as the "Data Fabric Software" by 360 Quadrants[33]. Of course, Informatica is one of the leaders in data management solutions and has multiple products and functionality. The challenge is that some of these solutions are leading, while other solutions only add value to the leading functionality.

So, you should be focused on what functionality you are looking for.

I think that the awareness of these challenges will assist you to be effective and successful in your choice of software.

At the end of this chapter, we focus on some features of software solutions related to data lineage. The categories of such solutions I mentioned in sub-chapter 11.1. For each solution category, I highlight the key requirements and functionality that could meet these requirements. In Additional materials, you find the overview of leading software solutions that relate to data lineage.

11.4 SOFTWARE SOLUTIONS FOR DOCUMENTING DATA LINEAGE

In this sub-chapter, I provide examples of the relationships between:
- Data lineage layers and components
- Data lineage requirements
- Software solutions and their products

The discussed requirements and functionalities are only examples you can use as a starting point to perform the analysis between the requirements of your company and solutions.

All references to Internet websites or software providers are only for demonstration purposes. I do not intend to recommend and demonstrate any particular preferences regarding software products. I am sure the proverb "Every Jack has his Jill" applies to every data lineage solution.

If you recall, we have identified four layers of data lineage:

- Business
- Data model, including:
  - Conceptual
  - Logical
  - Physical levels

We start the analysis of software with the business layer and its first component: the business process.

11.4.1 BUSINESS PROCESS MODELING SOLUTIONS

A business process is a data lineage component that belongs to the business layer. Business process modeling solutions focus on the documentation of business processes. The relationships between a data lineage component, requirements to solutions, and expected products/functionality can be seen in Figure 48.

Below are examples of the requirements to process modeling software:

- Ability to document business processes at different levels of abstraction
  Business processes can be documented at different levels of abstraction. The solution must allow building and linking processes at multiple levels of hierarchy.
- Collaboration
  The business processes should be available for different teams to work on. Therefore, a solution should maintain a central repository.
- Integration
  It should be possible to link business processes developed in the tool with artifacts produced in other software tools. For example, you should be able to link the repository of IT assets with business processes.

A business process modeling software should demonstrate the following functionalities or capabilities to meet the above-mentioned requirements:

- Hierarchy structure and drill-down and -up functionality
  A solution should maintain the modeling of business processes at different levels of abstraction. It should also allow business users to link business processes at different abstraction levels. A drill-down/up functionality should be in place.
- Standard diagrams and notations
  A solution should have different standardized diagrams for different types of business processes. It also should maintain different notations of the documentation.
- Integration
  A solution should allow two types of integration. The first type is the integration with other software solutions. The second one is the integration of different processes designed within the tooling. The last requirement is closely connected to the collaboration requirements.

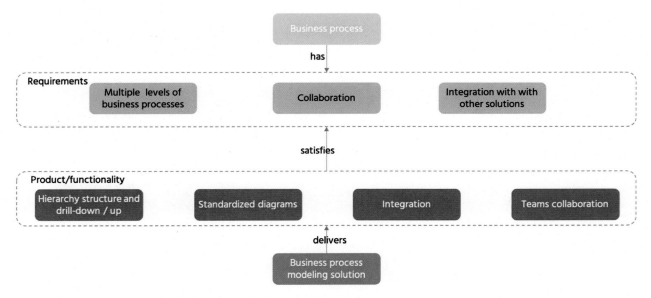

Figure 48: An example of requirements and solutions for a business process component.

- Teams collaboration
  Different teams should be able to work simultaneously on the same set of processes.

Business modeling software may not be complicated. Companies often use MS PowerPoint, MS Visio, or Lucidchart[34]. These software products have good visualization capabilities, but they lack a database repository. The ARIS[35] software is an example of a more complicated solution. Depending on the complexity of your company's business processes, there are plenty of different solutions on the market.

The business layer of data lineage next to processes includes other components such as business capability, for example. Let us consider solutions for the rest of the business layer's components.

11.4.2 ENTERPRISE ARCHITECTURE SOLUTIONS

The following data lineage components are part of the business layer:
- Business capability
- Value stream
- IT assets, including IT systems, applications, databases, etc.
- Application flow

Enterprise architecture solutions can assist in documenting these components.

The example of the requirements and functionality of an enterprise architecture solution can be seen in Figure 49.

You should think about the following basic requirements for enterprise architecture solution:
- Multiple levels of hierarchies
  For example, it is recommended to document the business capability map at least at three

135

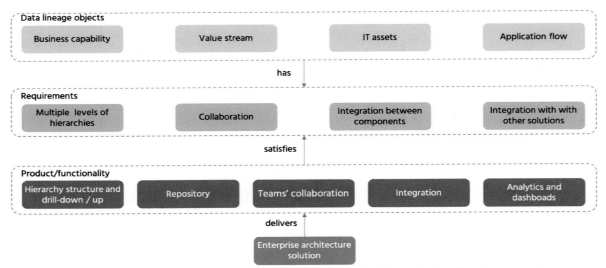

Figure 49: An example of requirements and solutions for the data lineage business layer's components.

levels of abstraction. Therefore, a solution should maintain a hierarchy structure of objects and have drill-down and drill-up functionality.

- Repository
  To manage company's assets, for example, IT assets, a central repository is needed.
- Teams' collaboration and integration
  These functionalities are similar to those that we have discussed for a business process modeling solution.
- Analytics and dashboards
  For the enterprise architecture solution, the capability to report and analyze information persisted in a repository is important.

I want to point out some challenges associated with this type of solution. Enterprise architecture, according to TOGAF® 9.2[36], includes four different types of architecture: business, data, application, and technology. The data lineage components mentioned in Figure 49 belong to business and application architecture. The challenge is that diverse software products support a different range of enterprise architectures. I randomly checked several enterprise architecture products published by Capterra[37]. For example, the Iris Business Architect[38] delivers only solutions for business architecture. Sparx Systems[39] offers not only the enterprise architecture functionalities but a wide range of other functionalities including, for example, business process management, document management, etc. Adaptive SRG[40] is also an integrated solution. Next to the enterprise architecture, it offers data quality, document management, compliance management, and other solutions. The choice of software depends on the extent to which your company has developed the enterprise architecture function and what kind of functionality it requires.

So, business process modeling and enterprise architecture solutions can cover to a great extent the documentation of data lineage at the business layer.

Now it is time to look at solutions that can document data lineage at the data model level.

11.4.3   DATA MODELING SOLUTIONS

Data models at different levels of abstractions are the next data lineage components that should be documented. For that, you need a data modeling solution. The example of the requirements and functionality of a data modeling solution you can see in Figure 50.

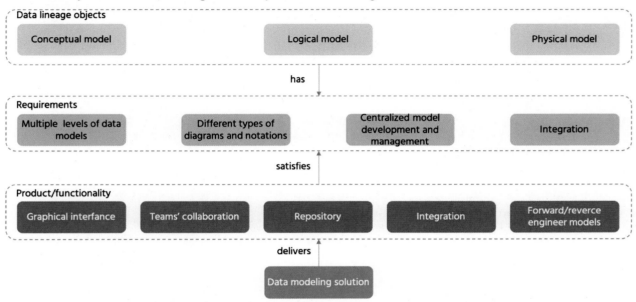

Figure 50: An example of requirements and solutions for the data modeling layer.

In sub-chapter 4.2, we discussed the challenges associated with data modeling. Some of these challenges come out when choosing the data modeling solutions and can be interpreted as requirements:

- Multiple levels of data models
  Software should be able to document data models at different abstraction levels and link them with each other. It means that software should have a functionality that can integrate data models at different levels.
- Different types of data models, data modeling diagrams, and notations

Software should maintain different types of data models, data modeling schemes, and corresponding diagramming notations.

Earlier, we discussed different approaches to data models. The classical approach recognizes conceptual, logical, and physical data models. New approaches focus, for example, on semantic-based data models. The choice of data modeling schemes and corresponding diagramming notations depends on the types of databases used within a company. Large companies definitely may use different types of databases. Therefore, data modeling solutions should be able to integrate different data models, and data modeling schemes with different diagramming notations.

- Centralized model development and management
  This requirement means that different teams across a company should have access to the

central repository of data models. A collaborative environment should allow different teams to exchange information and work on models simultaneously.

- Software should engineer models forward and in reverse
  Forward engineering means that a logical model can be transformed into a physical one. It means that a solution should model data from relational, NoSQL, big data, BI, and ETL sources. It also means that a physical model can be transformed into a physical database schema. Reverse engineering does the opposite. It focuses on the reconstructing of logical models from physical ones.

There are plenty of different data modeling solutions. If you need a light version, you can choose Archi[41], an open-source data modeling tool. I also want to mention some other solutions, such as the Sparx System Enterprise Architect[42], ER/Studio by Idera[43], and ERWIN[44]. There is one reason for mentioning them. These solutions are integrated. They offer some other solutions that are required for the documentation of data lineage.

We have investigated solutions that cover two key layers; business and data modeling. But these solutions mainly focus on descriptive data lineage. We need to examine solutions that offer automated methods to document data lineage at the physical level.

11.4.4 METADATA, DATA GOVERNANCE, AND DATA LINEAGE SOLUTIONS

I combine these three classifications of solutions in one paragraph. There are a couple of reasons for that. First, very often, the same software solutions have been classified in different contexts as "data governance," "metadata," and "data lineage." Collibra, Erwin, IBM, Informatica, Oracle, and SAS are the most prominent examples of that. The second reason is the definition of "metadata". The term "metadata" includes a wide range of different types of data. Even data lineage itself is metadata at a higher level of abstraction. Data models are also metadata. It brings a lot of confusion and challenges while talking about "metadata" solutions, repositories, etc. You always should go deep in detail to understand what these terms mean in a specific context. In this book, I discuss a metadata, data governance, and data lineage solutions to document the following data lineage components:

- Business metadata:
  - Business term and definition
  - Legislation, policies, information, and data requirements
- Technical metadata
  - Data definition
  - Description of databases
  - Business rules
  - Description of data processing at the physical level

In Figure 51, you will see the relationship between the above-mentioned data lineage components, requirements, software solutions, and products/functionality.

You should keep in mind the following requirements for the solutions:

- Different types of metadata
  We have just discussed that the term "metadata" has a different meaning in a different

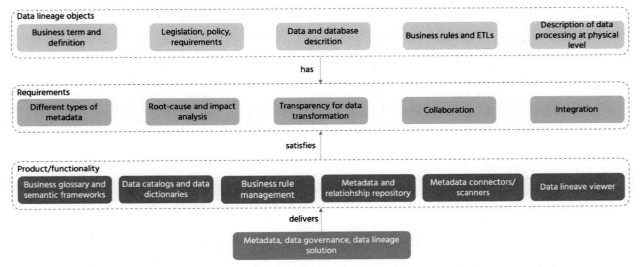

Figure 51: A relationship between data lineage objects and metadata, data governance, data lineage solutions.

context. For example, metadata about data sets differs from the metadata about tables and columns in databases. The solution should maintain the set of different repositories for different types of metadata.

- Ability to perform root-cause and impact analyses
  Data moves across the different systems, applications, databases along with data chains. Metadata describes these movements at different levels of abstraction. The solution should allow tracking the relationships between different metadata objects and performing root-cause and impact analysis.
- Transparency for data transformation
  Along with data chains, data undergoes different transformations. The transparency of such transformation is one of the key legislative requirements. To ensure the transparency of data transformation, a solution should maintain a repository of business rules applied to data.
- Collaboration and integration
  These requirements are similar to those that we discussed above.

To meet the above-described requirements, a solution should have a set of products and/or functionalities.

Sometimes it is difficult to make a comparison of products of different providers. Various providers put different meanings for the same product name. Let's take, for example, the solution of Solidatus[45]. Solidatus is a rapidly growing company that offers a data lineage solution. Please take a look at their solution description. You will find that the "data catalog" solution includes "business glossaries," "technical data descriptions," "assets inventory," policies and standards," and "other taxonomies"[46]. Octopai[47] provides a slightly different definition. In their opinion, "The data catalog is a tool that uses a completed business glossary and data dictionaries to locate data across the entire organization"[48]. In this book, I provide an example of the required solution products. While investigating a specific solution, you should dig deeper to understand the functionality behind different products. Below, you find some common terms that I use in this book to describe metadata-related solutions. As I mentioned, the definitions can vary among different solution providers. In this book, I apply the following definitions:

- **Business glossary**
  A business glossary is a collection of business terms and corresponding definitions.
- **Data dictionary**
  A data dictionary is a collection that contains metadata about data elements at the different levels of abstraction. It may include metadata about data entities and attributes at the logical level of a data model. It also may contain metadata about data elements at the physical level of data models or database levels.
- **Metadata repository**
  A metadata repository is a database that maintains a data dictionary.
- **Data catalog**
  A data catalog is a collection of the information about the location of data sets and data elements across an enterprise.
- **Business rule repository**
  A business rule repository is a database that collects business rules applied to data. In the best-case scenario, this repository also includes the representation of these rules in programming codes.
- **Data lineage viewer, metadata connectors, relationship repositories**
  Data lineage at the physical level requires a set of different capabilities. First, metadata should be read from different databases. Metadata connectors perform these tasks. Then metadata components and relations among them should be stored in a repository. A **data lineage viewer** is a tool that enables the visual representation of these metadata objects and relationships.

Some other solutions also have relations to the data lineage solutions.

11.4.5   DATA QUALITY AND KNOWLEDGE GRAPHS SOLUTIONS

I want to mention only two types of extra solutions you should pay attention to:

- Data quality solutions
  Some data lineage-related solutions integrated solutions for data quality. A data quality solution may include different functionalities. The first is data profiling, which allows examining data in different sources, investigating patrons, discovering irregularities and potential data quality issues. The second functionality may focus on the governance of data quality issues. Data lineage is the "must" condition for the successful governance of data quality. Therefore, the integrated data lineage and data quality solutions could deliver additional business benefits.
- Knowledge graphs solutions
  Knowledge graphs solutions explore the benefits of graphical databases. The technology allows connecting different sources of metadata. In this book, I have demonstrated that data lineage may be interpreted as a complex set of different metadata components. It may be challenging to find integrated software that includes all of the required solutions.

Therefore, the knowledge graph solution can be the best integration tool to integrate metadata that has been kept in different solutions.

11.4.6 THE HIGH-LEVEL OVERVIEW OF DATA LINEAGE-RELATED SOLUTIONS

The overview of different commercial Off-The-Shelf (COTS) solutions and corresponding functionality you find in Additional materials.

Some companies prefer to build their own solutions to capture data lineage. I have seen examples of data lineage solutions built using SQL and graphical databases. I am sure that the pros and contras between self-built and COTS data lineage solutions are similar to any type of software product.

In this book, I only focus on COTS solutions. I use different sources to compile the final list of providers and their solutions. I put the following assumptions into the formation of this list:

1. The list includes the following solutions:
    1. Business process modeling
       The solution offers the functionality to build business processes, as discussed in sub-chapter 11.4.1.
    2. Enterprise architecture
       The solution focuses on the design and maintenance of business, data, and application architecture artifacts needed for data lineage documentation, as explained in sub-chapter 11.4.2.
    3. Data modeling
       The solution includes functionalities to document and integrate data models at different levels of abstractions. The key features of the solution we discussed in sub-chapter 11.4.3.
    4. Data governance, including:
       - Stewardship
         This requirement means that a solution maintains the repository of data governance roles.
       - Policies and legislations
         A solution includes the repository of policies and legislations that can be linked to business data areas, data sets, and eventually, to data elements.

       These components correspond to the DAMA-DMBOK2's[49] definition of data governance.
    5. Metadata management:
       - Data catalog, business glossary, data dictionary, metadata repository
         These products maintain the description of metadata objects at different levels of abstraction.
       - Business rules manager
         This functionality represents the repository to store business rules applied to data transformation.
       - Automated data lineage at the physical level
         This functionality ensures the visual representation of metadata objects and relationships between them.

  - ○ Connectors
    Connectors allow automatic reading of codes to discover metadata objects and relationships between them.
    You can find more details about requirements to record metadata in sub-chapter 11.4.4.
  6. Data quality
    Data quality focuses either on data profiling or on the governance of data quality issues.
  7. Knowledge graphs
    The functionality allows linking different data lineage artifacts by using graph databases capabilities.
    For more details, check sub-chapter 11.4.5.
2. The list does not include a more detailed classification of products or functionalities.
  I made this choice for two reasons:
  1. New products and functionalities can be updated more frequently than the information in this book.
  2. The level of details about products provided at sites of different providers does not allow making a correct comparison.

  Therefore, the list gives only a high-level overview of the solutions. The detailed comparison of the products remains a challenge for the readers of this book.
3. The list includes only providers that deliver more than one capability required to document data lineage.
  The key reason for that is the necessity of an integrated solution to document multiple data lineage components.
  It means that I have not included providers that deliver only one capability. For example, a provider that offers only a data modeling solution.

By now, you know what kind of data lineage you are going to document. You also should have chosen the appropriate software. Now you are ready to proceed with the documentation.

SUMMARY OF CHAPTER 11

- Three steps lead you to choose a software solution:
    - Define business needs
    - Translate business needs into requirements
    - Find solutions, products, and functionality that meet the defined requirements
- To find out the information about software solutions, you should perform the following steps:
    - Check well-known and trustworthy sources
    - Create a list of vendors and solutions
    - Visit vendors' sites and map their products to your requirements
- During the investigation of software solutions, you should be aware of the following challenges:
    - Challenge 1: The classification terminology of solutions often does not match the generally accepted terminology. It is also not in sync at different sites.
    - Challenge 2: Even if the classification of solutions is similar, very often, the lists of software providers and/or products differ greatly.
    - Challenge 3: Software products with similar solutions have quite different functionalities.
    - Challenge 4: The criteria to define software as "the best" is unclear. Furthermore, the criteria used by different sources may differ greatly.
    - Challenge 5: The same product can be classified differently at different sources.
- To document the data lineage at the business layer, the following requirements should be met:
    - Multiple levels of hierarchies
    - Collaboration
    - Integration with other solutions
    - Integration between components
- Two types of software solutions can meet the requirements for the documentation at the business layer: business process modeling solutions and enterprise architecture solutions. These solutions should have the following functionality:
    - Hierarchy structure and drill-down/up functionality
    - Standardized diagrams
    - Integration capabilities
    - Teams' collaboration capability
    - Analytics and dashboard capabilities
- To document the data lineage at the level of data models, the following requirements should be met:
    - Multiple levels of data models
    - Different types of diagrams and notations
    - Centralized model development and management
    - Integration
- Data modeling solutions meet the requirements to document data lineage at the data model levels.
  The solution should have the following functionality:
    - Maintenance and integration of multiple data models

- - Graphical interface
  - Central repository and collaboration capabilities
  - Forward/reverse engineering
- The following requirements are valid for data lineate-related metadata:
  - Different types of metadata at the different levels of abstraction
  - Root-cause and impact analysis
  - Transparency for data transformation
  - Collaboration and integration
- Metadata, data governance, and data lineage solutions could meet the requirements for the documentation of metadata.
  The following functionality and/or products meet these requirements:
  - Business glossary and semantic frameworks
  - Data catalogs
  - Data dictionaries
  - Business rule management
  - Metadata and relationships repositories
  - Metadata connectors/scanners
  - Data lineage viewer
- Two additional solutions, data quality and knowledge graphs, can complement the requirements for data lineage.
- Multiple vendors offer different data-lineage solutions. From the broad spectrum of the solutions available on the market, you should choose one that best meets your company's requirements and resources.

12 | DOCUMENT DATA LINEAGE AND BUILD ANALYTICS

In Chapter 6, we discussed the key steps to performing a data lineage business case. So far, we have covered all steps required to start the implementation. Data lineage documentation and building analytical tools are the final steps that belong to the implementation itself. The better you made preparations; the easier implementation will be. But before you start, you should be aware of what key implementation steps to perform and the challenges you can expect.

In this chapter, we will:

- Discuss the practical aspects of data lineage documentation using descriptive and automated methods
- Examine the key steps of the documentation
- Talk about the common techniques used for the documentation and integration
- Discuss the necessity of building analytical tools above data lineage solutions

After reading this chapter, you will be able to:

- Lead the project of data lineage documentation
- Plan key steps of the implementation
- Deliver results that meet the requirements of different stakeholders

We have already discussed in sub-chapter 5.4 two key methods of data lineage documentation: descriptive and automated.

Descriptive data lineage is a method to record metadata data lineage manually in a metadata repository.

Automated data lineage is the method to record metadata data lineage by implementing automated processes to scan and ingest metadata into a metadata repository.

Each method is applicable for a specific set of data lineage components at the different levels of abstraction. One of the associated challenges is the integration of data lineage artifacts documented by different methods. Let us investigate which data lineage components you can document with one method or another.

12.1 KEY COMPONENTS FOR DESCRIPTIVE AND AUTOMATED DOCUMENTATION METHODS

The key components of data lineage were discussed in Chapter 4. Below, in Figure 52, you can see which components can be documented by which method.

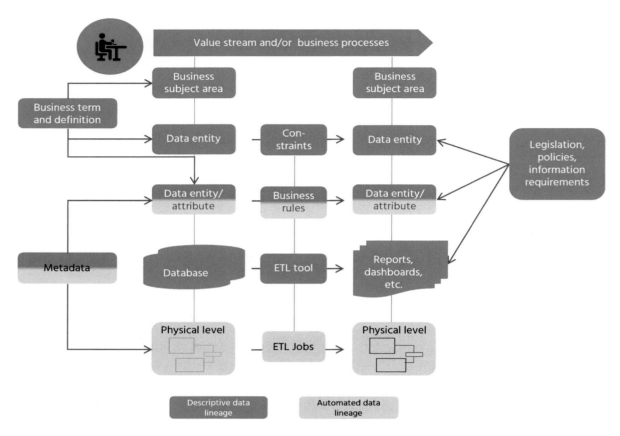

Figure 52: Data lineage components that can be documented by using descriptive and automated methods.

Descriptive data lineage

The components that can be documented by the descriptive method are marked in blue. These are:

- Business capability, business process
- IT asset flow
- Data set flow
- The conceptual and logical data model
- Business rules

Automated data lineage

All components at the physical level should be documented by using the automated method. They are marked in light grey in Figure 52.

Some data lineage components can be documented by either of these two methods. It depends on the company's resources and tools available. For example, logical data models and ETL scripts related to business rules. I also came across companies that tried to document physical data lineage manually.

The documentation of components should be performed in the logical order of some steps.

12.2 THE MAIN STEPS OF DATA LINEAGE DOCUMENTATION

There is no strict rule about the logical order in which you should document data lineage components. The most realistic is that different teams document diverse components simultaneously. The only thing that matters is the logic behind the relationships between these components. At some point in time, you should integrate the documentation of different data lineage components in one artifact: full-scope data lineage.

In this sub-chapter, we discuss the logic of the creation of the complete scope of data lineage. Three key phases are shown in Figure 53.

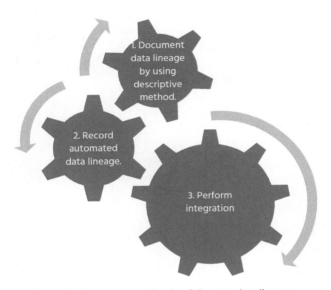

Figure 53: Key steps to delivering full-scope data lineage.

The key phases are:
1. Document data lineage by using the descriptive method
2. Record automated data lineage
3. Perform integration between artifacts of descriptive and automated data lineage

The phases seem to be very simple, but the performance of these phases is not. I have not seen any company so far that was able to complete all these steps, even within a limited scope. Such an initiative is both time and resource intensive. In the subsequent sub-chapters, I outline the key steps for each phase.

12.3 DOCUMENTATION USING A DESCRIPTIVE METHOD

The delivery of descriptive data lineage in full scope follows the logic shown in Figure 54. This logic demonstrates the way to integrate diverse artifacts of documented data lineage. Different teams can work simultaneously on the delivery of these artifacts.

Let's consider each of these steps in detail.

Figure 54: Steps to performing descriptive data lineage documentation.

Step 1: Document a business model.

The documentation of the business model may pursue different goals. From a data lineage perspective, the key goal is to discover:

- Business areas and associated data sets
- Data chains

You can use different techniques to document business models. To achieve the above-stated goal, I have developed a model that you can see in Figure 55. This model compiles two well-known models. The first one is the "business model canvas" technique. This model is one of the most effective techniques to do it. The description of the technique can be found in the paper "Business Models"[1] prepared by The Open Group Architecture Forum. The second model is a business capability map described in the "Business capabilities"[2] paper also written by The Open Group.

Let us take a deeper look at the model in Figure 55.

The concept of business capability and related definitions we have already discussed in sub-chapter 4.1. Business capabilities enable a business to achieve specific goals or deliver outcomes. Business processes ensure the delivery of the company's outcomes to customers. Business capabilities and processes are linked with each other.

Strategic capabilities represent the scope of strategic planning and control. Examples of such capabilities are strategic planning, risk management, policy management.

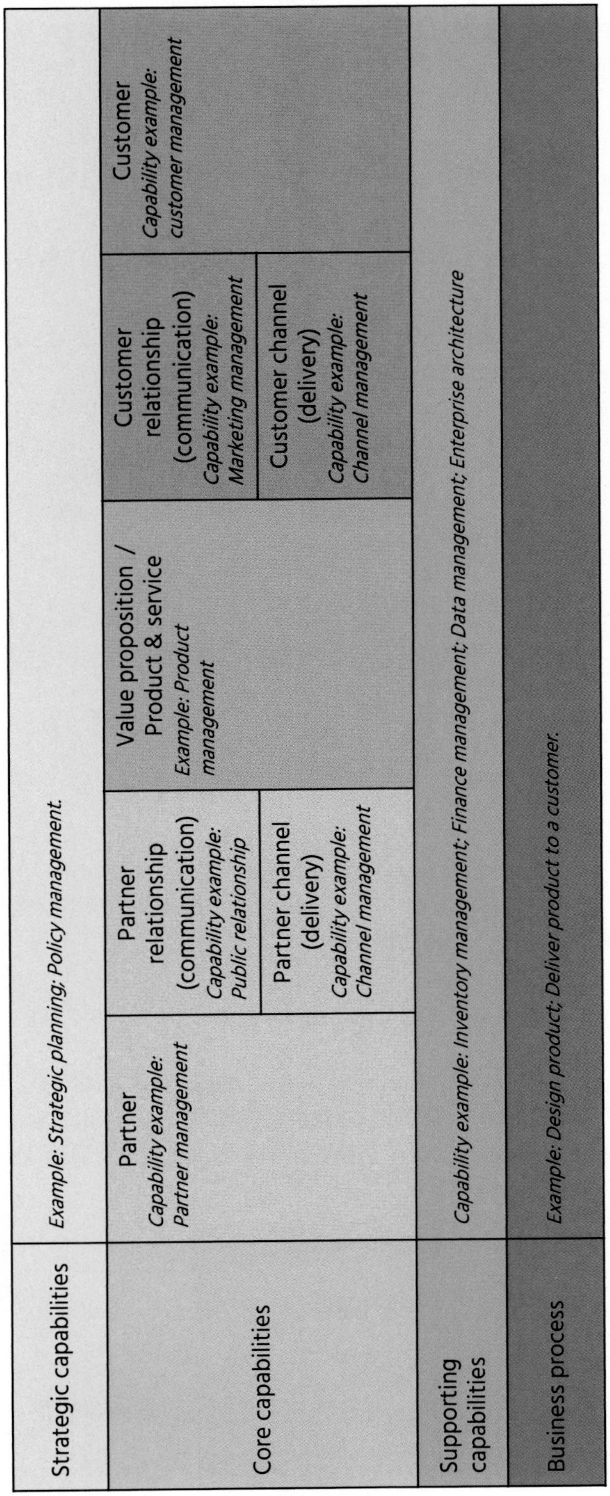

Strategic capabilities	*Example: Strategic planning; Policy management.*						
Core capabilities	**Partner** *Capability example: Partner management*	**Partner relationship (communication)** *Capability example: Public relationship*	**Value proposition / Product & service** *Example: Product management*	**Customer relationship (communication)** *Capability example: Marketing management*	**Customer** *Capability example: customer management*		
		Partner channel (delivery) *Capability example: Channel management*		**Customer channel (delivery)** *Capability example: Channel management*			
Supporting capabilities	*Capability example: Inventory management; Finance management; Data management; Enterprise architecture*						
Business process	*Example: Design product; Deliver product to a customer.*						

Figure 55: A model to document a business model.

Core capabilities focus on the delivery of a business value to customers. To deliver value, a company performs several steps. It purchases goods and services from partners, and then a company designs and produces new products and services. By doing this, it creates a value that is delivered to the company's customers.

Examples of core capabilities are partner management, product management, and customer management.

Supporting capabilities enable the functioning of the business. Finance management, inventory management are examples of such capabilities.

Business capabilities of a higher level should be decomposed into business capabilities of a lower level. For example, customer management can be decomposed into customer acquisition; customer consent management; customer complaints management, etc., as shown in Figure 56.

Figure 56: An example of a business capability decomposition.

One of the key goals of such a business analysis is the identification of key business subject areas.

Step 2: Identify key business subject areas.

The business model assists in understanding key business subject areas. In sub-chapter 4.5, we have already mentioned the concept of a business subject area. Two reasons lead to the necessity to identify business subject areas:

1. Critical business subject areas are the first candidates for the documentation of data lineage. The identification of critical business subject areas allows scoping your data lineage initiative.
2. Business subject areas provide the link between business and data models. The knowledge of business subject areas eases the development of data models.

The core business capabilities demonstrated in Figure 55 indicate the key business subject areas shown in Figure 57.

Figure 57: An example of a key subject area.

As we pointed out before, business processes link business capabilities. Therefore, the following step is the documentation of business processes.

Step 3: Document critical business processes.

Companies have different practices regarding business processes. For a smaller company, it is easier to document business processes. The larger the company, the more complicated this task becomes. The abstraction level to document business processes also differs per company. To make the exercise feasible, a company should concentrate only on the most critical processes. The definition of "criticality" is also company-dependent. A documented business process usually indicates roles that perform this process.

An example of the documented business process can be seen in Figure 58.

Figure 58: An example of a high-level business process.

This example provides an overview of high-level activities that a software company should perform to develop a new product. Each of these steps should be decomposed into activities at the lower levels of abstraction.

IT assets should be linked to business processes.

Step 4: Document data flows at the level of IT assets and data sets.

The next step is the documentation of IT assets. This step is a challenging exercise for large international companies. Such IT assets as a system, application, database, ETL tools deal with particular data sets. Business subject areas identified at Step 2 assist in the classification of data sets. The documentation of IT assets and data set flows takes place at a relatively high level of abstraction, as demonstrated in Figure 59.

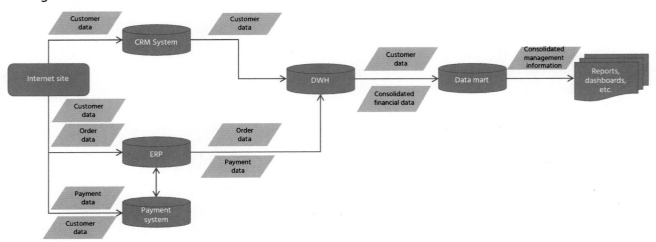

Figure 59: An example of the documentation of data lineage at the level of IT assets and data sets.

For example, the documentation of data lineage starts at the Internet site. From this point, data from internet sites flows to several locations. The data chain ends with reports. You can link particular data sets to IT assets. However, at this level of abstraction, you can specify data sets only at the high level of abstraction; for example, "customer data."

Conceptual and logical models assist in decomposing business subject areas and data sets into the lower levels of abstraction.

Step 5: Develop conceptual and logical data models.

We discussed data models and associated challenges in sub-chapter 4.5. Business subject areas should be worked out into data entities and attributes that are components of data models. An example of such elaboration you can see in Figure 60.

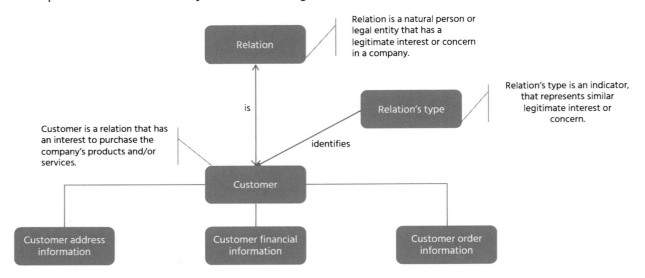

Figure 60: An example of a conceptual model.

The business subject domain "customer" receives an associated data entity "customer." This data entity has been decomposed into three other data elements as "customer address information," "customer financial information," and "customer order information." Such a decomposition should be continued to transform the conceptual model into the logical one.

This step of creating conceptual and logical models is the last step associated with the descriptive data lineage.

As I mentioned before, even the documentation of logical models can be automated by using the "forward or reverse engineering" capabilities of data modeling software.

Step 6: Map all artifacts from Step 2 to 5.

One of the biggest challenges in the documentation of data lineage is the mapping of data lineage components altogether. The way how you will do it depends on the tooling used for the documentation. If you use a tool with integration capabilities like Collibra, Informatica, Erwin, your task could be relatively easy. Such tools provide both integration and collaboration functionalities. In any case, the mapping of different artifacts is a time and resource-consuming process.

In my book "Data Management Toolkit"[3], I provided a detailed description of descriptive data lineage techniques and integration of data lineage components.

Now it is time to take a look at the recoding of automated data lineage.

12.4 DOCUMENTATION USING AN AUTOMATED METHOD

In the introduction of this book, I notified readers that this book is NOT for technical professionals. This subchapter aims to equip NON-technical professionals with the basic understanding of an automated data lineage solution and ease their communication with technical colleagues. Let us start with the basic concept.

Basic concept

Automated data lineage is metadata lineage at the physical level performed by means of automated software solutions. Table, column, and ETL job are examples of metadata lineage objects at this level. These are the basic objects. For instance, SAS data lineage for SAS applications can document more than 40 types of such objects.

Automated data lineage meets the requirement to document and visualize the movement of physical metadata between different tools. Data modeling, database design, ETL, and business intelligence tools are examples thereof.

Automated data lineage solution

The solution of the automated data lineage should include the following functionality:

- Read metadata components and relationships between them
  In this sub-chapter, I use the term "metadata" to mean the combination of metadata components as well as the relationships between them.
- Read metadata from different tools, such as data modeling and database design tools
- Read metadata from scripts written in different languages
  Some companies still use mainframes written in COBOL. Other companies have applications written in Python.
- Read metadata from tools from different providers and with different underlying technologies
  Think, for example, about metadata from relational, OLAP, graphical databases, etc.
- Move metadata between various tools
  For example, metadata from a relational database should be read and stored in a metadata repository.
- Visualize metadata movements
  The metadata movements should be available in graphical interfaces to ease the perception of information.
- Analyze metadata and deliver information in the form of reports and/or dashboards.
  We will discuss this requirement in the following subchapter.
- Aggregate metadata at different levels of abstraction and apply drill-up and drill-down functionality

For example, a user should be able to see the movement of data at an IT asset level, i.e., database level, and then drill it down to a table and column level.

To realize all of the above-mentioned functionalities, an automated data lineage solution may require the usage and integration of different products. Let us discuss the simplified model of the automated data lineage solution presented in Figure 61.

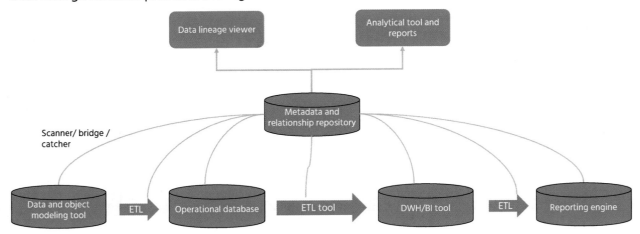

Figure 61: An example of metadata flow in automated data lineage solution.

Data flows through different databases and applications. A company wants to record and demonstrate the movement of metadata between data and object modeling tools, operational databases, data warehouse (DWH) and business intelligence (BI) tools, reporting engines, and ETL tools.

Scanners read metadata from these tools. Different solution providers use other names for scanners. You can come across the terms like "bridge," "connector," or "catcher." Every particular type of database, ETL tool, and coding language requires a separate type of scanner. A central metadata repository stores metadata from different sources and integrates it. A data lineage viewer visualizes data lineage components and relationships between them. Analytical tools above the metadata repository allow for analyzing the metadata.

Different methods to provide metadata for the automated data lineage also exist.

Different methods to provide metadata

The classification of the methods to get metadata indicates the availability of metadata and the feasibility of getting it. Two classifications of methods exist.

The first classification indicates the availability of metadata. Metadata can be retrieved "at run time" and "at design time."

"At design time" data lineage shows metadata that have been created or imported at some point of time for a particular data set. The update of data lineage takes place only when the database schema is changed.

"At run time" data lineage demonstrates metadata objects every time a particular data set has been processed.

The second classification distinguishes data lineage by the method metadata has been captured.

- Data lineage "as built"
  In this case, data lineage objects derive from the implementation code. The change in the implementation code will be immediately reflected in data lineage.
- Data lineage "as designed"
  The information about a data lineage component derives from the available documentation. Before the delivery into a metadata repository, such information should be hardcoded.

You may also face a situation with complex calculations performed within databases. In such a case, data lineage becomes too complex. In this case, the documentation about the calculations may be enough to meet business requirements.

In the end, I want to mention some challenges with the automated data lineage solutions.

Some challenges with an automated data lineage solution

Based on my practical experience, I would like to draw your attention to the following challenges:

- History control and auditability
  One of the key business requirements is the ability to trace the history of data processing. Very often, this requirement comes from the finance department. To explain the origin of some calculations, they need to take a look back at the history. The challenge is that metadata lineage solutions are not always capable of keeping such information. One of the key reasons is memory capacity.
  One of the work-around solutions can be the copying of metadata lineage information at the moment of new releases in databases.
- Excess of metadata data information and user unfriendliness
  Metadata lineage even for a limited architectural landscape includes hundreds of thousands of metadata objects and millions of relationships. For a business user, it is "too much". When they see the endless number of objects and relationships on a screen, their enthusiasm to work with data lineage disappears.
  Finally, a common business user has two requirements:

  - Know which data attributes at the source system have been used to derive a data attribute at the final destination, i.e. report
  - Know which transformations data have undergone on the way from the source to the final destination.

Analytics built above metadata repositories is one of the only solutions to meet these business requirements. Another option is to combine drill-down and drill-up functionalities with data lineage analytics.

- The necessity to build analytics above metadata repositories to prove the correctness of data lineage

If you think that documented data lineage is the end of the story, you'd be wrong. It's only the beginning. At this point, you should start building analytics above your metadata and relationship repositories.

The first reason we have just discussed. Metadata lineage is too complex for ordinary business users. They need simple Excel-like reports to use information. But the second reason is not so obvious. The question is "How can you prove the correctness of data lineage?" And if you think that it per definition is correct, you are again wrong. Different reasons can cause the incorrectness and incompleteness of data lineage. To some extent, it depends on the method to capture metadata. In any case, hardcoding is required to read metadata. To prove the data lineage is correct, you should have analytics above metadata repositories. The analysis of the relationships between the attributes at the start and end data points allows you to prove the correctness and completeness of data lineage. So, if you purchase a COTS solution, you should be sure that they have such analytical capabilities built in.

12.5 INTEGRATION OF ARTIFACTS OF DESCRIPTIVE AND AUTOMATED DATA LINEAGE

The intersection points between the descriptive and automated data lineage artifacts are the logical and physical data models correspondingly. Such integration is, in fact, the documentation of vertical lineage or linkage. Two approaches can be used to deliver an integration solution:

- Integration functionality within a data lineage solution
  Integration functionality may be a part of a data lineage solution, i.e., within data catalogs. There is one associated challenge you should be aware of. You should manually link multiple implemented physical data models to one logical model. Advanced solutions could offer the machine learning functionality to perform matching between physical and logical attributes. In any case, the mapping itself is a manual exercise. The only hope is that the rapidly developing technology will deliver more handy solutions in the foreseeable future.
- Use of a graph database to map metadata in different sources
  Graph database technologies enable mapping between different repositories and catalogs. The challenge with the mapping technique remains the same as discussed above.

By now, we have discussed all topics related to the documentation of metadata lineage at different levels of abstractions by using different methods and techniques. In the last sub-chapter, we discuss how to satisfy the needs of business users in data value lineage.

12.6 DOCUMENTATION OF DATA VALUE LINEAGE

I don't even recall how I came to the name of "data value lineage." While discussing the requirements of metadata lineage, we never thought that business stakeholders would not be happy with metadata lineage. It doesn't matter how often I explained the concept of metadata lineage to businesspeople, the first question I always get is, "Will I be able to trace the changes in data values from a report cell back to the original contracts?" At some point, we have even started a new stream of "data value lineage" within our project. The investigation of possible solutions did not bring any results. So far, I have not come across any COTS product that offered such functionality. I heard about some attempts to realize the concept with in-house solutions. The idea was to mark each data instance with a specific metadata stamp. For companies with huge volumes of data, it is not a feasible solution.

Later we have realized that two possible workaround solutions are feasible. The workarounds take off from assessing the real business need behind "data value lineage." Businesspeople, especially from the finance and risk departments, need to be able to reconcile data at different data points. So our solutions combined metadata lineage with some other solutions, such as:

- Drill-down and drill-back capability
  The drill-down capability allows zooming into from a higher level of aggregation to a lower one. The drill-back capability permits users to go back to the source of the data. Unfortunately, these capabilities are difficult to implement across several applications and along with extended data chains.
- Reconciliation reports in data points along with data chains
  Metadata lineage makes transparent the usage of data attributes required to produce final reports. The knowledge of metadata allows building analytical reports for known attributes at different data points to reconcile data.

Over the past seven chapters, we have discussed different approaches and methods to implement different types of data lineage. I want to end Part 2 by sharing my experience about key factors of a successful data lineage implementation.

SUMMARY OF CHAPTER 12

- Descriptive and automated methods to document data lineage apply to different layers and components of data lineage.
- Descriptive data lineage can be used to document:
  - Data lineage at the business layer for the following components:
    - Business capability, business process
    - IT asset flow
    - Data set flow
    - The conceptual and logical data model
    - Business rules
  - Data lineage at the level of data models:
    - Conceptual
    - Logical
- All components at the physical level should be documented by using the automated method.
- The main phases of the data lineage documentation are:
  1. Document data lineage by using the descriptive method.
  2. Record automated data lineage.
  3. Perform integration between artifacts of descriptive and automated data lineage.
- The documentation by using the descriptive method should be performed by following the next steps:

  Step 1: Document a business model.

  Step 2: Identify key business subject areas.

  Step 3: Document critical business processes.

  Step 4: Document data flows at the level of IT assets and data sets.

  Step 5: Develop conceptual and logical data models.

  Step 6: Map all artifacts from Steps 2 to 5.

- The solution for automated data lineage should include multiple functionalities to meet requirements such as:
  - Read metadata components and relationships between them
  - Read metadata from different tools
  - Read metadata from scripts written in different languages
  - Move metadata between various tools and repositories
  - Visualize metadata movements
  - Analyze metadata
  - Aggregate metadata
- Depending on the availability of metadata, data lineage can be "at run time" or "at design time."
- The feasibility to get metadata classifies data lineage into "as built" and "as designed" types.
- Challenges associated with the automated data lineage should be taken into account:
  - History control and auditability
  - Excess of metadata information and user unfriendliness

- o The necessity to build analytics above metadata repositories to:
    - Satisfy needs of ordinary business users
    - Prove the completeness and correctness of metadata lineage
- Two solutions allow integration of artifacts of descriptive and automated data lineage:
    - o Integration functionality within COTS products
    - o Usage of graph databases
- No COTS functionality exists for data value lineage.
- Two workaround solutions may assist in meeting data value lineage requirements:
    - o The combination of metadata lineage with drill-down and drill-up functionality
    - o Reconciliation reports in data points along with data chains

13 | KEY RISK AND SUCCESS FACTORS OF A DATA LINEAGE BUSINESS CASE

Like every project, a data lineage implementation project can either fail or succeed. Such a project has its risk factors and success factors.

In this chapter, we will:

- Discuss which risk factors to pay attention to
- Highlight success factors

After reading this chapter, you will be able to:

- Analyze risk factors applicable to your company to mitigate them
- Create conditions to realize success factors

13.1 RISK FACTORS

In this paragraph, I list risk factors that are common to many organizations. They arise from the background of the data lineage concept. Every organization could have some other industry or company-related risks. Let us discuss some examples of common risk factors:

- Data lineage is a complex concept.
  Data lineage remains an abstract, unknown subject for many business and data management professionals as they don't have much practical experience with it.
  To further the confusion, the concept of data lineage itself has no aligned definition within the professional community. It causes difficulties in communication and the identification of business needs and requirements.
- The implementation of data lineage in any case is time- and resource-intensive.
  It requires a lot of investments in software, hardware, and staff development. Even the implementation of data lineage with COTS solutions and an "out-of-the box" solution requires months and years of effort.
- Data lineage for legacy software remains a challenge.
  Many companies have legacy software, i.e., mainframes. One of the key challenges is the inability to read metadata automatically. Even products that have been brought to the market several years ago can remain a "black box" for data lineage purposes. Some vendors have solutions for legacy software, but the required efforts to implement them should not be underestimated.
- Many companies still don't have matured data management, data governance, and enterprise architecture functions.
  A data lineage initiative demands the combined efforts of experienced data management

and IT professionals with various backgrounds. Documented data lineage is the combination of the artifacts of diverse data management capabilities. Therefore, the implementation of data lineage requires a mature enough data management function in place.

The list of risk factors can be extended. However, the most important is to think about how to mitigate the risks and how to make the initiative successful.

13.2 SUCCESS FACTORS

To be successful with the data lineage business case, a company should focus on the following.

- Top management support
  You could get such support relatively quickly. Data lineage is considered to be one of the means to meet legislative requirements. So, it is not good will, but a high business necessity to have it in place. Top management should prioritize the company's resources and find resources to finance the project.
- Clear identification of business drivers, goals, and the project scope
  Diverse business drivers may require documentation of data lineage in different parts of a company. As previously discussed, GDPR requirements lead to data lineage for personal data. SOX compliance focuses attention on financial data. A focused approach assists in identifying a feasible scope for the initiative.
- Start "small"
  A pilot project is the best way to build knowledge and skills within the company in the area of data lineage. It also allows demonstrating the quick-wins to stakeholders, starting from the supervisory bodies and ending up with business users.
- Properly chosen metadata architecture and data lineage tooling
  I have worked for several years as a project manager for the implementation of two different ERP packages. Oftentimes, I observed that my clients were using only 20 percent of the functionality available in systems. A metadata architecture and data lineage solution should fit the company's needs and resources to use resources effectively.
- Well-established data management and data governance functions
  You may not have the well-established function of data management and governance at the beginning of the data lineage initiative. The data lineage initiative can enforce the development of these functions. In the last chapter of this book, we discuss this topic in greater depth.
- Active participation of business people
  Data lineage is often a technological feast. The challenge is that businesspeople have their own needs, requirements, and expectations for this functionality. Very often, such expectations are far from reality. It may be a great disappointment if nobody uses the data lineage as expected at the end of the project. Businesspeople should actively participate in the data lineage initiative from the early stages to prevent such a situation. Their voices and expectations should be heard and taken into account.

I hope that by now you are now ready to embark on the data lineage implementation adventure.

In Part 3, I demonstrate several business cases of data lineage usage.

SUMMARY OF CHAPTER 13

- Each data lineage project has its risk and success factors.
- The common risk factors are:
    - Data lineage is a complex concept.
    - The implementation of data lineage is time and resource-intensive.
    - Data lineage for legacy software remains a challenge.
    - Many companies still don't have matured data management, data governance, and enterprise architecture functions.
- The following factors could ensure the success of the data lineage initiative:
    - Top management support
    - Clear identification of business drivers, goals, and the project scope
    - Start small
    - Properly chosen metadata architecture and data lineage tooling
    - Well-established data management and data governance function
    - Active participation of businesspeople

SUMMARY OF PART 2

In Part 2, we have discussed the different practical aspects of the data lineage implementation.

The nine-step implementation methodology to build a data lineage business case has formed the framework for Part 2.

The nine-step methodology consists of the following steps:

1. **Identify key business drivers**
   Each data lineage initiative should start with the definition of key business drivers for this initiative. The chosen business drivers determine the feasible scope, deadlines, and resources needed.

2. **Buy-in support and involvement of key stakeholders**
   Data lineage initiative covers the needs of different stakeholders. It requires the participation of professionals with diverse backgrounds. It is a time and resource-intensive initiative. Therefore, close cooperation and the involvement of key stakeholders is one of the key success factors.

3. **Scope data lineage initiative**
   The following factors allow for limiting the data lineage initiative to the feasible level:
   - The scope of "enterprise"
   - The "length" of data lineage
   - The "depth" of data lineage
   - The sets of critical data elements
   - The number of data lineage components

4. **Define roles and accountabilities**
   Different business, data management, and IT roles perform the documentation of data lineage. Multiple factors influence the design of data management roles:
   - The type of data stewards
   - The dimensions of a business capability
   - Location of roles along with data chains
   - Data management sub-capabilities
   - Data architecture style
   - Approach to IT solution design
   - Data domain definition
   - The scope of "enterprise"

   The set of roles needed to document data lineage depends on the following characteristics of data lineage:
   - Data lineage layer
   - Data lineage components
   - Data management capabilities that are required to deliver data lineage outcomes

5. **Prepare data lineage requirements**
   Data lineage requirements depend on the chosen metamodel of data lineage and the types

of data lineage. Data lineage requirements aim to communicate the needs and expectations of stakeholders and fine-tune the scope of the initiative.

Metadata lineage requirements split into general requirements, requirements for horizontal and vertical data lineage.

Data value lineage requirements can include only general requirements and requirements for horizontal lineage.

6. **Choose an approach and methodology to implement data lineage**

Each company should choose its approach for the implementation of data lineage. Such an approach should fit the company's goals and resources. Different factors influence the choice of an approach:

- The "enterprise" coverage
- The method of data lineage documentation
- The scope parameters of data lineage
- The direction of documentation
- The project management style
- The maturity of metadata architecture

7. **Choose an appropriate data lineage solution**

Three steps to lead a company toward a software solution:

1. Define business needs
2. Translate business needs into requirements
3. Find out solutions, products, and functionality that meet the defined requirements

To find out more information about software solutions, a company should perform the following steps:

- Check well-known and trustworthy sources
- Create a list of vendors and solutions
- Visit vendors' sites and map their products to your requirements

During the investigation of software solutions, you should be aware of challenges. Multiple vendors offer different data-lineage solutions. From the broad spectrum of the solutions available on the market, you should choose one that best meets your company's requirements and resources.

8. **Document data lineage**

Descriptive and automated methods are key methods to document data lineage. These methods apply to different layers and components of data lineage.

Descriptive data lineage can be used to document:

- Data lineage at the business layer for the following components:
  - Business capability, business process
  - IT asset flow
  - Data set flow
  - The conceptual and logical data model
  - Business rules
- Data lineage at the level of data models:

The main phases of the data lineage documentation are:

1. Document data lineage by using the descriptive method
2. Record automated data lineage
3. Perform integration between artifacts of descriptive and automated data lineage

9. **Build analytical tools**

An analytical tool above metadata repositories and metadata lineage delivers the following values:

- It eases the usage of data lineage by business stakeholders.
- It assists in checking the data lineage completeness and correctness.

To succeed with the implementation of data lineage, a company should recognize and mitigate potential risk factors. It should take into consideration and explore key success factors in its practices.

Part 3
USING DATA LINEAGE

"The value of achievement lies in the achieving."

- Albert Einstein

In Part 1, we have agreed on the definition of data lineage and its metadata model, and in Part 2, we discussed the different aspects of data lineage implementation. Now it is time to examine some examples of data lineage usage. For many business users, data lineage could be a handy tool for their daily operations. At the same time, data lineage is not an easy tool to use. A company that has started a data lineage initiative should pay attention and involve business users in exploring data lineage. Business users should understand the usefulness and advantages of using this functionality.

Part 3 aims to guide data management, project management, and business practitioners on how to use data lineage in:

- Discovering critical data elements
- Identifying data quality requirements, checks, and controls
- Performing root-cause and impact analyses
- Implementing driver-based modeling and planning
- Implementing a data management framework

In the subsequent chapters, we will dive into each subject one by one.

14 | CRITICAL DATA

The concept of "critical data" has been on the agenda of data management professionals for many years. The key contributors to this concept are David Loshin, Rajesh Jugulum, DAMA-DMBOK publications, and legislative documents.

In this chapter, we will:
- Investigate contexts in which critical data concept is being used
- Discuss the definition of critical data (elements)
- Highlight the area of application of this concept
- Discuss techniques to define critical data elements

After reading this chapter, you will be able to:
- Assess the applicability of this concept in your company
- Identify the critical data elements relevant to your company's business

We start with the investigative contexts in which the critical data concept is used.

14.1 CONTEXTS FOR THE USAGE OF CRITICAL DATA

I have analyzed different sources and found out that the term "critical data (element)" (CDE) is being used in different contexts.

These four contexts demonstrated in Figure 62 are:
- Information technology (IT) operations
  In this context, critical data assists organizations in prioritizing IT work.
- Data protection and data security
  These two contexts are often used together. The best example of the data protection context is GDPR (The General Data Protection Regulation), known throughout the European Union. It focuses on the protection of personal data. In this case, all personal data is also considered as being critical data.
- Data management
  In this book, I focus mainly on this context. Critical data elements are important when dealing with data quality, master and reference data, and data governance.

Now it is time to specify the definition of critical data and critical data elements.

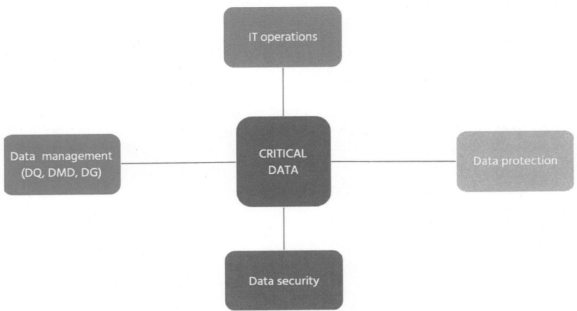

Figure 62: Contexts in which the concept of "critical data" is used.

14.2 THE DEFINITION OF CRITICAL DATA (ELEMENT)

In different sources, you will find two terms: "critical data" and "critical data element." Let us investigate to which extent they are similar.

DAMA-DMBOK2 specifies critical data as "[...] data that is most important to the organization and its customers"[1].

In standard number 239: "Principles for effective risk data aggregation and risk reporting" (BCBS 239 or PERDARR) by the Basel Committee on Banking Supervision, they provide several different definitions:

- "[...] data that is critical to enabling the bank to manage the risks it faces"[2]
- "[...] data critical to risk data aggregation and IT infrastructure initiative"[3]
- "[...] aggregated information to make critical decisions about risk"[4]

David Loshin, one of the first data management professionals, who started using this term, offers the two following definitions:

- "Critical data elements are those that are determined to be vital to the successful operation of the organization."[5]
- "Critical data elements are those on which the success of business processes and corresponding business applications rely."[6]

Rajesh Jugulum, a well-known specialist in data quality, explores the following definition:

"Critical data elements (CDEs) are defined as 'the data that is critical to success' in a specific business area (line of business, shared service, or group function), or "the data required to get the job done."[7]

To summarize the all-above cited definitions, critical data assists in:

- Managing risks
- Managing business decisions
- Successfully operating a business

So I offer the following definition of critical data. Critical data is data that is critical for managing business risks, making business decisions, and successfully operating a business.

The word "critical" in this definition still needs clarification. The criteria of "criticality" is the most important part of the definition. It is a state-of-the-art way to define which data elements are critical and which are not. The criteria of criticality differ by industry and per company. I have found several groups of criteria of criticality in the literature, as shown in Figure 63.

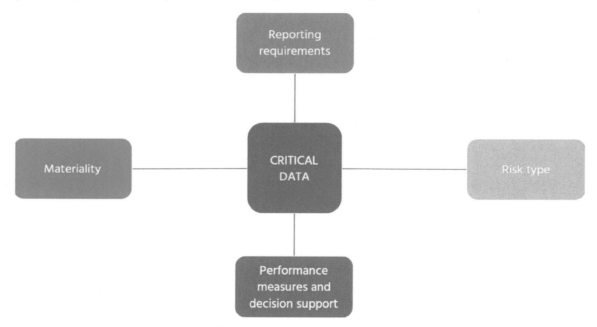

Figure 63: The key criteria of criticality.

Let us examine them one by one:
- Reporting requirements
  Critical data should be found in regulatory and financial reports, business policies, and business strategy.
- Type of risk
  In different industries, companies may classify risk differently. The most common types of risks are financial, credit, operational, reputational, etc.
- Performance management and decision support
  Critical data is data that is used in company performance management and decision support. In this respect, key management KPIs at different levels of the organization represent critical data.
- Materiality
  BCBS 239 standard has introduced the criteria of materiality concerning the concept of

critical data. The accounting approach to materiality can be used. The materiality concept has the following meaning: influence on economic decisions. This method is widely used in practice.

The final decision to identify data as critical remains the accountability of business experts. This approach is the most common method widely used in practice.

14.3 THE APPLICATION AREAS OF THE "CRITICAL DATA" CONCEPT

The concept of "critical data" can be used in two cases. The first one is the prioritization of data management initiatives. People often argue: is it prioritization or limitation? Assume a company has 10,000 elements, of which 1,600 are critical. Do you deal only with those 1,600 elements or deal with them as the first set of elements? In practice, you usually speak about prioritization, not limitation. The second case is building business cooperation and partnering with other business functions.

Several examples of the usage of "critical data" are demonstrated in Figure 64.

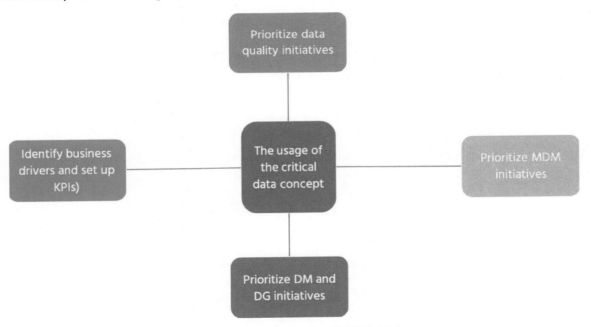

Figure 64: The areas of usage of "critical data."

Let's take a brief look at each of them.

- Prioritization of data quality (DQ) initiatives
  One of the key goals of a DQ initiative is to build data quality checks and controls for critical data elements. Designing, analyzing, and building data quality checks and controls is a time and resource-consuming exercise. Therefore, you need a mechanism to prioritize your data quality initiative. The critical data approach assists companies in such prioritization.
- Prioritization of master data management (MDM) initiatives
  The same idea is applicable to master and reference data initiatives. You need to take

control of all master data elements. But you can't do it at once. It would help if you had some prioritization tool. Therefore, the definition of critical data elements (CDE) is one of the best tools to do it.

- Prioritization of data management and data governance initiatives
  Chapter 7 discussed the key factors that assist in scoping data lineage initiatives to make them more feasible. The concept of critical data can also help with it, especially in the case of descriptive data lineage.
- Identification of business drivers and set up key performance indicators (KPIs)
  This area of application of critical data relates to the financial planning and analysis area. After some investigations, I concluded that data lineage could assist in identifying key elements of the driver-based models. We investigate this topic in-depth in Chapter 16.

Now it is time to discover how to implement the concept of critical data.

14.4 THE IMPLEMENTATION OF THE "CRITICAL DATA" CONCEPT

In this sub-chapter, I will share with you several practical recommendations regarding the implementation of this concept.

Recommendation 1: Physical data lineage should be in place.

To identify critical data at the end of the data chain, you should be able to trace and identify data back to its origin. This task is impossible without knowing data lineage. To perform such an analysis at the data entity and attribute level, physical data lineage is a "must" condition.

To explain this statement in-depth, let us use the simplified example of an application landscape shown in Figure 65.

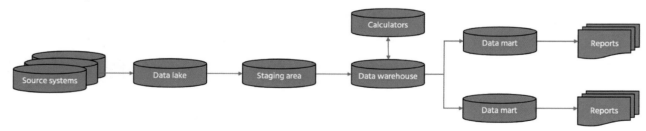

Figure 65: A simplified example of an application landscape.

Data flows from multiple source systems to a data lake. From the data lake, a set of integrated data goes through ETL processes to a staging area and then to a data warehouse (DWH). Additional to the DWH functionality, calculators perform calculations and read data back into the DWH. From the DWH, data flows to different data marts and reporting engines to produce different sets of reports.

In practice, depending on the company's size, the number of applications behind such a landscape varies from a couple of dozen to thousands.

When you start analyzing critical data along the data chain, you find out that critical data can be split into several categories.

This book elaborates on five different types of critical data elements (CDE), as shown in Figure 66. Let us consider them one by one.

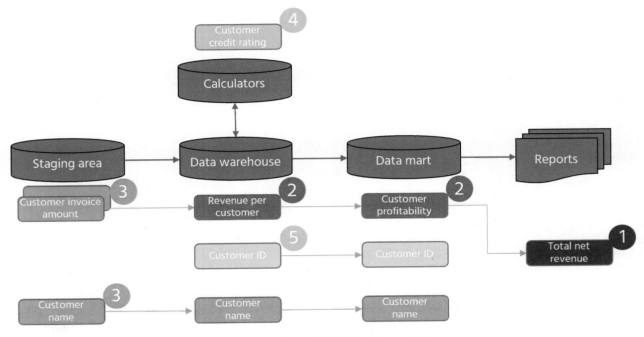

Figure 66: The example of critical data elements' types.

1. "Ultimate critical data element (CDE)"
   For the first type of critical data element, I use the title "the ultimate CDE". They are "ultimate" because they reside at the end of the data chain. Usually, their locations are reports or dashboards. The definition of ultimate CDEs corresponds to the definitions that we found in the literature. This type of CDEs makes the greatest impact on the company's profitability and performance. In our case, I used "Total net revenue" as an example of the "ultimate CDEs". Total net revenue is an aggregated figure. To derive the value of this CDE, you need to process and aggregate a bunch of other data elements. Some of them would be critical.

2. "Transitional calculated CDE"
   The title of this CDE includes two words: "transitional" and "calculated". They are "transitional" because they are located along with the data chain. They are "calculated" because some transformations should be applied to basic sourceable data elements to derive their values.

3. "Transitional sourceable CDE"
   These critical data elements also locate along with the data chain. These critical data elements either don't change along the chain or are used to enable calculations. The

173

example of the unchanged CDE is a "customer name". The element "customer invoice amount" is used for transformation and aggregation purposes.
4. "Business rule CDE"
The value of such critical data elements is not used directly in calculations. They are required for the execution of business rules.
5. "Technical CDE"
These critical data elements ensure the correct processing of data. Table keys are the example of such critical data elements.

Each of these critical data elements could be documented at different levels of data models.

Recommendation 3: Different types of CDEs should be documented at diverse levels of a data model.

In Part 2 of this book, we have discussed that the documentation of data lineage can take place at different levels of abstraction, such as:

- Business layer
- Data model level
  ○ Conceptual
  ○ Logical
  ○ Physical

The documentation of different types of critical data elements (CDEs) takes place at different levels of a data model, as shown in Figure 67.

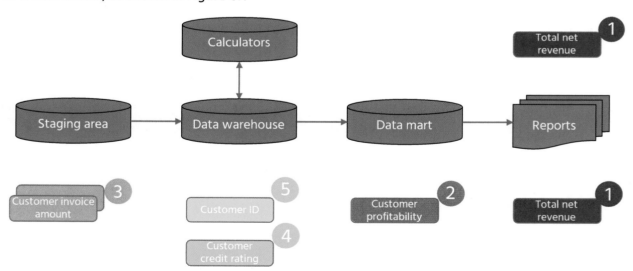

Figure 67: Critical data elements should be documented at the different levels of abstraction.

Let us consider each type of critical data elements in detail.

- "Ultimate critical data elements"
Ultimate critical data element (CDE) can be documented at any data model level. Take, for example, the "total net revenue." You can recognize this element as a business term.

You can create a business definition and document it at the conceptual level. Often, such elements are located in reports. In this case, they can also be documented at the logical level; this is more applicable for reports created manually in Excel. If reports are generated in some applications, the ultimate critical data element resides in a database. In this case, you document ultimate critical data elements at the physical level.

- "Transitional calculated CDE," "transitional sourceable CDE," "business rule CDE," and "technical CDE"
  All these types of critical data elements reside in databases or ETL tools. Therefore, they should be documented at the physical level of data models. I have seen attempts to document such elements at the logical level. There is one challenge with such an approach. At the logical level, you can only guess about the relationships between critical data elements. Only physical data lineage can provide correct information about the relationships among data elements along the data chain.

Different types of critical data elements and the abstraction level of their documentation require diverse criteria of criticality.

Recommendation 4: The criteria of criticality depend on the critical data element type.

The criteria of criticality vary depending on the critical data element (CDE) type and the level of a data model where it resides. Below we discuss the criteria in detail:

- "Ultimate critical data element (CDE)"
  The criteria of criticality are similar to those that we have already discussed in sub-chapter 14.2:
  - High-value impact on business performance
  - Subject to the attention of supervising institutions
  - Often used in external and internal reports
  - Used in strategic decision-making

  Let us use the "total net revenue" as an example. This data element meets all the requirements of criticality listed above.

- "Transitional calculated CDE" and "transitional sourceable CDE"
  For these types of elements, the main criticality criterion is the material impact on the value of an "ultimate critical data element." For example, without knowing the sourceable element, "customer invoice amount," and calculated element, "revenue per customer," you can hardly calculate the "total net revenue."
  In practice, the application of such criteria to define critical data elements is time- and resource-consuming.

- "Business rule CDE"
  The importance of this element for the calculation defines its criticality. Take, for example, a credit rating. This element determines, for example, the interest rate for a customer loan, but itself is not required in the calculation.

- "Technical CDE"
  The criticality of a technical CDE is specified by the importance of this data element for

calculating other CDE and is used for referential integrity. For example, without a value in a foreign key, a process of calculation will not be performed.

To achieve quick results, data management professionals should invent pragmatic approaches to identify critical data elements. Such an approach depends on the availability of data lineage.

Recommendation 5: Choose a pragmatic approach to define critical data elements.

The approach to defining critical data elements depends on the availability of physical data lineage, as shown in Figure 68.

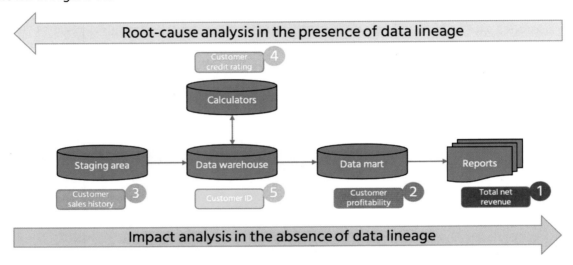

Figure 68: Pragmatic approaches to identify CDEs.

In an ideal world, when you have physical data lineage, you start with ultimate critical data elements (CDEs). The root-cause analysis allows you to discover all of the data elements needed for the calculation of CDEs. Then, by applying the chosen method of criticality, you can identify the critical data elements along data chains.

However, in the real world, not many companies have data lineage in place or data lineage in full scope. In this case, they can apply the impact analysis approach. Such an approach is based on knowledge. This method is applicable under two conditions:

- The set of sourcing elements is known, for example, in the form of sourceable formats.
- The data chain includes several applications or splits into several segments.

Below, I share with you examples of the application of both methods.

Impact analysis approach

The initial conditions for this example can be seen in Figure 69.

In this particular case, the sourcing format for a set of calculation engines and a set of final reports was known. It has included around 1,800 data elements. The identification of the sourceable critical data elements included two steps:

1. Limit sourceable elements to mandatory tables and fields.

It assisted in limiting 1,800 elements to 800.

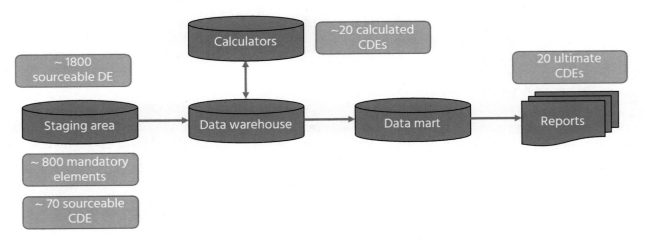

Figure 69: An example of the impact analysis approach.

2. Perform expert analysis.

Experts have identified around 70 sourceable critical data elements that, in their opinion, were critical to delivering the ultimate and calculated critical data elements.

Root-cause analysis

In this case, physical data lineage between the staging area and calculators and between the staging area and reports assisted in the identification of sourceable data elements. The results can be seen in Figure 70.

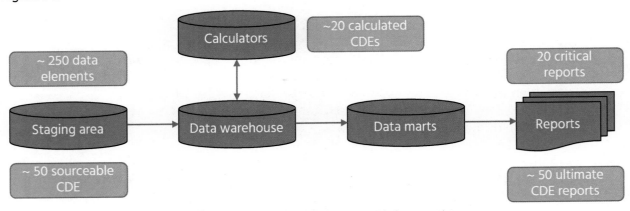

Figure 70: An example of the root-cause analysis approach.

The analysis included the following steps:

1. Identify critical reports
   From 160 reports, experts have chosen 20 as critical ones.
2. Analyze data elements in the critical reports
   Experts have identified around 50 critical ultimate data elements.
3. Analyze sourceable data elements
   Physical data lineage discovered around 250 sourceable data elements needed to calculate the chosen 50 ultimate data elements.
4. Involve experts for assessment
   Experts have scored 50 from sourceable data elements as the sourceable CDEs.

Every company may invent its own practical and pragmatic approaches to identifying critical data elements. Now it is time to discuss one of the key areas of the application of data lineage and critical data elements. This area is the data quality capability.

SUMMARY OF CHAPTER 14

- The concept of critical data can be found in different contexts, such as, for example:
  - Information technology (IT) operations
  - Data protection and data security
  - Data management
- Critical data is data that is critical for managing business risks, taking business decisions, and successfully operating a business.
- The criteria of criticality vary in different contexts. There are four key groups of the criteria of criticality:
  - Reporting requirements
  - Type of risk
  - Performance management and decision support
  - Materiality
- Within the data management context, the concept of critical data is used for:
  - Prioritization of data quality, master data, and data governance initiatives
  - Identification of business drivers and key performance indicators
- The following recommendations should be taken into account for the successful implementation of the critical data concept:
  1. Physical data lineage should be in place.
  2. Along with the data chain, you recognize several types of critical data.
  3. Different types of critical data elements should be documented at diverse levels of a data model.
  4. The criteria of criticality depend on the types of critical data elements.
  5. Choose a pragmatic approach to define critical data elements.

15 | DATA QUALITY

Data quality (DQ) is one of the key drivers for many companies to set up a data management initiative. Data quality is one of the data management capabilities. Setting up data quality requirements and designing DQ checks and controls are some of the keys DQ activities. Data lineage serves to perform these activities effectively.

In this chapter, we will:

- Provide recommendations for the usage of data lineage
- Demonstrate how to use the concept of critical data to scope DQ activities

After reading this chapter, you will be able to:

- Apply the concept of critical data to DQ activities within your company
- Align the scope of data lineage and DQ initiatives

15.1 SETTING UP DATA QUALITY REQUIREMENTS

Any of your data quality initiatives start with the definition of data quality requirements. Primarily, a company identifies data quality requirements for critical data elements. If you recall, in Chapter 14, we have identified five different types of critical data elements (CDEs), as shown in Figure 71:

1. Ultimate CDEs; "total net revenue" as an example
2. Transitional calculated CDEs; "customer profitability" as an example
3. Transitional sourceable CDEs; "customer invoice amount" as an example
4. Business rule CDEs; "customer credit rating" as an example
5. Technical CDE; "customer ID' as an example

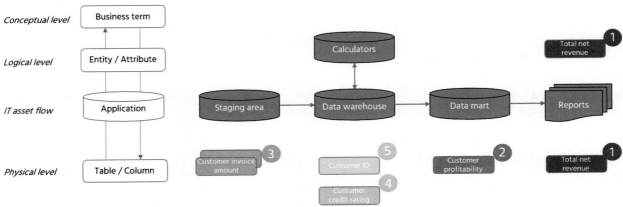

Figure 71: An example of setting up data quality requirements.

Business users set up their requirements for "ultimate critical data elements." In our case, it is "total net revenue." Business users usually identify their requirements at the conceptual or logical level of a data model. The key goal of data quality requirements is to build data quality checks and controls. For doing it, data quality requirements for the ultimate CDEs should be translated into requirements to other types of CDEs along with data chains. And all these requirements should be at the physical level. For that, the knowledge of physical data lineage becomes unavoidable.

Let us investigate in-depth the usage of data lineage for building DQ checks and controls.

15.2 DESIGNING AND BUILDING DATA QUALITY CHECKS AND CONTROLS

First, let us align terminology and identify the terms "check" and "control." In this book, I use the following definitions for these two terms:

Data quality check is a software code that checks the correspondence of a data instance or a data set to predefined requirements at some stage of data processing.

Data quality control is the process of controlling data. The set of data quality checks allow for performing the data quality control.

Data quality controls and checks are performed in multiple places along with data chains. In Figure 72, you can see an example of different locations of such controls.

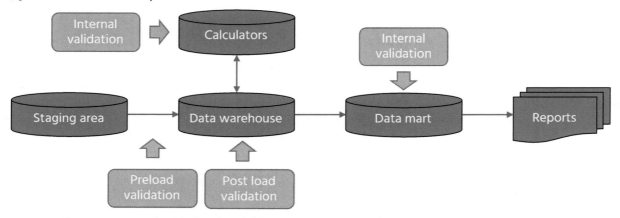

Figure 72: An example of the location of different types of DQ checks and controls along with the data chain.

Data quality controls reside either within applications or between applications within ETL processes.

Internal validations within calculators or data marts and post-load validations within a data warehouse are examples of checks within applications. Preload validations are performed during the ETL process while loading data into the data warehouse from the staging area.

Several challenges are associated with designing and building data quality checks and controls:

- The necessity to align data quality checks and controls along the chain
  Different stakeholders might have diverse data quality requirements for the same data elements. Similar checks and controls can also be built at different locations along the chain. The alignment of data quality checks and controls has to take place. Data quality

checks and controls should not contradict each other. They also have to be aligned and not repeated.

- The availability of the content of quality checks
  From the data lineage perspective, a company should have transparency regarding the content of validation rules applied to data. Depending on the location of data quality checks, the content of validation rules is not always accessible.
  Some data quality checks have been built within an application or ETL by using a business rule engine and accessible metadata. The content of such a rule is accessible.
  Other data quality checks are embedded in software code. It makes them untraceable.
- The necessity to know physical data lineage
  An effective system of data quality checks and controls can be built only if physical data lineage is known. Data quality checks and controls allow mitigating data quality errors and issues. If data quality issues have already taken place, then the root-cause analysis is a means to resolve these issues. A physical data lineage is also a precondition to perform a root-cause analysis.

SUMMARY OF CHAPTER 15

- Data quality requirements, building and designing data quality checks and controls are examples of data quality tasks that require knowledge of data lineage.
- Data quality requirements are set up at the different levels of data models along with the data chain. Mainly, such requirements have been specified at the physical level. Therefore, the knowledge of physical data lineage is highly demanded.
- Data quality check is a software code that checks the correspondence of a data instance or a data set to predefined requirements at some stage of data processing.
- Data quality control is a process of controlling data. The set of data quality checks allow performing data quality control.
- Building data quality checks and controls within databases and ETL tools along a data chain requires the knowledge of physical data lineage.
- Several challenges are associated with designing and building data quality checks and controls:
  - The necessity to align data quality checks and controls along the chain
  - The availability of the content of quality checks
  - The need to know a physical data lineage

16 | IMPACT AND ROOT-CAUSE ANALYSIS

Depending on business needs, data lineage assists in performing either an impact or root-cause analysis. We have briefly discussed these two types of analysis in sub-chapter 2.2.

Business change initiatives need to assess potential consequences if some changes take place in the application landscape, in database schemas, etc. An impact analysis is a means to do this.

The investigation of data quality issues and answering audit questions are the key reasons to perform root-cause analysis.

In this chapter, we will:
- Provide some practical recommendations about the performance of such analysis

After reading this chapter, you will be able to:
- Identify cases when impact and root-cause analysis should be accomplished
- Perform these two analyses

Let us recall the definitions of the impact and root-cause analysis.

Impact analysis allows one to track down the changes in data chains from their beginning to their end.

Root-cause analysis helps to track data origin back from the point of data usage.

Below, I have listed several recommendations regarding the usage of data lineage for these two types of analysis.

Recommendation 1: Different types of analysis require different data lineage components.

Data lineage eases the performance of both types of analysis. Depending on the goal and type of analysis, you may use diverse data lineage components. Let us consider two examples.

Example 1:

A company is planning to substitute a sourcing legacy software application, as shown in Figure 73. The legacy software is marked in red and resides at the beginning of the data chain.

The impact analysis could pursue the following goals:
- Assess the scope of changes along the data chain caused by the new database schema
- Estimate changes required in ETL jobs and tools
- Assess whether the new database schema contains all data attributes required for the sourcing of reports
- Plan the implementation of changes

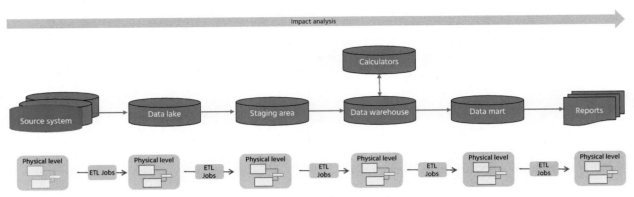

Figure 73: An example of impact analysis.

To perform such an analysis, the following horizontal data lineage components can be required:

- Application and data set flows
- Business rules
- Physical data lineage, including:
  - Physical data model
  - ETL jobs

The second example is for root-cause analysis.

Example 2:

New legislation requires a new set of reports. In Figure 74, this set is marked red.

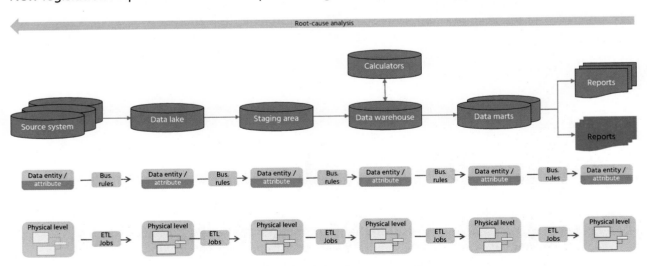

Figure 74: An example of root-cause analysis.

These reports include information that has not been provided so far. In this case, a root-cause analysis should assist achieving the following goals:

- Assess requirements for new sourcing data

- Estimate readiness of the existing data chains to proceed with and transform new data
- Evaluate changes that are needed to implement in the software applications, databases, ETL tools to perform the processing of new data.

To perform such an analysis, the following horizontal and vertical data lineage components can be required:

- Application and data set flows
- Conceptual and logical data models
- Business rules
- Physical data lineage, including:
  - Physical data model
  - ETL jobs

In these examples, we have investigated the impact and root-cause analysis for business change purposes. The usage of root-cause analysis for data quality and audit purpose next to data lineage may require some additional capabilities.

Recommendation 2: For root-cause analysis, data lineage may be combined with additional capabilities.

Fully documented metadata data lineage may not cover all needs of business users in some cases. The investigation of data quality issues and audit requirements to explain the origin of some figures in reports are key examples. In this case, business users next to metadata lineage may need some additional capabilities. We discussed these topics in sub-chapters 5.1 and 12.6 when we investigated data value lineage. Next to physical data lineage, business users may use drill-back and reconciliation capabilities.

The areas of metadata lineage applications discussed in Chapters 14 and 16 belong to the data management domain. Data lineage can also be of use in other business domains.

SUMMARY OF CHAPTER 16

- Depending on business needs, data lineage assists in performing either impact or root-cause analysis.
- Impact analysis allows one to track down the changes in data chains from their beginning to their end.
- Root-cause analysis helps to track data origin back from the point of data usage.
- A couple of recommendations assist in the performing of these two types of analysis:
  1. Different types of analysis require different data lineage components.
  2. For root-cause analysis, data lineage may be combined with additional capabilities.

17 | DRIVER-BASED MODELING

Metadata lineage can assist in performing some financial planning and analysis (FP&A) tasks. Driver-based modeling is one of the modern financial modeling techniques where the outcomes data lineage can be used.

In this chapter, we will:

- Investigate similarities between driver-based modeling and data lineage concepts
- Demonstrate the usage of data lineage for driver-based modeling

After reading this chapter, you will be able to:

- Communicate with your FP&A colleagues on the financial modeling subject
- Promote the usage of data lineage in the FP&A domain

Let's review the essence of driver-based modeling. Driver-based modeling focuses on identifying business drivers and linking them with financial results and key performance indicators (KPIs).

Business driver is an operational metric that:

- ensures a sustainable success and growth in the main areas of business for which the business was designed, and
- affects a company's earnings or the price of its stock

Key performance indicator (KPI) is a quantifiable metric used to evaluate the success of an organization, business function, employee, etc., in meeting objectives for performance.

Driver-based modeling aims to build mathematical models between business drivers and projected financial outcomes, i.e., revenue, costs, and other KPIs. Such models identify relationships between business drivers and financial outcomes, and KPIs. A driver-based model includes the set of drivers, financial outcomes, KPIs, and the relationships between them.

While working with FP&A professionals, I realized that what we data management professionals call critical data elements, finance professionals call "business drivers."

In this respect, critical data elements in data management and business drivers and KPIs in finance and performance management are similar concepts. Data management by using the CDE concept can assist finance in the specification of business drivers and KPIs.

A simplified example of the driver-based model can be seen in Figure 75.

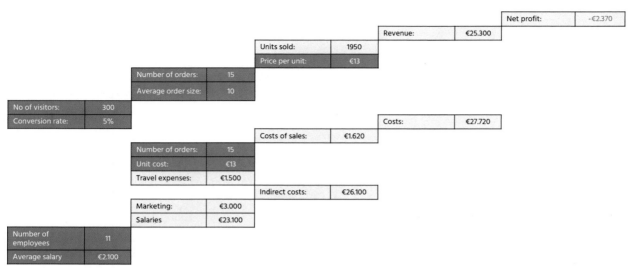

Figure 75: An example of a driver-based model.

Throughout the chain, business drivers influence a net profit, which is one of the key company's KPIs. Basic business drivers have been marked dark blue.

These business drivers represent data elements that have been processed to derive the calculated data elements and are marked in light-grey. Revenue, cost of sales, and net profit represent these calculated elements.

An example of data lineage at the conceptual level for this set of data elements is shown in Figure 76:

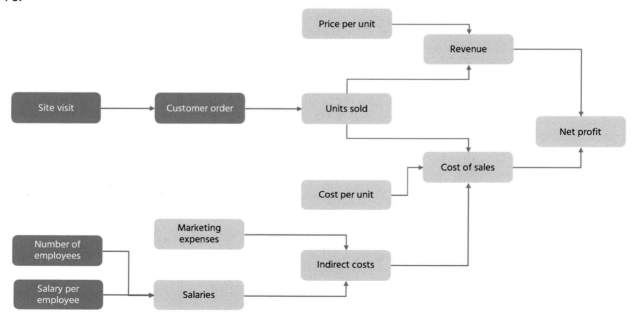

Figure 76: An example of data lineage at the conceptual level of a data model.

The demonstrated driver-based model and the conceptual data model illustrate many similarities.

Driver-based models are based on the assumptions derived as the results of the analysis. Data lineage delivers exact information which basic data elements influence the calculation of derived financial indicators. Thus, data lineage could save time for financial professionals to investigate relationships between business drivers and projected outcomes.

The example of driver-based modeling demonstrates that coordinated activities of finance and data management professionals can deliver mutual benefits for both functions.

SUMMARY OF CHAPTER 17

- Critical data elements in data management and business drivers and KPIs in finance/performance management are similar concepts. Through the use of the CDE concept, data management can assist finance in the specification of business drivers, KPIs, and relationships between them.
- The representation of the driver-based model and the conceptual data model demonstrates many similarities.
- Data lineage could assist in identifying relationships between business drivers and expected financial results and KPIs.

18 | THE SETUP OF A DATA MANAGEMENT FRAMEWORK

Data lineage and data management framework may seem like very different topics, but my practical experience made me conclude that they are very much related. The conclusion is this: *"The setup of a data management framework follows the logic of data lineage documentation."*

In this chapter, we will:

- Investigate similarities between the concepts of data lineage and a data management framework

After reading this chapter, you will:

- Be able to use the concept of data lineage to improve and extend the data management framework in your company
- Build data management capabilities required to document data lineage

To substantiate the conclusion mentioned above, I used the "Orange" model of data management[1] developed by Data Crossroads.

18.1 THE "ORANGE" MODEL OF DATA MANAGEMENT

This model considers data management as a business capability. The word "capability" stresses the ability of data management to deliver business value, reach goals, and deliver outcomes. The key business values that data management delivers are:

- Safeguarding the company's data resources
- Allowing a company to get economic values from data resources

Data management delivers these values by optimizing data value chains and establishing business capabilities that enable these chains.

A data value chain supports the business in creating business value, as shown in Figure 77.

The core data management sub-capabilities, such as data governance, data quality, data modeling, and information systems architecture, enable the design of data value chains. IT and other supporting capabilities enable the functioning of data value chains.

The data management capabilities form a framework in which data is being managed. The implementation of this framework follows a particular logic, and the relationships and dependencies between different data management capabilities define this logic.

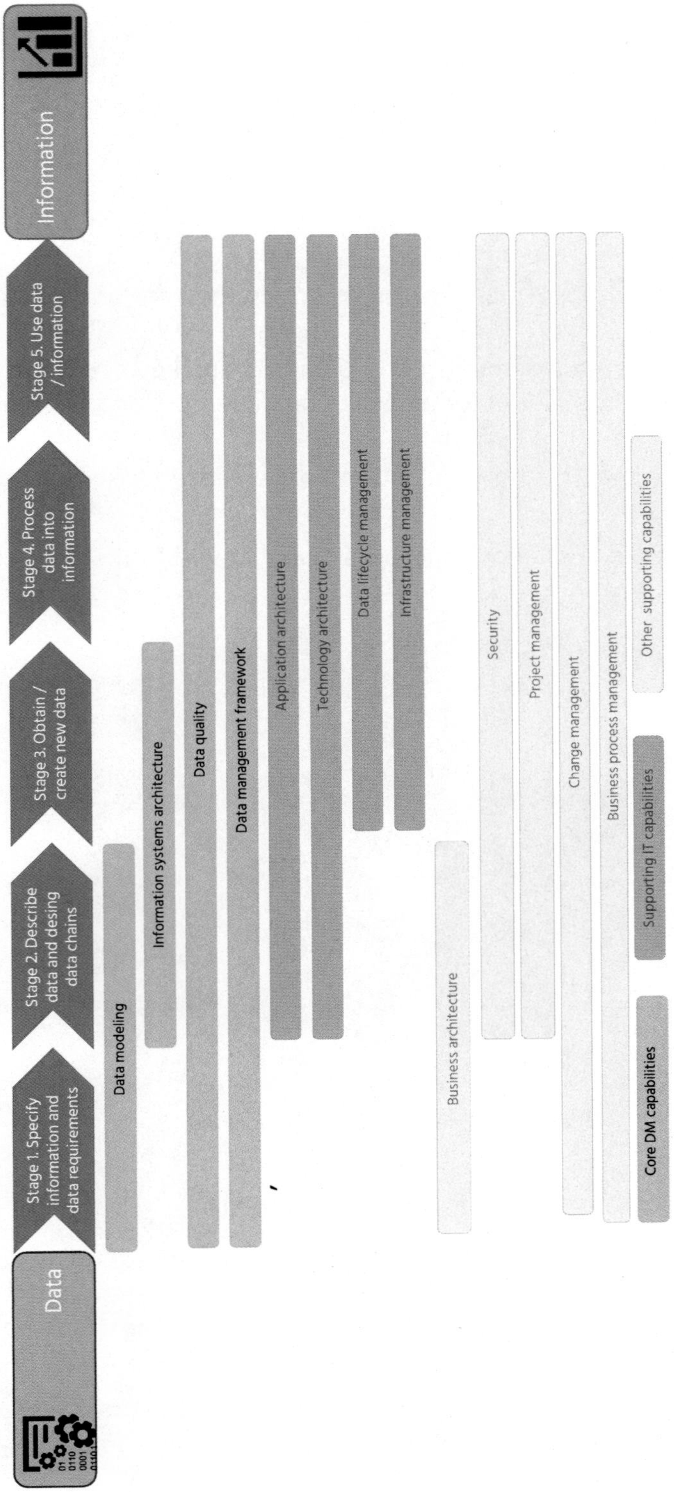

Figure 77: The "Orange" model of data management.

For example, a company can hardly successfully implement data quality without having information systems architecture and data modeling in place.

Let us consider the nature and essence of the similarities between data lineage and the implementation of a data management framework.

18.2 THE SETUP OF A DATA MANAGEMENT FRAMEWORK VS DATA LINEAGE DOCUMENTATION

The similarities between the setup of data management framework and documentation of data lineage can be found in:

- The deliverables of data management sub-capabilities and key components of data lineage
- The logical steps of the implementation of data management and documentation of data lineage

To demonstrate these similarities, I used the "data management star"[2] model developed by Data Crossroads, shown in Figure 78.

The model identifies five steps to implementing a data management framework. Let us consider each of these steps in-depth.

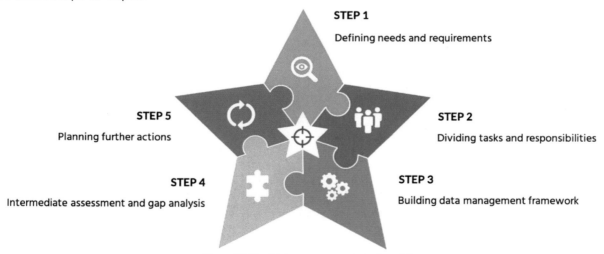

Figure 78: The "data management star" model.

Step 1: Defining needs and information requirements

In Step 1, a company determines the feasible scope of the data management framework. Business drivers, key stakeholders, their needs, and information requirements identify the scope of the data management framework. The list of deliverables includes a list of business drivers, stakeholders, and their most urgent information needs.

You start a data lineage initiative with the same step. The same factors, such as business drivers, stakeholders' needs, and requirements. define the scope.

Furthermore, the same business drivers often motivate a company to start both initiatives. Think, for example, about compliance with regulations.

When the scope is clear, the corresponding data management tasks and responsibilities should be defined.

Step 2: Dividing tasks and responsibilities

The data management framework defines the set of rules and roles. Rules include but are not limited to data management strategy, policies, standards, processes, procedures, plans. Roles should be linked to data management processes, tasks, and deliverables.

Data lineage is one of the deliverables of data management. Therefore, a company needs to specify and document its understanding of data lineage in the form of a data lineage metamodel. Depending on the model, different data management-related roles get accountabilities regarding data lineage documentation.

So, this step is also similar to both initiatives.

Step 3: Building the data management framework

The implementation of a data management framework follows several steps and requires different data management capabilities.

Step 3.1: Specify data requirements

As specified in Step 1, corresponding data should be found, delivered, and processed to meet information requirements. Very often, the relationship between raw data and information is not fully known. Data lineage is a means to fill in this gap. Usually, data lineage documentation starts with the specification of existing business processes. So the identification of data requirements demands the documentation of data lineage, at least at the business layer.

Step 3.2: Document business processes

Business process documentation is not considered to be a part of any of the data management sub-capabilities. Still, this is a required component of data lineage. The majority of companies begin their data lineage documentation with the analysis of business processes. Then related IT assets and business roles participated in the processes, and then data sets are mapped to those processes.

Step 3.3: Document system and application landscape

Data transformation usually takes place in IT assets such as systems, applications, etc. The documentation of an IT asset catalog and data flows are deliverables of the information systems architecture. At the same time, these flows are mandatory components of data lineage at the business layer.

Step 3.4: Develop conceptual, logical, and physical data models and link them

Data modeling delivers the set of data models at conceptual, logical, and physical levels. Data lineage can be documented at each of these levels. These models and the vertical links between them are components of data lineage.

Step 3.5: Identify critical data elements

The definition of critical data elements is a state-of-the-art task that was discussed in-depth in Chapter 14. The set of critical data elements is the deliverable of the data modeling sub-capability. The mandatory prerequisite to specify critical data elements is the knowledge of data lineage.

Data quality capability delivers data quality requirements, corresponding checks, and controls. We have demonstrated in Chapter 15 that it is practically impossible to do it without data lineage.

Step 3.6: Assemble data lineage

Only when all of the above-mentioned steps are complete can the data lineage be assembled. At this point, a company is ready with the implementation of its data management function.

Step 4: Perform Intermediate assessment and gap analysis

This step is required to compare the desired results specified in Step 1 with the achieved one. This step is also the point where a maturity assessment of data management can be performed. The same step you perform for the data lineage initiative.

Step 5: Plan further actions

As soon as the company has achieved the desired results, it might want to extend the scope of its data management initiative, including the scope of data lineage.

I hope that I have managed to convince you that the setup of a data management framework follows the logic of data lineage documentation.

This chapter completes Part 3 and the core content of this book. To demonstrate all that we have discussed, I have prepared a small case study.

SUMMARY OF CHAPTER 18

- Data lineage and data management frameworks may seem like very different topics, but they have a lot in common.
- The setup of the data management framework follows the logic of data lineage documentation.
- The "Orange" model of data management assists in demonstrating similarities between data lineage documentation and data management framework implementation.
- The "Orange" model identifies data management as a business capability that safeguards data resources and assists in getting economic value from them.
- Data management delivers its values by optimizing data value chains and establishing business capabilities that enable these chains.
- The data management capabilities form a framework in which data is being managed. The implementation of this framework follows a certain logic. The relationships and dependencies between different data management capabilities define this logic.
- The steps to setting up a data management framework defined by the "data management star" model are similar to the steps of documenting data lineage.

SUMMARY OF PART 3

In Part 3, we discussed different areas of the utilization of data lineage artifacts.

We have identified that data lineage can deliver value for different types of data management initiatives as well as assist other business functions in achieving their goals.

We have demonstrated the usage of data lineage for the following data management initiatives:

- Definition of critical data

Critical data is data that is critical for managing business risks, taking business decisions, and successfully operating a business.

Within the data management context, critical data is used for:

- ○ The prioritization of data quality, master data, data governance initiatives
- ○ The identification of business drivers and key performance indicators

To successfully implement the concept of critical data, the following conditions must be met:

- ○ Physical data lineage should be in place.
- ○ Along with the data chain, several types of critical data should be recognized.
- ○ Different types of critical data elements should be documented at diverse levels of a data model.
- ○ The criteria of criticality depend on the types of critical data elements.
- Data quality

Data quality requirements and building and designing data quality checks and controls are examples of a data quality initiative that requires the knowledge of data lineage:

- ○ Data quality requirements are set up at the different levels of data models along with the data chain.
- ○ Knowledge of physical data lineage is required to build data quality checks and controls within databases and ETL tools along with a data chain.
- Impact and root-cause analysis

Depending on business needs, data lineage assists in performing either impact or root-cause analysis.

The impact analysis allows tracking down the changes in data chains from their beginning to their end. The root-cause analysis helps to track data origin back from the point of data usage.

These two analyses are performed at different levels of abstraction.

- The setup of a data management framework or function

The same data management capabilities that form a data management framework are needed to document data lineage. The setup of a data management framework follows the same logic that we use to document data lineage. The key artifacts delivered by data management sub-capabilities create the basis for documented data lineage.

Part 4

CASE STUDY: "BUILD A DATA LINEAGE BUSINESS CASE"

We're done talking about the theory of data lineage metamodels, implementation, and how to use it, so now let's have fun with data lineage. Here you will read a short story about XYZ Company and its journey in documenting data lineage. XYZ is a fictitious company. Initially, I used this company in designing the case study for the book "Data Management Toolkit"[1] published in 2019. Since then, the business of XYZ has grown, and the company has faced new challenges.

XYZ is a software developer and provider of consulting services for software implementation. The company is established in one of the European Union (EU) countries and has several EU and the United States offices. The company has two business divisions.

The first division is the development center. There are two main software products the company develops. Product X serves the needs of entrepreneurs. Its customer segment, "Retail market segment," includes mainly sole proprietors or individuals. Product Y is oriented to meet the needs of small and medium enterprises. Its customer segment is called the "Corporate market segment." The second division is the consulting and hotline services. Product X does not require implementation support. Only hotline support is offered to retail customers. Product Y requires both implementation and hotline support.

Recently, the company's management faced some challenges with compliance with some regulations. Heads of data management and IT departments concluded that a data lineage may deliver the solution to meet these requirements. They decided to commence the data lineage initiative.

The Chief Data Officer came across the book "Data Lineage from Business Perspectives" and proposed exploring the book's methodology to scope the data lineage initiative. They organized the initiative group. The Chief Information Officer has chaired the group. Several heads of departments, including data management and IT, joined the group. To develop the business case, they decided to follow the methodology described in Chapter 6, "Build your data lineage case," of the aforementioned book.

STEP 1: IDENTIFY KEY DRIVERS

After some internal discussion, the data lineage initiative group concluded that they have two key drivers to proceed with the project. Both drivers relate to the necessity to comply with legislative requirements:

- General data protection regulation (GDPR) with a focus on personal retail customer data
- Sarbanes-Oxley Act (SOX) compliance with a focus on financial data and external reporting

Both drivers got the same priority. Therefore, the team decided to proceed with a further analysis taking into account both drivers.

STEP 2: BUY-IN SUPPORT AND INVOLVEMENT OF KEY STAKEHOLDERS

The top management of the company is fully aware of the necessity to comply with regulations. Top management delegated responsibility to the Chief Information Officer to:

- Prepare the business case
- Evaluate the required budget
- Inform the supervisory board of the company on progress regularly

The support to the initiative has been granted, and the initiative group has proceeded with the evaluation of the scope.

STEP 3: SCOPE DATA LINEAGE INITIATIVE

The group has defined the main goals of the scope evaluation. The scope of the initiative should ensure:

- Meeting the requirements at a "minimum acceptable level"
  The requirements of legislative acts don't provide direct instructions to have data lineage in place. The decision to use data lineage as a means to comply with regulations has been based on the experts' opinion. Therefore, the company by itself can define the minimum level of compliance.
- The alignment of legislative requirements with the requirements of business stakeholders
  Compliance with regulations is the key driver. But the deliverables of data lineage should also be used and valued by business users. Therefore, the requirements of business stakeholders should be considered and aligned with the legislative requirements. Data lineage must deliver business value for ordinary business users.
- The delivery of results within one year period
  The specialists within the company are aware that a data lineage initiative is a time and resource-consuming exercise. It can take months and years to implement it fully. But the company should first demonstrate its value. Therefore, the results should be delivered within a short period.

The initiative group decided to use the key dimensions of the scope identified in Chapter 7 of the "Data Lineage from Business Perspectives."

3.1. Identify the scope of "enterprise"

Enterprise architects developed a high-level overview of the architecture landscape, as shown in Figure 79.

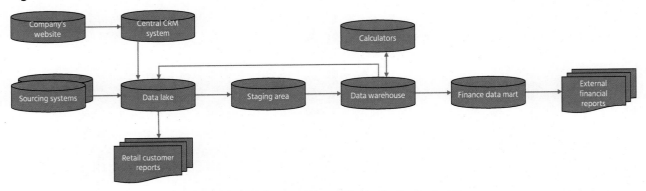

Figure 79: A high-level overview of the application landscape.

For scoping purposes, the initiative team decided to separate the landscape into two sectors, depending on the data sets in question. Then they identified the sectors of the landscape associated with the processing of:

- A set of retail customer personal data
- A set of financial data

The updated landscape can be seen in Figure 80. Applications used for the processing of personal data and financial data have been marked green and lilac correspondingly.

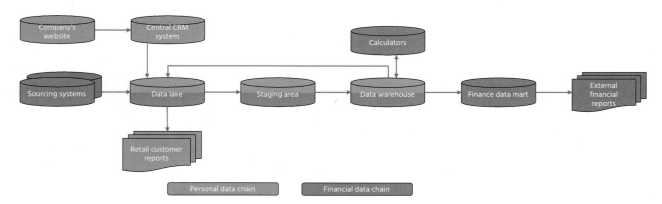

Figure 80: A simplified schema of the data application landscape with the indication for data sets.

Personal data processing

The data chain for personal data is marked green in Figure 80.

Retail customers provide their initial personal information at the company's website. The rest of the information has been gathered by account officers. All personal information goes to the central CRM system, which ingests the information into the company's data lake. Through the staging area, customer information goes to the central data warehouse (DWH). In a DWH, data undergoes integration and aggregation and is read back to the data lake. The retail customer reports have been generated based on the information received from the data lake.

Finance data processing

The data chain for personal data is marked in lilac in Figure 80.

Finance data sets stream from different source systems located in diverse offices into the data lake. From there, through some ETL processes, finance data flows to the data warehouse. For financial reporting, additional data should be calculated. Therefore, some data sets go to calculators. The calculated data is read back to the DWH. From DWH, data moves to finance data mart and then to reporting engines and reports.

After the "enterprise" scope has been identified, the data lineage team has proceeded with the definition of the data lineage "length" dimension.

3.2. Define the "length" of data lineage

The landscape drawn in Figure 81 demonstrates the full "length" of a data chain. Of course, the horizontal data lineage from the "golden" source to the "final" destination is the top goal of any data lineage initiative. The XYZ data lineage team has realized that the data chains are too long to document data lineage in one attempt. Therefore, they decided to split the chains into several segments. Data lineage for these segments should be documented in phases. The first draft of this proposal can be seen in Figure 81.

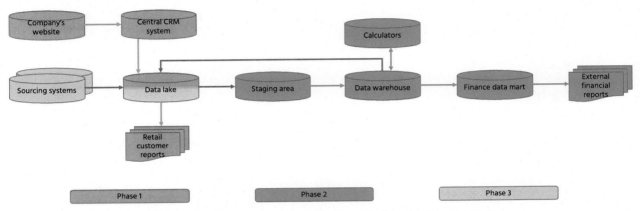

Figure 81: A simplified schema to scope the "length" of the data lineage initiative.

The team proposed the following phases for the documentation of data lineage:

Phase 1 - Document data lineage for the personal data set.

The set of applications in the scope is marked orange.

The team had several reasons to scope personal data for phase 1:

- The set of personal data includes a limited number of data attributes
- The chain consists of only several applications
- Phase 1 can be considered as a pilot project to develop the required skills within XYZ Company to document data lineage.

Phase 2 - Document data lineage for the financial data set, limited to the sector from the staging area to external financial reports.

One of the key reasons to define scope 2 was that this part of the landscape is owned and managed by the central finance function within XYZ Company.

Phase 3 - Document data lineage from source systems to the data lake and then from the data lake to the staging area. The ETL tools to ingest data from the data warehouse back to the data lake also form a part of phase 3.

To fine-tune these phases, the team proceeded with scoping the "depth" of data lineage.

199

3.3. Define the "depth" of data lineage

The "depth" of data lineage identifies the levels of data lineage documentation. The data lineage team realized they could document data lineage at four different levels, as described in Chapter 4 of this book:

- Business level
  The business level includes business capabilities, business processes, and roles that perform these processes, business subject areas, and IT asset and data set flows.
- The conceptual level of a data model
  Data lineage at the conceptual level of the data model demonstrates the movement of data at data entity levels.
- The logical level of a data model
  At the logical level of a data model, data lineage is documented at the level of data entities and attributes.
  Data lineage at the above-mentioned levels can be documented manually by applying "descriptive data lineage" techniques.
- The physical level of a data model
  By using the "automated data lineage" method at this level, data lineage can be documented at the level of tables and columns.

After careful considerations of the key goals of the data lineage initiative, the team has proposed the following "depth" of data lineage, as shown in Figure 82.

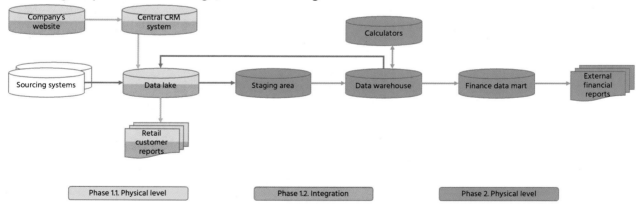

Figure 82: A simplified schema to scope the "depth" of the data lineage initiative.

The team has taken the following decisions:

1. Phase 1 for personal data has been split into two sub-phases:
   - Phase 1.1 focuses on the implementation of automated data lineage.
     During the implementation of the data management framework, XYZ performed a pilot project to document some artifacts related to the set of personal data. In detail, the project has been described in the case study "Data Management Toolkit"[2]. These artifacts form most of the part of the descriptive data lineage. Since then, some legacy applications have been substituted. However, the artifacts that belong to the business, conceptual, and logical layers remain valid. Therefore, during phase 1.1, only

physical data lineage will be documented by using an automated method.
- Phase 1.2 aims to implement the vertical data lineage.
This phase is the integration between the data lineage components and objects at physical and logical levels of data models. The integration between objects at the business, conceptual, and logical levels has been performed during the descriptive data lineage. The integration between these layers has been completed using MS office applications.
2. Phase 2 for the financial data set concentrates on the recording of the automated data lineage.

The team believes that automated data lineage can deliver results in a shorter period.

The decision about the next steps is postponed until the completion of the implementation of phases 1.1, 1.2, and 2.

The last step in the exercise is the specification of data lineage components and objects to be documented.

3.4. Define the key data lineage components and objects

The data lineage team has provided the proposal regarding data lineage components and objects to be documented, as shown in Table 14.

For phase 1.1, the team decided to implement horizontal data lineage at the physical level. Data lineage should include the following objects: tables, columns, ETL jobs.

Phase 1.2 focuses on the integration of data lineage at physical and logical data model levels.

As mentioned earlier, some artifacts of descriptive data lineage have been already documented during previous data management initiatives. The documentation includes the following already-documented components of horizontal data lineage:
- Business processes and associated roles
- IT asset flows
- Business subject areas and data entities with corresponding definitions
- Constraints applied to data entities
- Data attributes with corresponding definitions
- Business rules that are applied to data entities

Data set	Phase	Data lineage component	Data lineage object	Status
Personal data	Phase 1.1	Horizontal data lineage Physical data model	• Table • Column • ETL job	To do
	Phase 1.2	Horizontal data lineage Business process	• Business process • Role	Done
		Horizontal data lineage Application flow	• Application	Done
		Horizontal data lineage Conceptual data model	• Business subject area • Data entity • Terms and definitions • Constraints	Done
		Horizontal data lineage Logical data model	• Data entity • Data attribute • Terms and definitions • Business rule	Done
		Vertical lineage Link between physical and logical levels	• Table ~ data entity • Column ~ data attribute	To do
Financial data	Phase 2	Horizontal data lineage Physical data model	• Table • Column • ETL job	To do

Table 14: The scope of data lineage components and objects for the phases 1.1, 1.2, and 2.

202

The goal of phase 1.2 is to document mapping between tables and data entities, and columns and data attributes. The link between ETL jobs and business rules is beyond the scope.

Phase 2 aims at the documentation of horizontal data lineage at the physical level. The key data lineage objects are physical tables, columns, and ETL jobs.

The proposed scope has been presented and agreed upon. The initiative group has moved with the business case development.

The next step is the definition of roles and accountabilities.

STEP 4: DEFINE ROLES AND ACCOUNTABILITIES

The data management function has already been set up within XYZ Company. Therefore, the existing teams of data management and technical stewards will perform the implementation.

The data lineate initiative group has decided to involve data management and business stewards to define the requirements for data lineage.

STEP 5: PREPARE DATA LINEAGE REQUIREMENTS

As a result of multiple interviews with business and data management stakeholders, the data lineage initiative team came up with the requirements document. To develop the requirements, the initiative group used Template 1 presented in additional materials of the book. The summary of the metadata lineage general requirements for phases 1.1, 1.2, and 2 in the tabular form can be found in Table 15.

The requirements have been identified for:
- All three phases of data lineage implementation
- Data lineage layer such as business, conceptual, logical, and physical
- Data lineage components per each layer.

In Table 15, when a requirement is applicable for a specific phase, data lineage level, and component, the intercection cell is marked in dark blue.

Next to the general requirements, the team has prepared additional requirements for the automated data lineage solution that have to be implemented in phases 1.1 and 2. An example of the template for such requirements can be seen in Table 16.

Data lineage requirement	Data lineage type	Project phase	Data lineage level / components and data lineage objects				
			Business • Business process • Application	Conceptual • Business subject • Data entity & attribute	Logical • Data entity & attribute	Physical • Application • Table, column • ETL job	
Graphical representation of data lineage as a chain of linked metadata objects and relationships between them	Horizontal	Phase 1.1 Phase 1.2 Phase 2					
Visualize metadata elements for metadata object	Horizontal	Phase 1.1 Phase 1.2 Phase 2					
Ability to trace the link between metadata objects in two directions: from source to destination and vice versa	Horizontal	Phase 1.1 Phase 1.2 Phase 2					
Zoom in (drill up and drill down) capability to move between different level of abstractions	Vertical	Phase 1.1 Phase 1.2 Phase 2					
Ability to maintain versioning control and archive data lineage for auditability purposes	Horizontal Vertical	Phase 1.1 Phase 1.2 Phase 2					
Maintain data lineage objects and corresponding metadata in a central repository	Horizontal	Phase 1.1 Phase 1.2 Phase 2					
Link data lineage objects within a data lineage level	Vertical	Phase 1.1 Phase 1.2 Phase 2					
Link data lineage objects between levels:							
• Business level to conceptual	Vertical	Phase 1.2					
• Conceptual to logical	Vertical	Phase 1.2					
• Logical to physical	Vertical	Phase 1.1 Phase 2					

Table 15: Metadata lineage general requirements.

Requirement	Central CRM system	ETL to data lake	Data lake
Database type	MS SQL server		Snowflake
ETL tool type		Azure data factory	
Level of automation	Fully automated	Fully automated	Fully automated

Table 16: An example of the additional requirements for automated data lineage.

When the requirements have been discussed and approved, the data lineage initiative team has proceeded to the next step in business case development.

STEP 6: CHOOSE AN APPROACH AND METHOD TO DOCUMENT DATA LINEAGE

At this stage, XYZ Company management has confirmed the proposed approaches and methods to document data lineage. The approaches and methods vary depending on the chosen scope:

Personal data sets

- "Enterprise coverage"
  Data lineage will be documented for the set of applications demonstrated in Figure 82.
- Method of documentation
  The physical data lineage will be documented using the automated method.
  For data lineage at the business, conceptual, and logical layers, descriptive data lineage has already been applied.
- The direction of documentation
  The company has opted for the hybrid approach to document data lineage. Descriptive data lineage has already been documented at earlier stages. After the completion of physical data lineage documentation, logical and physical levels will be integrated.
  For the integration between logical and physical levels, the company intends to use a semi-automated solution.

Financial data sets

- "Enterprise coverage"
  The scope of data lineage covers the set of applications shown in Figure 82.
- Method of documentation
  Only physical data lineage has been taken into the defined scope. The intention is to implement an automated solution.
- The direction of documentation
  The decision regarding data lineage documentation at other layers will be made after the successful completion of the physical data lineage.

The company's management has also decided to proceed with the centralized approach to managing data lineage implementation within the company.

This approach means the following:

- The company uses the common metadata model of data lineage.
  The company supports the metadata model lineage that consists of business layers and three layers of data models.
  For individual implementation initiatives, the set of metadata objects can vary depending on data lineage needs.
- The company will invest in one data lineage solution that can be used at multiple locations and for different data lineage initiatives.
  The solution should include an integration capability. It means the possibility to integrate different levels of data lineage. The tool should support different technologies.

After these decisions have been made, a data lineage initiative team moved to the next step to analyze different data lineage solutions.

STEP 7: CHOOSE APPROPRIATE DATA LINEAGE SOLUTION

The data lineage initiative team has proceeded with the choice of a software solution. They decided to proceed only with COTS (commercial-of-the-shelf) solutions. They found a list of data lineage solutions. Primarily, they simply decided to compile the shortlist of requirements and compare different solutions based on the information available at the providers' sites. Only after such an analysis would they proceed with a shortlist of candidates. The team has prepared a long list of solutions available at the market. They investigated the sites of providers and completed the comparison. The example of the template the team has prepared can be seen in Table 17.

The team used the MoSCoW[3] method to prioritize the importance of solution functionality. They compared two different solutions. In case a solution meets the requirements, the cell is marked in dark blue. If the information at the vendor's site was unclear, the cell is marked In yellow. In case they could not find a reference to the requirement, the cell remains unmarked.

After completing the preliminary analysis, the team has created a shortlist and proceeded with the planning demonstrations.

After choosing a software solution, the implementation phase has started.

I hope this small case-study has assisted you in assimilating the information about data lineage provided in this book. Of course, the reality would be much more complicated. Still, I believe that this book will assist you in making your data lineage business case successful.

N	Requirement	MoSCoW (Must/Should/ Could/Would)	Data lineage Solution 1	Data lineage Solution 2
1	A solution includes a catalog/repository to document:			
	• Business process at different abstraction level	C		
	• Role	C		
	• Legislations and policies	W		
	• IT assets	M		
	• Business glossary	M		
	• Data catalog	M		
	• Data dictionary	M		
	• Business rules	S		
	• Relationship repository	M		
2	A solution has:			
	• Metadata lineage viewer	M		
	• Ready to use scanners for the defined list of databases, ETL tools, programming languages	M		
3	Additional visualization requirement for data lineage capability:			
	• Graphical representation of data lineage as a chain of linked metadata objects and relationships between them	M		
	• Visualize metadata elements for metadata object	M		
	• Ability to trace the link between metadata objects in two directions: from source to destination and vice versa	M		
	• Zoom in (drill up and drill down) capability to move between different level of abstractions	M		
4	Print document function in order to able to get printed evidences about data lineage	M		
5	Ability to maintain versioning control and archive data lineage for auditability purposes	M		
6	Data modeling capabilities, including:			
	• Maintain conceptual, logical, and physical data models	S		
	• Different types of diagrams and notations	S		
	• Forward- and reverse engineer models	S		
7	Collaborative environment	M		
8	Integration capabilities:			
	• Vertical mapping between business and conceptual level	C		
	• Conceptual and logical data models	S		
	• Logical and physical data models	S		
9	Additional capabilities:			
	• Business architecture	W		
	• Data quality	W		

Table 17: A template to compare data lineage requirements with the solutions' functionalities.

AFTERWORD

I initially planned this book as a compilation of some of my initial articles and presentations about data lineage. All of them have received good feedback from readers worldwide. The process of writing this book has taken just over a year. During this period, I continuously developed my knowledge in the area of data lineage. So, the scope of the book has been grown substantially compared to the initial plan. The book includes all my hands-on experience with data lineage that I have gained so far.

I sincerely hope that I have succeeded in explaining the theory and sharing experience in the implementation and use of data lineage. I am aware that this book still may not answer all your questions about this topic.

Data lineage is a rapidly growing capability within data management. In my opinion, data lineage is one of the most challenging tasks for data management professionals. It offers many opportunities to increase the efficiency of data management practices. In return, data lineage requires a lot of effort, resources, and dedication of all data-related stakeholders. I am very optimistic about technological developments in data lineage solutions.

I am sure that within the next few years more and more companies will develop this capability and elaborate on the new areas of its usage.

Hopefully, the reading of this book has motivated you to step into the "data lineage world".

For me, data lineage has opened a lot of new perspectives in professional development. Dealing with this topic has forced me to deepen my knowledge in various areas of data management. It has also motivated me to renew my view on data management. It resulted in the development of the "Orange" model. The "Orange" model represents the practical method to design and implement a data management framework. Data lineage plays a key role in this model. It allows demonstrating and taking into consideration the dynamic nature of data within the business lifecycle.

I am sure that dealing with data lineage will also boost your career and professional development.

I wish you good luck on your data lineage adventure!

Acknowledgements

I got my initial experience in the area of data lineage during the implementation of the SAS data lineage solution in ABN AMRO Bank B.V. I would like to express my gratitude to all of my colleagues from ABN AMRO B.V. and SAS who encouraged and supported me in developing my expertise.

ADDITIONAL MATERIALS

TEMPLATE 1: DATA LINEAGE REQUIREMENTS

This template demonstrates the key requirements for data lineage. It includes several columns:

- The requirements type
  The requirement type recognizes two types of requirements.
  General requirements are applied to all components of data lineage. The general requirements may differ per data lineage type.
  Requirements per data lineage layer assist in identifying which components should be documented at each layer.

- Data lineage requirement
  In this column, you should indicate the essence of the requirement.

- Data lineage type
  Vertical and horizontal lineage may have different general requirements. Therefore, in this template, we indicate their applicability.

- Requirement (Yes/No)

The template includes the complete set of components that belong to the metamodel of data lineage. For your business case, you should limit this set to the required minimum.

Requirement type	Data lineage requirement	Data lineage type	Requirement (Yes/No)
General	Graphical representation of data lineage as a chain of linked metadata objects and relationships between them	Horizontal	
General	Visualize metadata elements for metadata object	Horizontal	
General	Ability to trace the link between metadata objects in two directions: from source to destination and vice versa	Horizontal	
General	Zoom in (drill up and drill down) capability to move between different level of abstractions	Vertical	
General	Ability to maintain versioning control and archive data lineage for auditability purposes	Horizontal Vertical	
General	Maintain data lineage objects and corresponding metadata in a central repository	Horizontal	
General	Link data lineage objects within a data lineage level	Vertical	
General	Link data lineage objects between levels:		
General	• Business level to conceptual	Vertical	
General	• Conceptual to logical	Vertical	
General	• Logical to physical	Vertical	
Business layer	Document the following components at the business layer:		
	• Business capability		
	• Process		
	• Role		
	• Business subject area		
	• IT asset		
Conceptual layer	Document the following components at the conceptual layer:		
	• Data entity		
	• Relationship		
	• Business rule		
Logical layer	Document the following components at the logical layer:		
	• Data attribute		
	• Relationship		
	• Business rule		
Physical layer	Document the following components at the physical layer:		
	• Table		
	• Column		
	• ETL mapping		
	• ETL content		

TEMPLATE 2: THE SCOPE AND PROGRESS OF A DATA LINEAGE INITIATIVE

This template assists in communicating the scope of data lineage initiatives. It is also a good tool to demonstrate the progress of implementation.

The template includes the following columns:

- Data lineage layer
  In this column, you indicate layers at which data lineage will be documented.

- Data lineage component
  Each layer constitutes corresponding components.
  It could happen that data lineage will be documented along the data chain at different layers and with different components.

- IT assets that constitute the data chain in question
  In the rest of the columns, you indicate IT assets that are in the scope of your data lineage initiative.
  In the body of the template for each IT asset, layer, and corresponding components, you can indicate the following information:
    - Scope
    - Deadline for delivery
    - Progress status

Data lineage layer	Data lineage component	Application 1	ETL 1	Application 2
Business	• Business capability	Scope/ Deadline/ Completeness	Scope/ Deadline/ Completeness	Scope/ Deadline/ Completeness
	• Process			
	• Role			
	• Business subject area			
	• IT asset			
Conceptual	• Data entity			
	• Relationship			
	• Business rule			
Logical	• Data attribute			
	• Relationship			
	• Business rule			
Physical	• Table			
	• Column			
	• ETL mapping			
	• ETL content			

OVERVIEW OF DATA LINEAGE SOLUTIONS

This overview provides an analysis of the software solutions currently available in the market. The research includes solutions that cover more than one data lineage component identified by the metamodel of data lineage. The overview is only for informational purposes. I don't provide any preferences regarding a particular solution.

Name of the software vendor company	Business process modeling	Enterprise architecture	Data modeling	Data governance (stewardship, legislation, policies)	Metadata management				Data quality	Knowledge graphs
					Business glossary, data catalogue, data dictionary, metadata and relationship repository	Business rules manager	Automated data lineage at physical level	Connectors		
AB Initio[1]									X	
AboutDataGovernance[2]					X					
Adaptive[3]		X						X		
Alation[4]					X			X	X	
Alex Solution[5]					X		X			
ASG Technologies[6]					X		X	X		
Ataccama[7]					X		X	X	X	
Atlan[8]					X		X	X		
CluedIn[9]									X	
Collibra[10]				X	X		X	X	X	X
Data advantage group[11]				X	X		X	X		
dataworld[12]					X		X	X		X
Dataedo[13]			X		X		X	X		
Erwin[14]	X	X	X	X	X	X	X	X		
Global IDs[15]							X	X	X	
IBM[16]	X			X	X	X	X	X	X	
INFOGiX[17]				X	X		X	X		
Informatica[18]				X	X	X	X	X	X	X
IO-TAHOE[19]					X		X	X		
Manta[20]							X	X		
Octopai[21]					X		X	X		
Oracle[22]					X		X	X	X	
Orion Governance[23]	X			X			X	X		X
OvalEdge[24]				X	X		X	X	X	
SAP[25]					X		X	X		
SAS[26]					X		X	X	X	
Semantic Web Company[27]					X					X
Smartlogic[28]					X					X
Solidatus[29]				X			X	X		X
Syniti[30]				X	X		X	X	X	X
Talend[31]					X		X	X	X	
TopQuadrant[32]				X	X		X	X		X
Truedat[33]				X	X		X	X	X	X
Zeenea Data Catalogue[34]					X		X	X	X	X

TEMPLATE 3: COMPARE DATA LINEAGE SOLUTIONS

This template assists in performing a comparative analysis of different software solutions for data lineage documentation. It includes the key software functionalities to be compared.

This template includes the following columns:

- Requirement
  This column includes requirements for a data lineage solution. The business requirements that were identified by using Template 1 have been translated into the required products/ functionality.

- MoSCoW
  MoSCoW indicates your company's priorities of having some functionality/products.

- Data lineage solution 1 and 2
  In these columns, you can compare functionality offered by each of the solutions you considered.

N	Requirement	MoSCoW (Must/Should/ Could/Would)	Data lineage Solution 1	Data lineage Solution 2
1	A solution includes a catalog/repository to document:			
	• Business process at different abstraction level			
	• Role			
	• Legislations and policies			
	• IT assets			
	• Business glossary			
	• Data catalog			
	• Data dictionary			
	• Business rules			
	• Relationship repository			
2	A solution has:			
	• Metadata lineage viewer			
	• Ready to use scanners for the defined list of databases, ETL tools, programming languages			
3	Additional visualization requirement for data lineage capability:			
	• Graphical representation of data lineage as a chain of linked metadata objects and relationships between them			
	• Visualize metadata elements for metadata object			
	• Ability to trace the link between metadata objects in two directions: from source to destination and vice versa			
	• Zoom in (drill up and drill down) capability to move between different level of abstractions			
4	Print document function in order to able to get printed evidences about data lineage			
5	Ability to maintain versioning control and archive data lineage for auditability purposes			
6	Data modeling capabilities, including:			
	• Maintain conceptual, logical, and physical data models			
	• Different types of diagrams and notations			
	• Forward- and reverse engineer models			
7	Collaborative environment			
8	Integration capabilities:			
	• Vertical mapping between business and conceptual level			
	• Conceptual and logical data models			
	• Logical and physical data models			
9	Additional capabilities:			
	• Business architecture			
	• Data quality			

GLOSSARY

Automated data lineage is the method to record metadata lineage by implementing automated processes to scan and ingest metadata into a repository.

Business data steward is a data steward with significant knowledge, skills, and experience in one or more business domains.

Business glossary is a collection of business terms and corresponding definitions.

Business driver is an operational metric that:
- ensures a sustainable success and growth in the main areas of business for which the business was designed, and
- affects a company's earnings or the price of its stock

Business role is a role that contributes to organizational performance through the application of skills, knowledge, experience, or abilities.

Business rule repository is a database that collects business rules applied to data. In the best-case scenario, this repository also includes the representation of these rules in programming codes.

Business subject area is a data element that describes data at the highest level of abstraction.

Context is a set of conditions that identifies boundaries for a particular physical object, concept, process, phenomenon, etc.

Critical data is data that is critical for managing business risks, making business decisions, and successfully operating a business.

Data is the physical or electronic representation of signals "in a manner suitable for communication, interpretation, or processing by human beings or by automatic means"

(United Nations Statistical Commission and Economic Commission for Europe. Terminology on Statistical Metadata. United Nations. Geneva, 2000., https://unece.org/fileadmin/DAM/stats/publications/53metadaterminology.pdf, p.8. Accessed 16 Feb.2021).

Data attribute is a metadata component in a logical data model that identifies, describes or measures a data entity.

Data catalog is a collection of the information about the location of data sets and data elements across an enterprise.

Data dictionary is a collection that contains metadata about data elements at the different levels of abstraction.

Data chain is the physical realization of a data lifecycle.

Data element "is the smallest identifiable unit of data within a certain context for which the definition, identification, permissible values and other information is specified by means of a set of attributes" (United Nations Statistical Commission and Economic Commission for Europe. Terminology on Statistical Metadata. United Nations. Geneva, 2000., https://unece.org/fileadmin/DAM/stats/publications/53metadaterminology.pdf, p.8. Accessed 16 Feb.2021).

Data element is a "unit of data that is considered in context to be indivisible" (DAMA International.

The DAMA Dictionary of Data Management, Second Edition: Technics Publications, 2011, p.215).

Data entity is a metadata object in a logical data model that identifies, describes, or measures a business subject area.

Data instance is a particular value of a data element valid at a point in time.

Data lifecycle is the set of processes that move and transform data from the moment of its creation to the moment of its archiving and/or destruction.

Data lineage is a model that describes a data chain at different levels of abstraction.

Data lineage viewer is a tool that enables the visual representation of these metadata objects and relationships.

Data management is a business capability that safeguards data assets and delivers business value from them.

Data management framework is a business capability that delivers the structure in which other data management capabilities operate.

Data management role is a business role that performs data management related tasks and delivers intended data management outcomes.

Data management steward is a data steward with knowledge, skills, and experience in one or more data management domains.

Data model is the model that represents data at different levels of abstraction.

Data modeling is a business capability that delivers data models "[...] a) to define and analyze data requirements; b) design logical and physical structures that support these requirements; and c) define business and technical meta-data"

(DAMA International. The DAMA Dictionary of Data Management, Second Edition: Technics Publications, 2011, p.81).

Data quality is a business capability that enables the delivery of data and information of required quality.

Data quality check is a software code that checks the correspondence of a data instance or a data set to predefined requirements at some stage of data processing.

Data quality control is the process of controlling data. The set of data-quality checks allow for performing data-quality control.

Data steward is a steward that manages data assets.

Database is the "collection of interrelated data stored together in one or more computerized files"

(ISO/IEC/IEEE 24765:2017(en) Systems and software engineering — Vocabulary. https://www.iso.org/obp/ui#iso:std:iso-iec-ieee:24765:ed-2:v1:en:term:3.445).

Descriptive data lineage is a method to record metadata data lineage manually in a repository.

Functional requirement is a requirement that specifies what the system should do.

Functional role is a data management role that is defined by the organizational structure of an organization.

Information is data in a context that permits the explanation of its meaning and specification of relational connections.

Information systems architecture is a business capability that enables the delivery of data and application architecture required for designing data and information value chains.

Information Technology (IT) Application is software that supports one or more related business capabilities.

Information Technology (IT) system is a system composed from "[...] one or more computers, associated software, databases, peripherals, terminals, human operations, physical processes, information transfer means, that form an autonomous whole, capable of performing information processing and/or information transfer"

(ISO/IEC 14662:2010(en) Information technology — Open-edi reference model; https://www.iso.org/obp/ui#iso:std:iso-iec:14662:ed-3:v1:en).

Key performance indicator (KPI) is a quantifiable metric used to evaluate the success of an organization, business function, employee, etc., in meeting objectives for performance.

Metadata is data that defines and describes other data in a particular context.

Metadata repository is a database that maintains a data dictionary.

Metamodel is a model that describes the metadata needed to specify other models.

Metamodel of data lineage is the metamodel that describes metadata needed to document the data lineage model.

Model is an abstract representation of something, such as a physical object, process, phenomenon, etc.

Non-functional requirement is a requirement that identifies how the system should do it.

Process owner is a business role that defines and maintains a process as well as manages the process's performance and change.

Role is "the position or purpose that someone or something has in a situation, organization, society, or relationship"

("Role." Dictionary.cambridge.org, Cambridge Dictionary, https://dictionary.cambridge.org/dictionary/english/role. Accessed 16 Feb. 2021.)

Signal is "something that shows that something else exists or might happen or exists in the future" ("Signal." Dictionary.cambridge.org, Cambridge Dictionary, https://dictionary.cambridge.org/dictionary/english/signal. Accessed 16 Feb. 2021).

Stakeholder is an individual or a group of individuals with particular concerns and interests in the outcomes of the data lineage initiative.

Steward is a business role assigned to an employee that manages the organization's assets on behalf of the organization.

System is a combination of interacting elements organized to achieve one or more stated purposes.

System or application owner is "a business role that is accountable for a system lifecycle" (ISO/IEC/IEEE 24765:2017(en) Systems and software engineering — Vocabulary. https://www.iso.org/obp/ui#iso:std:iso-iec-ieee:24765:ed-2:v1:en:term:3.445).

Technical data steward is a data steward with knowledge, skills, and experience in one or more information technology (IT) and/or security domains.

Virtual role is a data management role that is not defined by the organizational structure of an organization and can be assigned to a functional role.

LIST OF FIGURES

LIST OF TABLES

REFERENCES

Introduction

1. Frisendal, Thomas. *Graph Data Modeling for NoSQL and SQL: Visualize Structure and Meaning.* Technics Publications, 2016, p.83.

2. "What Is a Concept Map: Definition & Tutorial." *MindMaster*, www.mindmaster.io/article/what-is-a-concept-map.html#:~:text=So what is a Concept,concepts in a graphical format.

PART 1. CLARIFYING THE CONCEPT OF DATA LINEAGE

Chapter 1. Analysis of existing views and approaches to data lineage

1. DAMA International. *DAMA-DMBOK: Data Management Body of Knowledge, Second Edition.* Bradley Beach, N.J.: Technics Publications, 2017.

2. *The TOGAF® Standard, Version 9.2*, 2018, pubs.opengroup.org/architecture/togaf9-doc/arch/.

3. DAMA International. *The DAMA Dictionary of Data Management, Second Edition*: Technics Publications, 2011, p.78.

4. Mosley, Mark., and Michael Brackett. *The DAMA Guide to the Data Management Body of Knowledge (DAMA-DMBOK Guide), First Edition.* Bradley Beach, N.J.: Technics Publications, 2010, p.83.

5. Mosley, Mark., and Michael Brackett. *The DAMA Guide to the Data Management Body of Knowledge (DAMA-DMBOK Guide), First Edition.* Bradley Beach, N.J.: Technics Publications, 2010, p.81.

6. DAMA International. *DAMA-DMBOK: Data Management Body of Knowledge, Second Edition.* Bradley Beach, N.J.: Technics Publications, 2017, p.28.

7. DAMA International. *DAMA-DMBOK: Data Management Body of Knowledge, Second Edition.* Bradley Beach, N.J.: Technics Publications, 2017, p.107.

8. DAMA International. *The DAMA Dictionary of Data Management, Second Edition*: Technics Publications, 2011, p.90.

9. DAMA International. *The DAMA Dictionary of Data Management, Second Edition*: Technics Publications, 2011, p.90.

10. DAMA International. *DAMA-DMBOK: Data Management Body of Knowledge, Second Edition.* Bradley Beach, N.J.: Technics Publications, 2017, p.28.

11. DAMA International. *The DAMA Dictionary of Data Management, Second Edition*: Technics Publications, 2011, p.75.

12. DAMA International. *The DAMA Dictionary of Data Management, Second Edition*: Technics Publications, 2011, p.75.

13. DAMA International. *DAMA-DMBOK: Data Management Body of Knowledge, Second Edition.* Bradley Beach, N.J.: Technics Publications, 2017, p.104.

14. DAMA International. *DAMA-DMBOK: Data Management Body of Knowledge, Second Edition.* Bradley Beach, N.J.: Technics Publications, 2017, p.104.

15. DAMA International. *DAMA-DMBOK: Data Management Body of Knowledge, Second Edition.* Bradley Beach, N.J.: Technics Publications, 2017, p.107.

16. DAMA International. *DAMA-DMBOK: Data Management Body of Knowledge, Second Edition.* Bradley Beach, N.J.: Technics Publications, 2017, p.108.

17. DAMA International. *The DAMA Dictionary of Data Management, Second Edition*: Technics Publications, 2011, p.68.

18. Mosley, Mark., and Michael Brackett. *The DAMA Guide to the Data Management Body of Knowledge (DAMA-DMBOK Guide), First Edition.* Bradley Beach, N.J.: Technics Publications, 2010, p.79.

19. DAMA International. *The DAMA Dictionary of Data Management, Second Edition*: Technics Publications, 2011, p.68.

20. DAMA International. *The DAMA Dictionary of Data Management, Second Edition*: Technics Publications, 2011, p.141.

21. Mosley, Mark., and Michael Brackett. *The DAMA Guide to the Data Management Body of Knowledge (DAMA-DMBOK Guide), First Edition.* Bradley Beach, N.J.: Technics Publications, 2010, p.64.

22. Mosley, Mark., and Michael Brackett. *The DAMA Guide to the Data Management Body of Knowledge (DAMA-DMBOK Guide), First Edition.* Bradley Beach, N.J.: Technics Publications, 2010, p.66.

23. Mosley, Mark., and Michael Brackett. *The DAMA Guide to the Data Management Body of Knowledge (DAMA-DMBOK Guide), First Edition.* Bradley Beach, N.J.: Technics Publications, 2010, p.83.

24. Mosley, Mark., and Michael Brackett. *The DAMA Guide to the Data Management Body of Knowledge (DAMA-DMBOK Guide), First Edition.* Bradley Beach, N.J.: Technics Publications, 2010, p.64.

25. DAMA International. *The DAMA Dictionary of Data Management, Second Edition*: Technics Publications, 2011, p.78.

26. DAMA International. *DAMA-DMBOK: Data Management Body of Knowledge, Second Edition.* Bradley Beach, N.J.: Technics Publications, 2017, p.110.

27. DAMA International. *The DAMA Dictionary of Data Management, Second Edition*: Technics Publications, 2011, p.18.

28. DAMA International. *The DAMA Dictionary of Data Management, Second Edition*: Technics Publications, 2011, p.68.

29. *The TOGAF® Standard, Version 9.2*, 2018, pubs.opengroup.org/architecture/togaf9-doc/arch/.

30. *The TOGAF® Standard, Version 9.2*, 2018, pubs.opengroup.org/architecture/togaf9-doc/arch/.

31. *TOGAF® Series Guide: Business Capabilities*, 2016, publications.opengroup.org/g161, p.4.

32. "Health Informatics – Trusted end-to-end information flows - ISO/TS Standard No. 21089:2018." *International Organization for Standards*, www.iso.org/obp/ui#iso:std:iso:ts:21089:ed-1:v1:en:term:3.44, Accessed 15 Feb.2021.

33. *TOGAF® Series Guide: Business Capabilities*, 2016, publications.opengroup.org/g161, p.4.

34. *TOGAF® Series Guide: Business Capabilities*, 2016, publications.opengroup.org/g189, p.4.

35. DAMA International. *The DAMA Dictionary of Data Management, Second Edition*: Technics Publications, 2011, p.36.

36. DAMA International. *DAMA-DMBOK: Data Management Body of Knowledge, Second Edition.* Bradley Beach, N.J.: Technics Publications, 2017.

37. DAMA International. *DAMA-DMBOK: Data Management Body of Knowledge, Second Edition.*

Bradley Beach, N.J.: Technics Publications, 2017, p.100.

38. DAMA International. *DAMA-DMBOK: Data Management Body of Knowledge, Second Edition.* Bradley Beach, N.J.: Technics Publications, 2017, p.287.

39. DAMA International. *DAMA-DMBOK: Data Management Body of Knowledge, Second Edition.* Bradley Beach, N.J.: Technics Publications, 2017, p.382.

40. DAMA International. *DAMA-DMBOK: Data Management Body of Knowledge, Second Edition.* Bradley Beach, N.J.: Technics Publications, 2017, p.419.

41. DAMA International. *DAMA-DMBOK: Data Management Body of Knowledge, Second Edition.* Bradley Beach, N.J.: Technics Publications, 2017, p.287.

42. DAMA International. *DAMA-DMBOK: Data Management Body of Knowledge, Second Edition.* Bradley Beach, N.J.: Technics Publications, 2017, p.108.

43. DAMA International. *DAMA-DMBOK: Data Management Body of Knowledge, Second Edition.* Bradley Beach, N.J.: Technics Publications, 2017, p.153.

44. DAMA International. *DAMA-DMBOK: Data Management Body of Knowledge, Second Edition.* Bradley Beach, N.J.: Technics Publications, 2017, p.153.

45. DAMA International. *DAMA-DMBOK: Data Management Body of Knowledge, Second Edition.* Bradley Beach, N.J.: Technics Publications, 2017, p.111.

46. DAMA International. *DAMA-DMBOK: Data Management Body of Knowledge, Second Edition.* Bradley Beach, N.J.: Technics Publications, 2017, p.288.

47. DAMA International. *DAMA-DMBOK: Data Management Body of Knowledge, Second Edition.* Bradley Beach, N.J.: Technics Publications, 2017, p.159.

48. DAMA International. *DAMA-DMBOK: Data Management Body of Knowledge, Second Edition.* Bradley Beach, N.J.: Technics Publications, 2017, p.159.

49. DAMA International. *DAMA-DMBOK: Data Management Body of Knowledge, Second Edition.* Bradley Beach, N.J.: Technics Publications, 2017, p.159.

Chapter 2. Key business drivers to document data lineage

1. Basel Committee on Banking Supervision. *Principles for effective risk data aggregation and risk reporting.* Bank for International Settlements 2013. https://www.bis.org/publ/BCBS 239.pdf

2. "General Data Protection Regulation (GDPR) ". *General Data Protection Regulation (GDPR)*, 2018, https://gdpr-info.eu/. Accessed 16 Feb 2021.

3. European Central Bank. Banking supervision. *ECB Guide to internal models.* October 2019. https://www.bankingsupervision.europa.eu/ecb/pub/pdf/ssm.guidetointernalmodels_consolidated_201910~97fd49fb08.en.pdf

4. IAS plus. IFRS 17 - *Insurance Contracts* [online]. 18 May 2018. [Accessed 16 February 2021]. Available from: https://www.iasplus.com/en/standards/ifrs/ifrs-17

5. Basel Committee on Banking Supervision. *Principles for effective risk data aggregation and risk reporting.* Bank for International Settlements 2013. Principle 3, par.39. https://www.bis.org/publ/BCBS 239.pdf

6. Basel Committee on Banking Supervision. *Principles for effective risk data aggregation and risk reporting*. Bank for International Settlements 2013. Principle 2, par.34. https://www.bis.org/publ/ BCBS 239.pdf

7. Basel Committee on Banking Supervision. *Principles for effective risk data aggregation and risk reporting*. Bank for International Settlements 2013. Principle 2. https://www.bis.org/publ/BCBS 239. pdf

8. "General Data Protection Regulation (GDPR) ". *General Data Protection Regulation (GDPR)*, 2018, https://gdpr-info.eu/. Accessed 16 Feb 2021. Art.30.

9. Basel Committee on Banking Supervision. *Principles for effective risk data aggregation and risk reporting*. Bank for International Settlements 2013. Principle 6, par.37. https://www.bis.org/publ/BCBS 239.pdf

10. Basel Committee on Banking Supervision. *Principles for effective risk data aggregation and risk reporting*. Bank for International Settlements 2013. Principle 8, par.67. https://www.bis.org/publ/ BCBS 239.pdf

11. Basel Committee on Banking Supervision. *Principles for effective risk data aggregation and risk reporting*. Bank for International Settlements 2013. Principle 7, par.53b. https://www.bis.org/publ/ BCBS 239.pdf

12. Basel Committee on Banking Supervision. *Principles for effective risk data aggregation and risk reporting*. Bank for International Settlements 2013. Principle 7, par.53b. https://www.bis.org/publ/ BCBS 239.pdf

13. Basel Committee on Banking Supervision. *Principles for effective risk data aggregation and risk reporting*. Bank for International Settlements 2013. Principle 2, par.33. https://www.bis.org/publ/BCBS 239.pdf

14. "General Data Protection Regulation (GDPR) ". *General Data Protection Regulation (GDPR)*, 2018, https://gdpr-info.eu/. Accessed 16 Feb 2021. Art.30.

15. "General Data Protection Regulation (GDPR) ". *General Data Protection Regulation (GDPR)*, 2018, https://gdpr-info.eu/. Accessed 16 Feb 2021. Art.17.

16. "General Data Protection Regulation (GDPR) ". *General Data Protection Regulation (GDPR)*, 2018, https://gdpr-info.eu/. Accessed 16 Feb 2021. Art.18.

17. "General Data Protection Regulation (GDPR) ". *General Data Protection Regulation (GDPR)*, 2018, https://gdpr-info.eu/. Accessed 16 Feb 2021. Art.20.

18. Basel Committee on Banking Supervision. *Principles for effective risk data aggregation and risk reporting*. Bank for International Settlements 2013. Principle 3, par.40. https://www.bis.org/publ/ BCBS 239.pdf

19. Basel Committee on Banking Supervision. *Principles for effective risk data aggregation and risk reporting*. Bank for International Settlements 2013. Principle 4, par.43. https://www.bis.org/publ/ BCBS 239.pdf

20. Basel Committee on Banking Supervision. *Principles for effective risk data aggregation and risk reporting*. Bank for International Settlements 2013. Principle 3, par.36a. https://www.bis.org/publ/ BCBS 239.pdf

21. Basel Committee on Banking Supervision. *Principles for effective risk data aggregation and risk*

reporting. Bank for International Settlements 2013. Principle 7, par.53c. https://www.bis.org/publ/BCBS 239.pdf

22. "General Data Protection Regulation (GDPR) ". *General Data Protection Regulation (GDPR)*, 2018, https://gdpr-info.eu/. Accessed 16 Feb 2021. Art.32.

Chapter 3. The concept of a metamodel

1. AZ Quotes: Quotes for All Occasions. *AZ Quotes* [online]. [Accessed 16 February 2021]. Available from: https://www.azquotes.com/

2. DAMA International. *The DAMA Dictionary of Data Management, Second Edition*: Technics Publications, 2011, p.66.

3. DAMA International. *The DAMA Dictionary of Data Management, Second Edition*: Technics Publications, 2011, p.66.

4. *"Information technology — Metadata registries (MDR) — Part 1: Framework*. - ISO/IEC Standard No. 11179-1:2015." International Organization for Standards, https://www.iso.org/obp/ui/#iso:std:iso-iec:11179:-1:ed-3:v1:en, Accessed 15 Feb.2021.

5. *The TOGAF® Standard, Version 9.2*, 2018, pubs.opengroup.org/architecture/togaf9-doc/arch/.

6. "Data." *Merriam-Webster.com Dictionary*, Merriam-Webster, https://www.merriam-webster.com/dictionary/data. Accessed 16 Feb. 2021.

7. DAMA International. *The DAMA Dictionary of Data Management, Second Edition*: Technics Publications, 2011, p.121.

8. "Fact." *Merriam-Webster.com Dictionary*, Merriam-Webster, https://www.merriam-webster.com/dictionary/fact. Accessed 16 Feb. 2021.

9. Pedro de Buyckere. The difference between data, information, knowledge and wisdom. *From experience to meaning...* [online]. 30 June 2018. [Accessed 16 February 2021]. Available from: https://theeconomyofmeaning.com/2018/06/29/the-difference-between-data-information-knowledge-and-wisdom/

10. "Signal." Dictionary.cambridge.org, Cambridge Dictionary, https://dictionary.cambridge.org/dictionary/english/signal. Accessed 16 Feb. 2021.

11. United Nations Statistical Commission and Economic Commission for Europe. Terminology on Statistical Metadata. United Nations. Geneva, 2000., https://unece.org/fileadmin/DAM/stats/publications/53metadaterminology.pdf, p.8. Accessed 16 Feb.2021.

12. DAMA International. *The DAMA Dictionary of Data Management, Second Edition*: Technics Publications, 2011, pp.166-167.

13. DAMA International. *DAMA-DMBOK: Data Management Body of Knowledge, Second Edition*. Bradley Beach, N.J.: Technics Publications, 2017, pp.422-423.

14. DAMA International. *DAMA-DMBOK: Data Management Body of Knowledge, Second Edition*. Bradley Beach, N.J.: Technics Publications, 2017, p.423.

15. DAMA International. *DAMA-DMBOK: Data Management Body of Knowledge, Second Edition*. Bradley Beach, N.J.: Technics Publications, 2017, p.423.

16. DAMA International. *DAMA-DMBOK: Data Management Body of Knowledge, Second Edition.* Bradley Beach, N.J.: Technics Publications, 2017, p.423.

17. DAMA International. *DAMA-DMBOK: Data Management Body of Knowledge, Second Edition.* Bradley Beach, N.J.: Technics Publications, 2017, p.423.

18. DAMA International. *DAMA-DMBOK: Data Management Body of Knowledge, Second Edition.* Bradley Beach, N.J.: Technics Publications, 2017, pp.422-423.

19. DAMA International. *The DAMA Dictionary of Data Management, Second Edition*: Technics Publications, 2011, pp.167.

20. *The TOGAF® Standard, Version 9.2*, 2018, pubs.opengroup.org/architecture/togaf9-doc/arch/.

21. *The TOGAF® Standard, Version 9.2*, 2018, pubs.opengroup.org/architecture/togaf9-doc/arch/.

22. "Information technology – Metadata registries (MDR) – Part 1 : Framework – ISO/IEC Standard No. 11179:2004." *International Organization for Standards*, https://www.iso.org/obp/ui/#iso:std:iso-iec:11179:-1:ed-2:v1:en. Accessed 16 Feb.2021.

Chapter 4. The metadata of data lineage

1. *The TOGAF® Standard, Version 9.2*, 2018, pubs.opengroup.org/architecture/togaf9-doc/arch/.

2. *TOGAF® Series Guide: Business Capabilities*, 2016, publications.opengroup.org/g189.

3. *TOGAF® Series Guide: Business Capabilities*, 2016, publications.opengroup.org/g189, p.2.

4. *TOGAF® Series Guide: Business Capabilities*, 2016, publications.opengroup.org/g189, p.9.

5. *TOGAF® Series Guide: Business Capabilities*, 2016, publications.opengroup.org/g189.

6. "Role." Dictionary.cambridge.org, Cambridge Dictionary, https://dictionary.cambridge.org/dictionary/english/role. Accessed 16 Feb. 2021.

7. *The TOGAF® Standard, Version 9.2*, 2018, pubs.opengroup.org/architecture/togaf9-doc/arch/. Accessed 16 Feb. 2021.

8. "*Systems and software engineering — Vocabulary – ISO/IEC/ IEEE Standard No. 24765:2017.*" International Organization for Standards, https://www.iso.org/obp/ui#iso:std:iso-iec-ieee:24765:ed-2:v1:en:term:3.445]. Accessed 16 Feb. 2021.

9. "*Information technology — Open-edi reference model* ISO/IEC Standard No. 14662:2010." International Organization for Standards, https://www.iso.org/obp/ui#iso:std:iso-iec:14662:ed-3:v1:en. Accessed 16 Feb. 2021.

10. "*Systems and software engineering — Vocabulary – ISO/IEC/ IEEE Standard No. 24765:2017.*" International Organization for Standards, https://www.iso.org/obp/ui#iso:std:iso-iec-ieee:24765:ed-2:v1:en:term:3.445]. Accessed 16 Feb. 2021.

11. DAMA International. *DAMA-DMBOK: Data Management Body of Knowledge, Second Edition.* Bradley Beach, N.J.: Technics Publications, 2017, p.145-148.

12. Frisendal, Thomas. *Graph Data Modeling for NoSQL and SQL: Visualize Structure and Meaning.* Technics Publications, 2016, p.83.

13. EVANS, Eric. *Domain-driven design reference: definitions and patterns summaries.* Indianapolis, IN

: Dog Ear Publishing, 2015.

14. DAMA International. *DAMA-DMBOK: Data Management Body of Knowledge, Second Edition.* Bradley Beach, N.J.: Technics Publications, 2017, p.136.

15. Mosley, Mark., and Michael Brackett. *The DAMA Guide to the Data Management Body of Knowledge (DAMA-DMBOK Guide), First Edition.* Bradley Beach, N.J.: Technics Publications, 2010, p.75.

16. DAMA International. *DAMA-DMBOK: Data Management Body of Knowledge, Second Edition.* Bradley Beach, N.J.: Technics Publications, 2017, p.106.

17. DAMA International. *The DAMA Dictionary of Data Management, Second Edition*: Technics Publications, 2011, p.81.

18. "Semantic data model." Technopedia.com, Technopedia, https://www.techopedia.com/definition/30489/semantic-data-model. Accessed 16 Feb. 2021.

19. Frisendal, Thomas. *Graph Data Modeling for NoSQL and SQL: Visualize Structure and Meaning.* Technics Publications, 2016.

20. Frisendal, Thomas. *Graph Data Modeling for NoSQL and SQL: Visualize Structure and Meaning.* Technics Publications, 2016.

21. DAMA International. *DAMA-DMBOK: Data Management Body of Knowledge, Second Edition.* Bradley Beach, N.J.: Technics Publications, 2017, p.81.

22. DAMA International. *The DAMA Dictionary of Data Management, Second Edition*: Technics Publications, 2011, p.74.

23. DAMA International. *The DAMA Dictionary of Data Management, Second Edition*: Technics Publications, 2011, p.127.

24. "Space data and information transfer systems — Data entity dictionary specification language (DEDSL) — Abstract syntax – ISO Standard No.21961:2003." International Organization for Standards, https://www.iso.org/obp/ui#iso:std:iso:21961:ed-1:v1:en. Accessed 16 Feb. 2021.

25. DAMA International. *The DAMA Dictionary of Data Management, Second Edition*: Technics Publications, 2011, p.69.

26. DAMA International. *DAMA-DMBOK: Data Management Body of Knowledge, Second Edition.* Bradley Beach, N.J.: Technics Publications, 2017, p.133.

27. "Health Informatics – Trusted end-to-end information flows – ISO/TS Standard No.21089:2018." International Organization for Standards. https://www.iso.org/obp/ui#iso:std:iso:ts:21089:ed-1:v1:en:term:3.44. Accessed 16 Feb. 2021.

28. Frisendal, Thomas. *Graph Data Modeling for NoSQL and SQL: Visualize Structure and Meaning.* Technics Publications, 2016.

29. DAMA International. *DAMA-DMBOK: Data Management Body of Knowledge, Second Edition.* Bradley Beach, N.J.: Technics Publications, 2017, p.133.

30. DAMA International. *The DAMA Dictionary of Data Management, Second Edition*: Technics Publications, 2011, p.215.

31. DAMA International. *The DAMA Dictionary of Data Management, Second Edition*: Technics Publications, 2011, p.60.

32. DAMA International. *The DAMA Dictionary of Data Management, Second Edition*: Technics Publications, 2011, p.60.

33. "Intelligent transport systems – System architecture – 'Use Case' pro-forma template – ISO/TR Standard No. 25102: 2008." International Organization for Standards. https://www.iso.org/obp/ui#iso:std:iso:tr:25102:ed-1:v1:en:term:2.2. Accessed 16 Feb. 2021.

34. ROSS, Ronald. What Is a 'Business Rule'? : Commentary : Business Rules Community / Business Rules Journal. BRC [online]. [Accessed 16 February 2021]. Available from: http://www.brcommunity.com/articles.php?id=b005

35. Object Management Group ®. *Semantics of Business Vocabulary and Business Rules TM. Version 1.5.* An OMG® Semantics of Business Vocabulary and Business Rules TM Publication. OMG Document Number: formal/2019-10-02 [SMSC/19-10-02]. https://www.omg.org/spec/SBVR/1.5/PDF. Accessed 16 Feb. 2021.

PART 2. IMPLEMENTING DATA LINEAGE

Chapter 6. Build your data lineage case by following 9-step methodology

1. STEENBEEK, Irina. *The Data Management Toolkit: A Step-by-Step Implementation Guide for the Pioneers of Data Management.* Amsterdam, The Netherlands : Data Crossroads, 2019, p.24.

2. STEENBEEK, Irina. *The Data Management Toolkit: A Step-by-Step Implementation Guide for the Pioneers of Data Management.* Amsterdam, The Netherlands : Data Crossroads, 2019, p.30.

Chapter 7. Scope your data lineage initiative

1. *The TOGAF® Standard, Version 9.2,* 2018, pubs.opengroup.org/architecture/togaf9-doc/arch/. Accessed 16 Feb. 2021.

Chapter 8. Data lineage-related roles

1. "Role." Dictionary.cambridge.org, Cambridge Dictionary, https://dictionary.cambridge.org/dictionary/english/role. Accessed 16 Feb. 2021.

2. STEENBEEK, Irina. *The "Orange" Model of Data Management.* Amsterdam, The Netherlands : Data Crossroads, 2019.

3. DAMA International. *The DAMA Dictionary of Data Management, Second Edition*: Technics Publications, 2011, p.81.

4. RACI Matrix. *Project Smart* [online]. [Accessed 16 February 2021]. Available from: https://www.projectsmart.co.uk/raci-matrix.php

Chapter 11. Choose a suitable software solution

1. International Institute of Business Analysis. A Guide to the Business Analysis Body of Knowledge (BABOK guide), version 2.0, Toronto. : International Institute of Business Analysis, 2009, p.12.

2. International Institute of Business Analysis. A Guide to the Business Analysis Body of Knowledge (BABOK guide), version 2.0, Toronto. : International Institute of Business Analysis, 2009, p.15.

3. International Institute of Business Analysis. A Guide to the Business Analysis Body of Knowledge (BABOK guide), version 2.0, Toronto. : International Institute of Business Analysis, 2009, p.12.

4. "Systems and software engineering – Life Cycle Management – Part 5: Software development planning – ISO/IEC/IEEE Standard No. 24748-5:2017." International Organization for Standards, https://www.iso.org/obp/ui#iso:std:iso-iec-ieee:24748:-5:ed-1:v1:en:term:3.18. Accessed 16 Feb. 2021.

5. "Intelligent transport systems — Cooperative ITS — Part 4: Minimum system requirements and behaviour for core systems – ISO/TR Standard No. 17427-4:2015." ." International Organization for Standards. https://www.iso.org/obp/ui#iso:std:iso:tr:17427:-4:ed-1:v1:en:term:2.20. Accessed 16 Feb. 2021.

6. BOOGAARD, Kat. An explanation of SMART goals and how to write them. *Work Life by Atlassian* [online]. 5 January 2021. [Accessed 16 February 2021]. Available from: https://www.atlassian.com/blog/productivity/how-to-write-smart-goals.

7. DAMA International. *DAMA-DMBOK: Data Management Body of Knowledge, Second Edition.* Bradley Beach, N.J.: Technics Publications, 2017, p.67.

8. DAMA International. *DAMA-DMBOK: Data Management Body of Knowledge, Second Edition.* Bradley Beach, N.J.: Technics Publications, 2017, p.69.

9. STEENBEEK, Irina. Data Management & Data Governance 101: The Yin and Yang Duality. *Data Crossroads* [online]. 9 July 2020. [Accessed 16 February 2021]. Available from: https://datacrossroads.nl/2019/09/22/data-management-data-governance-101-the-yin-and-yang-duality/.

10. 10+ Best Data Governance Tools To Fulfill Your Data Needs In 2021. *Software Testing Help* [online]. 15 February 2021. [Accessed 16 February 2021]. Available from: https://www.softwaretestinghelp.com/data-governance-tools/

11. Best Data Governance Software 2021: Reviews of the Most Popular Tools & Systems. *Best Data Governance Software 2021 | Reviews of the Most Popular Tools & Systems* [online]. [Accessed 16 February 2021]. Available from: https://www.capterra.com/data-governance-software/.

12. MORRIS, Evan. Top 5 Data Governance Framework Tools To Look Out For. *Medium* [online]. 17 July 2019. [Accessed 16 February 2021]. Available from: https://towardsdatascience.com/top-5-data-governance-framework-tools-to-look-out-for-8d753ab314de.

13. Best Data Governance Tools & Software 2021. *Datamation* [online]. 28 January 2021. [Accessed 16 February 2021]. Available from: https://www.datamation.com/big-data/data-governance-tools/.

14. 10+ Best Data Governance Tools To Fulfill Your Data Needs In 2021. *Software Testing Help* [online]. 15 February 2021. [Accessed 16 February 2021]. Available from: https://www.softwaretestinghelp.com/data-governance-tools/.

15. Best Data Governance Software 2021: Reviews of the Most Popular Tools & Systems. *Best Data Governance Software 2021 | Reviews of the Most Popular Tools & Systems* [online]. [Accessed 16 February 2021]. Available from: https://www.capterra.com/data-governance-software/.

16. MORRIS, Evan. Top 5 Data Governance Framework Tools To Look Out For. *Medium* [online]. 17 July 2019. [Accessed 16 February 2021]. Available from: https://towardsdatascience.com/top-5-data-governance-framework-tools-to-look-out-for-8d753ab314de.

17. Best Data Governance Tools & Software 2021. *Datamation* [online]. 28 January 2021. [Accessed 16 February 2021]. Available from: https://www.datamation.com/big-data/data-governance-tools/.

18. 10+ Best Data Governance Tools To Fulfill Your Data Needs In 2021. *Software Testing Help* [online]. 15 February 2021. [Accessed 16 February 2021]. Available from: https://www.softwaretestinghelp.com/data-governance-tools/.

19. Best Data Governance Software 2021: Reviews of the Most Popular Tools & Systems. *Best Data Governance Software 2021 | Reviews of the Most Popular Tools & Systems* [online]. [Accessed 16 February 2021]. Available from: https://www.capterra.com/data-governance-software/.

20. MORRIS, Evan. Top 5 Data Governance Framework Tools To Look Out For. *Medium* [online]. 17 July 2019. [Accessed 16 February 2021]. Available from: https://towardsdatascience.com/top-5-data-governance-framework-tools-to-look-out-for-8d753ab314de.

21. Best Data Governance Tools & Software 2021. *Datamation* [online]. 28 January 2021. [Accessed 16 February 2021]. Available from: https://www.datamation.com/big-data/data-governance-tools/.

22. *Top Software at Capterra | Software & Software Reviews For Business & Nonprofit* [online]. [Accessed 16 February 2021]. Available from: https://www.capterra.com/

23. Information Governance Software - a.k.a.® Homepage. *a.k.a. Information Governance Software* [online]. [Accessed 16 February 2021]. Available from: https://www.a-k-a.co/

24. *Alfresco* [online]. [Accessed 16 February 2021]. Available from: https://www.alfresco.com/

25. Email Security, DNS Filtering and Email Archiving. *Email Security and DNS Filtering Vendor* [online]. [Accessed 16 February 2021]. Available from: https://trust.titanhq.com/

26. Free Software Testing & Development Courses. *Software Testing Help* [online]. [Accessed 16 February 2021]. Available from: https://www.softwaretestinghelp.com/

27. 10+ Best Data Governance Tools To Fulfill Your Data Needs In 2021. *Software Testing Help* [online]. 15 February 2021. [Accessed 16 February 2021]. Available from: https://www.softwaretestinghelp.com/data-governance-tools/

28. *Top Software at Capterra | Software & Software Reviews For Business & Nonprofit* [online]. [Accessed 16 February 2021]. Available from: https://www.capterra.com/

29. 2020 Gartner Magic Quadrant for Metadata Management Solutions - PPC. *Collibra* [online]. [Accessed 16 February 2021]. Available from: https://www.collibra.com/download/2020-gartner-magic-quadrant-leader-ppc?utm_source=Google-Ads

30. Gartner 2020 Magic Quadrant for Metadata Management Solutions. *Informatica* [online]. [Accessed 16 February 2021]. Available from: https://www.informatica.com/nl/metadata-management-magic-quadrant.html

31. 10+ Best Data Governance Tools To Fulfill Your Data Needs In 2021. *Software Testing Help* [online]. 15 February 2021. [Accessed 16 February 2021]. Available from: https://www.softwaretestinghelp.com/data-governance-tools/

32. MORRIS, Evan. Top 5 Data Governance Framework Tools To Look Out For. *Medium* [online]. 17 July 2019. [Accessed 16 February 2021]. Available from: https://towardsdatascience.com/top-5-data-governance-framework-tools-to-look-out-for-8d753ab314de.

33. Best Data Fabric Software in 2021. in *2021* [online]. [Accessed 16 February 2021]. Available from:

https://www.360quadrants.com/software/data-fabric-software

34. Online Diagram Software & Visual Solution. *Lucidchart* [online]. [Accessed 16 February 2021]. Available from: https://www.lucidchart.com/

35. Jumpstart your processes journey. *ARIS Cloud* [online]. 4 January 2021. [Accessed 16 February 2021]. Available from: https://ariscloud.com/

36. *The TOGAF® Standard, Version 9.2,* 2018, pubs.opengroup.org/architecture/togaf9-doc/arch/. Accessed 16 Feb. 2021.

37. Best Enterprise Architecture Software 2021: Reviews of the Most Popular Tools & Systems. *Best Enterprise Architecture Software 2021 | Reviews of the Most Popular Tools & Systems* [online]. [Accessed 16 February 2021]. Available from: https://www.capterra.com/enterprise-architecture-software/

38. Home - IRIS Business Architect collaborative software. *IRIS Business Architect* [online]. 31 July 2012. [Accessed 16 February 2021]. Available from: https://biz-architect.com/

39. Public eTrainings. *UML, SysML, BPMN, Togaf, Updm united in Enterprise Architect from Sparx Systems* [online]. [Accessed 16 February 2021]. Available from: https://www.sparxsystems.eu/

40. Identify and Manage your Governance, Risk and Compliance Challenges. *AdaptiveGRC* [online]. [Accessed 16 February 2021]. Available from: https://adaptivegrc.com/

41. *Archi* [online]. [Accessed 16 February 2021]. Available from: https://www.archimatetool.com/

42. Public eTrainings. *UML, SysML, BPMN, Togaf, Updm united in Enterprise Architect from Sparx Systems* [online]. [Accessed 16 February 2021]. Available from: https://www.sparxsystems.eu/

43. *IDERA Software* [online]. [Accessed 16 February 2021]. Available from: https://www.idera.com/

44. Data Governance: Enterprise Modeling & Data Intelligence. *erwin, Inc.* [online]. 26 January 2021. [Accessed 16 February 2021]. Available from: https://erwin.com/

45. Solutions Overview - Solidatus - Award-Winning Data Lineage Solution. *Solidatus* [online]. [Accessed 16 February 2021]. Available from: https://www.solidatus.com/solutions/

46. Solidatus for Data Catalog - A component of modern data management. *Solidatus* [online]. [Accessed 16 February 2021]. Available from: https://www.solidatus.com/data-catalog/

47. Automated Data Lineage & Data Discovery. *Octopai* [online]. 17 January 2021. [Accessed 16 February 2021]. Available from: https://www.octopai.com/

48. What is the difference between a business glossary, a data dictionary and a data catalog? *Octopai* [online]. 12 February 2020. [Accessed 16 February 2021]. Available from: https://www.octopai.com/question/what-is-the-difference-between-a-business-glossary-a-data-dictionary-and-a-data-catalog/

49. DAMA International. *DAMA-DMBOK: Data Management Body of Knowledge, Second Edition.* Bradley Beach, N.J.: Technics Publications, 2017, p..67.

Chapter 12. Document data lineage and build analytics

1. *TOGAF® Series Guide: Business Models,* 2018, publications.opengroup.org/g18A, p.5.

2. *TOGAF® Series Guide: Business Capabilities,* 2016, publications.opengroup.org/g189, p.9.

3. STEENBEEK, Irina. *The Data Management Toolkit: A Step-by-Step Implementation Guide for the Pioneers of Data Management.* Amsterdam, The Netherlands : Data Crossroads, 2019.

PART 3. USING DATA LINEAGE

Chapter 14. Critical data

1. DAMA International. *DAMA-DMBOK: Data Management Body of Knowledge, Second Edition.* Bradley Beach, N.J.: Technics Publications, 2017, p.454.

Chapter 18. The setup of data management framework

1. STEENBEEK, Irina. *The "Orange" Model of Data Management.* Amsterdam, The Netherlands : Data Crossroads, 2019.

2. STEENBEEK, Irina. *The Data Management Toolkit: A Step-by-Step Implementation Guide for the Pioneers of Data Management.* Amsterdam, The Netherlands : Data Crossroads, 2019.

PART 4. CASE-STUDY "BUILD A DATA LINEAGE BUSINESS CASE"

1. STEENBEEK, Irina. *The Data Management Toolkit: A Step-by-Step Implementation Guide for the Pioneers of Data Management.* Amsterdam, The Netherlands : Data Crossroads, 2019, p.180.

2. STEENBEEK, Irina. *The Data Management Toolkit: A Step-by-Step Implementation Guide for the Pioneers of Data Management.* Amsterdam, The Netherlands : Data Crossroads, 2019, p.180.

3. What is MoSCoW Prioritization?: Overview of the MoSCoW Method. *ProductPlan* [online]. 1 October 2020. [Accessed 16 February 2021]. Available from: https://www.productplan.com/glossary/moscow-prioritization/

ATTACHMENTS

Attachment 3. The list of data lineage solution providers

1. *Ab Initio* [online]. [Accessed 16 February 2021]. Available from: https://www.abinitio.com/

2. ....Unleash the power of your metadata with the most effective Reversal Data Lineage Solution. *About Data Governance* [online]. [Accessed 16 February 2021]. Available from: https://www.aboutdatagovernance.com/

3. Metadata Management and Enterprise Architecture Solutions. *Adaptive* [online]. 29 July 2014. [Accessed 16 February 2021]. Available from: https://www.adaptive.com/

4. Enterprise Data Catalog & Data Governance. *Alation* [online]. 10 February 2021. [Accessed 16 February 2021]. Available from: http://www.alation.com/

5. Alex Solutions - Global Leader. Alex [online]. [Accessed 16 February 2021]. Available from: http://alexsolutions.com.au/

6. Read More ASG Sees Significant Momentum in 2020 with its IT Systems and Information Management Solutions. *ASG Technologies: Information Access, Management and Control* [online]. 26 January 1970. [Accessed 16 February 2021]. Available from: https://www.asg.com/

7. ATACCAMA. Self-Driving Data Management & Governance. *Ataccama* [online]. [Accessed 16 February 2021]. Available from: https://www.ataccama.com/

8. Home for Data Teams. *Atlan* [online]. [Accessed 16 February 2021]. Available from: https://atlan.com/

9. The Smart Data Fabric. *CluedIn* [online]. [Accessed 16 February 2021]. Available from: https://www.cluedin.com/

10. Trusted data for your entire organization. *Collibra* [online]. [Accessed 16 February 2021]. Available from: https://collibra.com/

11. Enterprise Metadata Management & Data Governance Solutions. *Data Advantage Group* [online]. [Accessed 16 February 2021]. Available from: https://www.dag.com/

12. The Cloud-Native Data Catalog. *data.world* [online]. 5 February 2021. [Accessed 16 February 2021]. Available from: https://data.world/

13. Single Source of Truth About Your Data. *Dataedo* [online]. [Accessed 16 February 2021]. Available from: https://dataedo.com/

14. Data Governance: Enterprise Modeling & Data Intelligence. *erwin, Inc.* [online]. 26 January 2021. [Accessed 16 February 2021]. Available from: https://erwin.com/

15. Enterprise Data Management, Understand Meaning & Flow Enterprise Data. *Global IDs* [online]. [Accessed 16 February 2021]. Available from: https://www.globalids.com/

16. Drive real business transformation. *IBM* [online]. 1 October 2015. [Accessed 16 February 2021]. Available from: https://ibm.com/

17. Data Governance and Management Solutions. *Infogix* [online]. 26 January 2021. [Accessed 16 February 2021]. Available from: https://www.infogix.com/

18. Informatica. *Enterprise Cloud Data Management* [online]. [Accessed 16 February 2021]. Available from: https://www.informatica.com/

19. Big Data Automation for Enterprises to Operate More Efficiently. *Io* [online]. 4 February 2021. [Accessed 16 February 2021]. Available from: https://www.iotahoe.com/

20. Data Lineage Done Right. *MANTA* [online]. 15 January 2021. [Accessed 16 February 2021]. Available from: https://getmanta.com/

21. Automated Data Lineage & Data Discovery. *Octopai* [online]. 17 January 2021. [Accessed 16 February 2021]. Available from: https://www.octopai.com/

22. Integrated Cloud Applications and Platform Services. *Oracle* [online]. [Accessed 16 February 2021]. Available from: https://www.oracle.com/

23. Information governance: spark data science: Data fabric tools. *Enterprise Information Intelligence - Orion Governance* [online]. [Accessed 16 February 2021]. Available from: https://www.oriongovernance.com/

24. A comprehensive data cataloging and governance solution. *OvalEdge* [online]. [Accessed 16 February 2021]. Available from: https://ovaledge.com/

25. SAP Software Solutions: Business Applications and Technology. *SAP* [online]. [Accessed 16 February 2021]. Available from: https://www.sap.com/

26. *SAS* [online]. [Accessed 16 February 2021]. Available from: https://www.sas.com/

27. Semantic Web Company Home. *Semantic Web Company* [online]. 6 September 2019. [Accessed 16 February 2021]. Available from: https://semantic-web.com/

28. Smartlogic's Semantic AI Platform Semaphore. *Smartlogic Semaphore - Semantic AI Platform* [online]. [Accessed 16 February 2021]. Available from: https://www.smartlogic.com/

29. An Award-Winning Data Lineage Solution. *Solidatus* [online]. [Accessed 16 February 2021]. Available from: https://www.solidatus.com/

30. *Syniti* [online]. 2 February 2021. [Accessed 16 February 2021]. Available from: https://www.syniti.com/

31. Talend - A Cloud Data Integration Leader (modern ETL). *Talend Real-Time Open Source Data Integration Software* [online]. 4 February 2021. [Accessed 16 February 2021]. Available from: https://www.talend.com/

32. TopQuadrant - Enterprise Data Governance. *TopQuadrant, Inc* [online]. [Accessed 16 February 2021]. Available from: https://www.topquadrant.com/

33. The Data Governance Open Source Solution. *Truedat* [online]. 1 October 2019. [Accessed 16 February 2021]. Available from: https://www.truedat.io/

34. Zeenea Data Catalog Software - Be(come) data fluent ! *Zeenea* [online]. 5 February 2021. [Accessed 16 February 2021]. Available from: https://zeenea.com/

OTHER BOOKS BY IRINA STEENBEEK

THE DATA MANAGEMENT TOOLKIT

This book is the step-by-step guide for the implementation of data management. This guide describes in detail the key phases of implementing a data management framework. It explains in-depth the "Data Management Star" method developed by Data Crossroads. The extended set of templates allows documenting the key deliverables. A case study demonstrates the example of such an implementation performed by a fictitious company XYZ.

This book is for those practitioners who implement a data management framework in their companies

THE DATA MANAGEMENT COOKBOOK

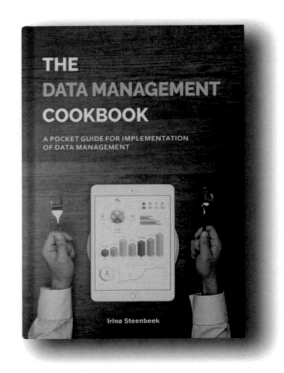

This small book is a pocket guide for the implementation of data management. It highlights the key steps of the method developed by Data Crossroads. This method, called "Data Management Star," is the summary of practical implementation experience.

This book is for those professionals who want to start a data management initiative and become familiar with the main phases of such an endeavor.

DATA CROSSROADS SERVICES

Data Crossroads is a coaching enterprise in data management. The key areas of expertise are:

- Data management maturity assessment
- Implementation of a data management framework
- Data lineage business case

Data Crossroads delivers its services using the "Orange" framework - the collection of ready-to-use models, techniques, and templates for building a fit-for-purpose data management framework.

The "Orange" model allows a customer to quickly and effectively achieve the goals of its data management initiative by using one of the following services:

PERFORM A PRELIMINARY FREE-OF-CHARGE DATA MANAGEMENT ASSESSMENT AND GET A FREE REPORT

Go to: **datacrossroads.nl/maturity**

COMPARE THE RESULTS WITH PEERS IN THE INDUSTRY BY DOWNLOADING A FREE DM MATURITY REVIEW

Go to: **datacrossroads.nl/maturity-review-2020**

ARRANGE A 30-MINUTE FREE STRATEGY SESSION TO DISCUSS EXISTING CHALLENGES

Go to: **datacrossroads.nl/free-strategy-session**

TRAIN INTERNAL STAFF TO PERFORM THE DATA MANAGEMENT INITIATIVE

Go to: **datacrossroads.nl/workshop**

PERFORM A CUSTOMIZED MATURITY ASSESSMENT, DEVELOP A ROADMAP, AND IMPLEMENT OR OPTIMIZE DATA MANAGEMENT:

- Do-It-Yourself Approach

  Go to: **datacrossroads.nl/dm-toolkit**

- Benefit from our coaching or consulting support

  Go to: **datacrossroads.nl/consulting**

Made in the USA
Las Vegas, NV
17 October 2023

79270969R00145